THE SEASONS IN MAHĀKĀVYA LITERATURE

THE SEASONS IN MAHĀKĀVYA LITERATURE

DANIELLE FELLER

Eastern Book Linkers
DELHI :: INDIA

Published by
EASTERN BOOK LINKERS
5825, New Chandrawal, Jawahar Nagar
Delhi-110007

First Published : 1995

ISBN 681-86339-24-8

Price RS. 350-

Published by : Shamlal Malhotra for Eastern Book Linkers, 5825, New Chandrawal, Delhi-110007 and Printed at Suman Printers, Maujpur, Delhi-110053.

This book is dedicated

to

My parents,

TONY AND ELISABETH FELLER

ACKNOWLEDGMENTS

In the first place, I am deeply indebted to Prof. J. Bronkhorst from Lausanne University (Switzerland), who was my guide for my degree dissertation on which this work is based. Now again, in spite of his many obligations, he has taken the time to read this manuscript and offer many valuable suggestions, for which I would like to thank him sincerely.

Many thanks also go to Dr. R.P. Goswamy, the Librarian CASS Library (Pune) for painstakingly reading the manuscript of this book and drawing my attention to many blunders and omissions.

I also wish to thank Dr. Jan Houben from Leiden (Netherlands) who was so kind as to read this manuscript and make helpful remarks about it.

I would like to thank, if this were not too weak a term, my husband Dr. J. Sudhakar. This work was started on his suggestion and it could be brought to completion only thanks to his readiness at any time of the day or night to discuss it and offer his help and suggestions, as well as his sometimes severe but always objective criticisms. Thanks to his thorough acquaintance with Indian poetics, his help proved particularly invaluable in translating the 18th *adhyāya* of Rājaśekhara's Kāvyamīmāṁsā. Thanks for everything !

Finally, I am grateful to Mr. Sham Lal Malhotra proprietor, Eastern Book Linkers, for his willingness to print this book.

DANIELLE FELLER

CONTENTS

PART III

Introduction

Season descriptions seem to have been a popular theme in Indian literature, for we find them in the most diverse literary as well as non-literary genres, such as lyrical poetry, dramas, prose *kāvyas*, *Mahākāvyas*, and epics as well as *purāṇas*, *alaṁkāra-śāstra*, epigraphic inscriptions, didactic literature, medical treatises, Buddhist and Jaina religious literature, and so on. Moreover, season descriptions form a separate genre by themselves, the *ṣaḍṛtuvarṇana*s, or descriptions of the six seasons, of which the best known is Ṛtusaṁhāra.

It is not my aim here, nor would it be within the limits of my capacity, to deal with all these *ṛtu* descriptions, which are moreover not limited to Sanskrit texts, but also appear in Pāli and in various Prākrits. To my knowledge, there exist two more general and comprehensive studies on the seasons, both concerned with Sanskrit literature, namely L. Renou's 'Un théme littéraire en sanskrit : les saisons' and V. Raghavan's *Ṛtu in Sanskrit Literature*.[1] L. Renou's work is a simple article, and thus by necessity enumerative and descriptive in nature. V. Raghavan's study is more comprehensive and voluminous, and he dwells more in details on various season descriptions.

As the title of this book shows, we shall deal here only with the season descriptions of *Mahākāvya* literature. But within this genre, a selection had to be made again, for *Mahākāvyas*

1. Renou, Louis : Un theme litteraire en sanskrit : les saisons', in *Sanskrit et culture : l'apport de l'Inde a la civilisation humaine*, Paris, 1950.
Raghavan, V. : *Ṛtu in Sanskrit Literature*, Delhi, 1972.

are extremely numerous, their production extending up to nearly contemporary times, and they are not only composed in Sanskrit but in various Prākrits as well.[2] That is why we have chosen to study only those works which the tradition considers as the six principal *Mahākāvyas* namely Kālidāsa's Kumārasaṁbhava and Raghuvaṁśa, Bhaṭṭi's Bhaṭṭikāvya or Rāvaṇavadha, Bhāravi's Kirātārjunīya, Māgha's Śiśupālavadha and Śrīharṣa's Naiṣadhacarita or Naiṣadhīyacarita.[3]

These works are of course very well-known, but in spite of this we shall briefly say a few words about their authors and contents. The Kumārasaṁbhava and Raghuvaṁśa were both written by Kālidāsa, who probably lived in Ujjain during the fifth century A.D., and they are both mainly based on Purāṇic material. The Kumārasaṁbhava is usually considered to have been written first, whereas the Raghuvaṁśa passes for Kālidāsa's last work. The Kumārasaṁbhava is composed in 8 *sargas*, which is rather short for *Mahākāvya*, and it tells the well-known love-story of Śiva and Pārvatī. As for the Raghuvaṁśa, it tells in 19 *sargas* the story of Raghu's dynasty, starting with king Dilīpa, Raghu's father and ending with Agnivarṇa.

The date of Bhaṭṭi, the author of the Bhaṭṭikāvya, is quite uncertain, but he seems to have lived in Valabhī, between the beginning of the sixth and the middle of the seventh centuries A.D. His only known work is the Bhaṭṭikāvya or Rāvaṇavadha, which retells in 22 *sargas* the story of Rāma based on the Rāmāyaṇa, starting with Viṣṇu's descent or *Avatāra*, and ending with Rāma's and Sītā's return to Ayodhyā. The aim of the Bhaṭṭikāvya is not only to tell the story of Rāma, but also at the same time to illustrate certain grammatical and stylistic rules. Thus, this work is actually a *śāstra-kāvya*.[4]

2. See Lienhard, Siegfried : 'A history of classical poetry Sanskrit—Pali—Prakrit, in *A History of Indian Literature*, Vol. 3, Wiesbaden 1984, p. 196ff.

3. Sometimes, the Bhaṭṭikāvya is not included in this list, and sometimes the Meghadūta figures in it. But the latter work should rather be considered as a long lyrical poem than as a *Mahākāvya*.

4. A *śāstra-kāvya* is a poetic text whose subject-matter is taken from the epics or from the Purāṇas, but which has at the same time a didactic aim, mostly taken from the field of grammar or poetics.

Bhāravi must have lived at approximately the same date, or somewhat later than Bhaṭṭi, in the course of the sixth century. According to the tradition, he lived in South India at the court of Kāñcīpuram. His only known work is the Kirātārjunīya, which retells in 18 *sargas* the Mahābhārata episode of the fight between Arjuna and Śiva in the disguise of a Kirāta.

Māgha was probably from North India, and his dates are as usual uncertain. But it is sure that he lived after Bhāravi, probably during the seventh or eighth centuries A.D. The *Śiśupālavadha*, which seems to be his only work, is composed in 20 *sargas* and tells the Mahābhārata story of Kṛṣṇa's slaying of Śiśupāla, the Cedi king.

From the ninth century onwards, *Mahākāvyas* proliferate. Śrīharṣa is the last great figure to emerge from this multitude of authors. Śrīharṣa, who should not be confused with king Harṣa, the author of three well-known dramas, seems to have lived at the court of Kānyakubja (Kanauj) during the second part of the twelfth century A.D., but the numerous Bengalisms of his work show that he was probably originally from Bengal. He is also considered to be the author of the Khaṇḍanakhaṇḍakhādya, a polemical philosophical work. His *Mahākāvya*, the Naiṣadhacarita, tells in 22 *sargas* the well-known Mahābhārata story of Nala and Damayantī, but only up to the point of their marriage.

Apart from these six works, we shall also deal with the Rāmāyaṇa season descriptions. Of course, the Rāmāyaṇa is not a *Mahākāvya*, but one of the two great epics. But at the same time, it is traditionally considered as the *ādi-kāvya*, or first poetic work, and it had a considerable influence on later poems. This is certainly the case as far as its season descriptions are concerned.

The season descriptions appear in the following passages of the seven above-mentioned works :

Rāmāyaṇa : winter (III, 15)
spring (IV, 1)
the rainy season (II, 57, 10-14 & IV, 27)
autumn (IV, 29)

Kumārasaṁbhava : spring (III, 23-40)

Raghuvaṁśa : autumn (IV, 14-24)

	spring (IX, 24-48)
	summer (XVI, 43-53)
	cycle of seasons (XIX, 37-47)
Bhaṭṭikāvya :	autumn (II, 1-20)
	spring (VI, 73-86)
	the rainy season (VII, 1-13)
	autumn (VII, 14-17)
Kirātārjunīya :	autumn (*sarga* IV)
	cycle of seasons (X, 18-38)
Śiśupālavadha :	cycle of seasons (sarga VI)
Naiṣadhacarita :	all the seasons (I, 76-106)

From now on, we shall designate these seven works by the following abbreviations, taken from the Monier-Williams dictionary : Rāmāyaṇa=R; Kumārasaṁbhava=Kum; Raghuvaṁśa=Ragh.; Bhaṭṭikāvya=Bhaṭṭ.; Kirātārjunīya=Kir.; Śiśupālavadha=Śiś.; Naiṣadhacarita=Naiṣ.; the Ṛtusaṁhāra, to which we shall by necessity refer often, will be abbreviated as Ṛtus.

In the first part of our work, we shall deal with certain topics which will help us to understand the nature of these season descriptions, such as the number of Indian seasons and their names, the history and origin of this theme and what the *ālaṁkārikas* have to say on it.

In the second part, we shall deal with the season descriptions themselves, describing them from a formal point of view and also underlining some of their general characteristics.

The third part will be dedicated to the thematic analysis of these passages.

Thus, by studying the season descriptions in the abovementioned works, we hope to be able to trace the development of this topic in the course of the centuries, in the context of one and the same genre, the *Mahākāvyas*, and of their model, the Rāmāyaṇa.

In this book, unless mentioned otherwise, all the translations are our own.

Part I

CHAPTER I

THE NUMBER OF INDIAN SEASONS AND THEIR NAMES

The most ancient layer of Vedic literature reflects a division of the year into three seasons[1] : summer, the rains and winter. Thus in RV I, 164, 2 and I, 164, 48, the year is likened to a wheel and the seasons to the three navel—like holes in the centre of that wheel (*tri-nābhi—*, *trīṇi nabhyāni*). The beginning of each of these three main periods of the year was marked by the *cāturmāsya* sacrifices marking the beginning of a period of four months.

The later Ṛg-vedic *saṁhitās* already speak of five seasons : spring, summer, the rains, autumn and winter : *vasanta*, *gharma*, *prāvṛṣ*, *śarat* and *hemanta*. *Śiśira* was not yet counted as a separate season. But it was mentioned along with *hemanta* in a compound *hemanta-śiśira*, to designate winter.[2] According to H. Zimmer, the introduction of autumn as a season may have been due to the change from a pastoral activity to an agricultural one : autumn, the season of the harvest, is an important time for a society of agriculturers.[3] Still according to the same

1. For this discussion on the number of seasons, see Raghavan, V. : *Ṛtu in Sanskrit Literature*, Delhi, 1972, pp. 2-3, and additional note 1), as well as Zimmer, Heinrich : *Altindisches Leben*. Berlin, 1879; re-ed. 1973, Hildesheim-New Work, pp. 371-374.
2. E.g. in Yajur Veda, I, 6, 2, 3 and IV, 3, 3, 2.
3. see Zimmer, H. : *op. cit.*, p. 372.

author, *vasanta*, spring, must have been the last season to appear, for its name figures only twice in the RV, and that too in the tenth *maṇḍala*, which is considered to be a later one (X, 90, 6 and X, 161, 4).[4]

Finally, six seasons are recognized in the Yajur Veda and in the Brāhmaṇas, including *śiśira* : *ṣaḍ vā ṛtavaḥ saṁvatsare* (Taittirīya Saṁhitā V, 4, 2, 2). According to Zimmer, the sixth season, *śiśira*, was introduced in order to have a regular repartition of two months per season.[5] This is of course a somewhat artificial division. But the natural reality is sometimes reflected in the texts : thus the rains are referred to as *catvāro vārṣikā māsāḥ* (R. IV, 29, 32) : the four months of the rains, and not two. Inversely, *śiśira* is called *śiśira-māsa* (Śiś. VI, 65) : the month of *śiśira*, a singular and not a dual, and similarly spring bears the name of *puṣpa-māsa* (e.g., R. IV, 1, 19) : the month of flowers, again singular.

Among modern authors, we find different opinions concerning the varying number of seasons in different Vedic passages. According to Zimmer,[6] the shift from three to five seasons was due to the climatic changes that the Aryans met with while penetrating further into the south-east of India. But what Raghavan remarks seems more probable : "In one and the same Vedic text, it is quite common to find the Ṛtus spoken of as five in some context and as six in others; when they are counted as five, Hemanta and Śiśira are clubbed together. The real basis of giving 5 or 6 as the number is the idea on hand to reinforce which the Ṛtus are brought in as *arthavāda*; if the thing dealt with is 5 in number, the text would say *pañca vā ṛtavaḥ* but if the thing is 6 in number it would say *ṣaḍ vā ṛtavaḥ*."

"A similar exigency is responsible when some other Vedic text wants to emphasise a thing which is primarily threefold and says that the real Ṛtus are only three, *Grīṣma*, *Varṣā* and *Hemanta*."[7]

About the division into six seasons, Renou remarks : "Non qu'il y ait nulle part en Inde six saisons tranchées. Mais ces six

4. see Zimmer, H, : *op. cit.*, pp. 372-3.
5. see Zimmer, H. : *op. cit.*, p. 373.
6. see Zimmer, H. : *op. cit.*, p. 373.
7. Raghavan, V. : *op. cit.*, additional note 1, p. 169.

fragmentent une division premiere en trois." (Not that there are anywhere in India six well-defined seasons. But these six fragment a first division into three.)[8] And this is indeed the idea which is expressed for instance in the Jaiminīya Brāhmaṇa (III, 1), in which it is said that *vasanta*, *śarat* and *śiśira* are but secondarily derived from *grīṣma*, *varṣāḥ* and *hemanta* respectively.

In classical times, the most usual number of seasons is six,[9] and this is also what we find in our texts.[10] Thus the Kir. and Śiś. cycles both describe six seasons, and this was already the case of the Ṛtus. before them. Kālidāsa's position is somewhat more delicate to define : in his Ragh. cycle, he dedicates two verses to each season, but only one to *hemanta* and one to *śiśira*, grouping these two seasons together, which evokes the compounded *hemanta-śiśira* season of certain Vedic passages.

The term *ṛtu* (season) derives from the same Indo-European root *ar— as its twin *ṛta*.[11] *Ṛtu* has for its meanings : any settled point of time, fixed time; time appointed for any action (esp. sacrifices), right or fit time; an epoch, period (esp. a division or part of the year), and hence, *season*.[12] *Ṛta*, to which Pokorny ascribes the primary meanings of "adapted", "suitable", is translated by J. Gonda as "cosmic order, law, truth, reality."[13]

About the relation between *ṛtu* and *ṛta*, Raghavan remarks : "From the order of Nature and regularity with which things in Nature move and progress, the idea of moral order and truth grew from the word Ṛta. Ṛtu and Ṛta go together as two aspects of action or movement of the same root 'Ṛ' 'to go' ...

8. Renou, Louis : *op. cit.*, p. 145 (footnote).

9. We find of course still different numbers mentioned. For instance seven, the seventh season representing the intercalary month, or twelve, the seasons thus corresponding to the months, or even thirteen or twenty four.

10. Of course, this can be categorically affirmed only in the case of those texts which contain a cycle of seasons.

11. see Pokorny, Julius : *Indogermanisches etymologisches Wörterbuch*, Bern, 1959, p. 56.

12. see Sir Monier-Williams, Monier, *A Sanskrit-English Dictionary*, Oxford 1979 (9th ed,), p. 224, under *ṛtu*.

13. see Gonda, Jan : "Vedic Literature" in *A History of Indian Literature*, vol. I, Wiesbaden, 1975, p. 97.

While Ṛta was the abstract aspect, Ṛtu was the active aspect. It is from these ideas that Ṛtu came to mean the form in which Nature expressed itself in an orderly sequence in particular, specific and patent forms, in short, the Seasons".[14]

The seasons themselves bear the following names, which appear already in the Vedas : *vasanta* (spring), *grīṣma* or *gharma* (summer), *varṣāḥ* or *prāvṛṣ* (the rains), *śarat* (autumn), *hemanta* (winter) and *śiśira* (the cool season).

Vasanta, m : spring. This term is of Indo-European origin, deriving from the form *ues-en-to- of the root *ues-ṛ-, from which derives also for instance Latin *ver* (spring). Moreover, *vasanta* is probably apparented with the Sanskrit root VAS-, to shine. Thus, *vasanta* is the "shining season".[15]

Grīṣma, m : summer. The origin of this word is uncertain. It might come from *grī- (strong, violent) and *sma- (from samā, the year, the season). Thus, summer would be the violent season, a probable allusion to its violent heat.[16]

Gharma, m : summer. This term comes from the Indo-European root *guher-, meaning "hot", "warm".[17]

Varṣāḥ, f. plur. or *prā-vṛṣ* f : the rainy season. These two terms belong to the same family as the Sanskrit root VṚṢ' to rain, which derives from the Indo-European root *uer-s- (rain), an enlargement of the root *ūr-, *auer-.[18]

Śarat, f : autumn. This term seems to derive from the same Indo-European root *kel- as *śiśira*.

14. Raghavan, V, : *op. cit.*, p. 1.

15. see Pokorny, J. : *op. cit.*, p. 1174.

16. see Mayrhofer, Manfred : *Kurzgefasstes etymologisches Wörterbuch des Altindischen* Heidelberg, 1956, p. 354.

17. see Pokorny, J. : *op. cit.*, p. 493.

18. see Pokorny, J. : *op. cit.*, p. 81.

This root has two different and even opposed meanings : (1) cold, to freeze, (2) hot, the link between both being probably the meaning of "burning". *Śarat* is supposed to come from the second meaning, that of "hot", thus belonging to the same family as for instance Latin *calidus* (hot) or *calor* (heat).[19] This seems to be somewhat surprising, for autumn, even in India, is not really a hot season.

Hemanta, m : winter. *Hemanta* derives from the same Indo-European root *ghei-, meaning "winter", "snow" as for instance Latin *hiems* (winter).[20]

Śiśira, m : the cool season. Derives from the same Indo-European root *kel- as *śarat*, but from its first meaning of "cold", "to freeze".[21]

To each one of these six seasons, two months are attributed. Thus, to *vasanta* correspond the months of Madhu (March-April) and Mādhava (April-May). To *grīṣma* the months of Śukra (May-June) and Śuci (June-July). To *varṣāḥ* the months of Nabhas (July-August) and Nabhasya (August-September). To *śarat* the months of Iṣa (September-October) and Ūrja (October-November). To *hemanta* the months of Sahas (November-December) and Sahasya (December-January), and finally to *śiśira*, the months of Tapas (January-February) and Tapasya (February-March).

As we see, most of these names allude to the most prominent characteristics of each season. Madhu and Mādhava refer to the sweetness of spring ; Śukra and Śuci to the burning light of summer ; Nabhas and Nabhasya to the clouds of the monsoon ; Iṣa and Ūrja to the sap, fertility and vigour of autumn ; Sahas and Sahasya probably to strength of the cold in winter. Tapas and Tapasya, with their meaning of "heat", seem to be

19. see Pokorny, J. : *op. cit.*, p. 551.
20. see Pokorny, J. : *op. cit.*, p. 425.
21. see Pokorny, J. : *op. cit.*, p. 551.

more difficult to explain for *śiśira*, the "cool season". The Śatapathabrāhmaṇa,[22] which gives the list of the names of the months, explains these two terms in the following way : *yad etayor baliṣṭhaṁ syāyati teno haitaṁ tapaś ca tayasyaś ca* (because it freezes very strongly during these two months, for this reason ,they are called Tapas and Tapasya), which does not seem to throw much light on the problem. Raghavan explains these terms in the following way "and *Tapa* and *Tapasya* (relate) perhas to the way earth is scorched up by the withering of vegetation and barren-ness."[23]

The above-listed set of names of the seasons can be found for instance in the Taittirīya Saṁhitā (I, 4, 14) or in the Śatapathabrāhmaṇa (IV, 3, 1, 14-19). According to Raghavan,[24] these names are more ancient than the other well-established names of the months, which derive from the name of the constellation in which their full moon is placed. Thus we have the months of Caitra and Vaiśākha for spring, Jyaiṣṭha and Āṣāḍha for summer, Śrāvaṇa and Proṣṭhapāda for the monsoon, Āśvina and Kārttika for autumn, Mārgaśīrṣa and Pauṣa for winter and Māgha and Phālguna for *śiśira*. In *Mahākāvya* literature, both sets of names are used to designate the months.

Apart from the above-listed names, the seasons themselves have a number of other names. We shall now enumerate all the names by which the seasons are designated in the texts we are studying here, starting with the most frequently used ones.[25]

Thus spring bears the following names :

madhu, m : "sweet, pleasant". This name appears in the following passages : Kum. III, 24, 27, 30 and 34. Ragh. IX, 24, 26, 30, 32 and 38. Kir. X, 36. Śiś. VI, 15, 17, 20, 68 and 69. Naiṣ. I, 105.

22. in IV, 3, 1, 19.
23. Raghavan, V. : *op. cit.*, p. 5,
24. see Raghavan, V. : *op. cit.*, p. 4.
25. We are only listing here the names given to the seasons which appear in the six *Mahākāvyas* which form the object of our study, and in the R. It goes without saying that the seasons may have other names too.

This is by far the most common name of spring, appearing even more frequently than *vasanta* itself. It is moreover the name of the first spring-month (Caitra) before being that of spring itself. On the one hand, it is propably for reasons of metrics that this term is used so frequently, being a short word of only two short syllables, which can be easily inserted in the most diverse meters. On the other hand, and this reason is certainly even more weighty, the term *madhu* allows a host of associations of ideas and even puns, due to its other meanings : as an adjective, it means 'sweet', 'pleasant' "delicious". As a noun, it designates "honey", "liquor" or "wine". It can also be found in compound words designating the bees, such as *madhu-lih*, *-leha*, or *-lehin* (honey-licker) or *madhu-kara* (honey-maker). All these meanings of *madhu* are of course in perfect harmony with the atmosphere of spring, a sweet and pleasant season in which honey, bees and wine abound.

vasanta, m : spring. This is the "real" name of spring, and can be found in the following passages : R. IV, 1 12. Kum. III, 29. Kir. X, 31. Śiś. VI, 67.

surabhi, m : "perfumed". Spring probably deserves this appellation due to the perfume of its flowers. This term allows of course puns on *surabhi* "perfumed" and *surabhi* "spring". It appears in the following passages : R. IV, 1, 6. Kir. X, 30. Śiś. VI, 2.

puṣpamāsa, m : "the month of flowers". This name refers to the most characteristic aspect of

		spring, its abundant flowers. It can be found in R. IV, 1, 19 and 42. Kir. X, 35.
mādhava, m	:	This is also the name of the second month of spring, Vaiśākha. It is found in R. IV, 1, 4, and Kum. III, 23.
śiśira-atyaya, m	:	"the end of *śiśira*" (R. IV, 1, 20)
hima-anta, m	:	"the end of winter" (R. IV, 1, 42)
hima-vyapāya, m	:	"the end of winter" (Kum. III, 33)
śiśira-apagama, m	:	"the departure of *śiśira*" (Ragh. IX, 27)
apa-tuṣāra-tā, f	:	"coldlessness" (Ragh. IX, 39)

All these last five designations of spring, which occur only once each, designate spring by referring to the preceeding season. Except the last one, *apa-tuṣāra-tā*, which is also the only feminine term to designate this season, they are all based on the same scheme : name of winter, plus a name signifying "end" or "departure", with variations in the vocabulary. As we can see, the texts indifferently mention winter or *śiśira* as the season which immediately preceeds spring. As the context shows in each case, these terms do not designate the actual "end" of winter, or the passage from winter to spring, as we might think, but the fully developed spring-season.

Summer bears the following names :

gharma, m	:	"heat" (R. IV, 27, 7 and Ragh. XVI, 43)
śuci, m	:	"the shining one". This is also the name of the second month of summer, Āṣāḍha. It can be found in the following passages: Śiś. VI, 22 and 71.
grīṣma, m	:	"summer" (Ragh. XIX, 45)
ā-tapa, m	:	"heat" (Ragh. XVI, 49)
nidāgha-avadhi, m	:	"the time of heat" (Ragh. XVI, 52)
nidāgha-kāla, m	:	"the time of heat" (Kir. X, 36)
madhu-nirgama, m	:	"the departure of spring" (Ragh. XIX, 46).
vasanta-atyaya, m	;	"the departure of spring" (Ragh XVI, 50)

Most of the names of summer have for meaning "heat", being derived from roots such as TAP, GHṚ or DAH, meaning "to burn" or ŚUC, meaning "to shine, to burn". The expression "departure of spring", parallel to the expression "departure of winter" to designate spring, is also found twice. Most of the names of summer are found in the Ragh., for it is the only one among our texts which dedicates a description to this season.

The terms designating the rainy season are the following :

prā-vṛṣ, f : "the rains" (R. II, 57, 10. Ragh. XIX, 37. Bhaṭṭ. VII, 13)

varṣāḥ, f. plur. : "the rains" (R. IV 27, 14. Bhaṭṭ. VII, 1).

varṣa-rātra, m : "the night of the rains" (R. IV, 29, 1)

varṣuka-kāla, m : "the rainy season" (Bhaṭṭ. VII, 18)

catvāro vārṣikā māsāḥ, m. plur. : "the four rainy months" (R. IV, 29, 32)

jala-āgama, m : "the approach of the water" (R. IV, 27, 2)

jala-da-kāla, m : "the time of the water-givers" (i.e.: of the clouds) Śiś. VI, 41)

ghana-āgama, m : "the approach of the clouds" (Kir. IV, 22)

ghana-samaya, m : "the season of clouds" (Kir. X, 24)

kadamba-anila, m : "(the season wherein blows) the wind (perfumed by) *kadambas*" (Kir. IV, 24)

Prā-vṛṣ and *varṣāḥ* are the usual names of the monsoon. *Varṣuka-kāla* and *catvāro vārṣikā māsāḥ* are periphrastic expressions to designate this season. *Varṣa-rātra* signifies in fact "night of the rains", an allusion to the darkness of the cloudy monsoon-sky, but this metaphorical meaning has faded and it simply means "rainy season". The terms *jalāgama*, *jaladakāla*, *ghanāgama* and *ghanasamaya* are also metaphors referring to the most prominent characteristics of the monsoon, its rain and clouds, but they are immediately comprehensible.

Kadambānila on the other hand designates the rainy season

only in this Kir. verse. Otherwise, it simply means "wind (perfumed by) *kadambas*", an can also be found in this sense in other passages of the Kir.

As for autumn, it has only one basic name :

śarat, f : (R. III, 15, 1; IV, 27, 46; IV, 29, 12 and 28. Ragh. IV, 14 and 24. Bhaṭṭ. II, 1. Kir. IV, 2; 9; 12; 20 (twice); 21; X, 24. Śiś. VI, 42; 44; 51; 52 and 54.

Otherwise, we find two very indirect ways of designating this season in the Śiś., but they are poetic expressions which are peculiar to Māgha:

kāle...anīcakāśe (loc.) : "the time when the *kāśa*-grass is high" (VI, 74)

samayena... rasamāna-sārasena (I) : "the season when the *sārasa*-birds cry" (VI, 75)

Winter bears the following names :

hima, m : "cold, frost, the cold season, winter" (Kir. X, 30. Śiś. VI, 58 and 59)

hemanta, m : "winter" (R. III, 15, 1)

hima-ṛtu, m : "the season of the cold" (Sis. VI, 61)

tusāra-kāla, m : "the time of the snow" (Kir. X, 21)

As we see, all the terms designating winter are composed of words meaning "cold", "frost" or "snow".

As for the last season, *śiśira*, the "cool season", it is always called *śiśira*, certainly in order to distinguish it clearly from *hemanta*. We find this term in the following passages: Ragh. XIX, 42. Kir. X, 30. Śiś. VI, 62. We also find *śiśira-māsa*, m: the month of *śiśira*, in Śiś. VI, 65.

Thus we see that most of the seasons bear an impressive number of names.[26] This is undoubtedly due to the amazing

26. The notable exceptions are *śiśira* and autumn. We can easily understand why *śiśira* has only one name, for any metaphorical name alluding to its cold could be mistaken for *hemanta*. The case of autumn on the other hand is more mysterious, and it seems unexplainable why this season, which is often described and has moreover many typical characteristics, bears only one name (with the exception of Māgha's own two invented names for it).

richness of the Sanskrit language, as well as to the freedom it allows of coining compound nouns. Apart from their "real" names, the seasons have a host of other, often metaphorical names, but whose metaphorical sense must have been largely lost. Thus they can be considered as dead metaphors. The term *varṣa-rātra*, the "night of the rains", which we discussed above, is a case in point. Moreover, the poets themselves did not hesitate to invent new names for the seasons, whenever the necessity arose. Most remarkable in this respect are Bhāravi's *kadambānila* (IV, 24) to designate the monsoon, and Māgha's *kāle ...anīcakāśe* (VI, 74) and *samayena ...rasamānasārasena* (VI, 75) to designate autumn. These last two expressions must have been invented by the poet due to the compulsion of respecting the *yamaka* which consists in having identical second and fourth *padas* in these verses.

CHAPTER II

A SHORT HISTOY OF THE THEME OF THE SEASONS

In this section, we shall attempt to trace the origins of the theme of season descriptions as they appear in *Mahākāvyas*. *Mahākāvyas* are a composite genre, and we shall have to investigate the early history of this genre in order to obtain information about the probable origin of the motif which concerns us here. Before doing so, we shall turn to the oldest layer of Indian literature, the Veda, and see what it has to offer on the seasons.

At a first glance, it seems that we can indeed find in the Ṛg-Veda passages which can be called "season descriptions". But we cannot fail to notice immediately the differences which exist between the Vedic seasons descriptions and those which occur later in *kāvya* literature. The fundamental difference resides in the fact that in *kāvya* literature, the seasons are a poetic motif by themselves: when a poet describes a season, or all the seasons, he does not have any other extraneous aim than this description. In the Veda, on the other hand, the context is always religious, and whatever season descriptions may occur, they are always inscribed in, and subordinated to, the religious thought, which is absolutely lacking in *kāvya* season descriptions.

To illustrate this, the famous hymn to Parjanya (RV. V, 83) is a perfect example. Parjanya, a form of Indra, is the cloud dispensing water, fertility and life, and this hymn describes the onslaught of the monsoon :

achā vada tavaṣaṁ gīrbhir ābhiḥ stuhi parjanyaṁ namasā vivāsa /
kanikradad vṛṣabho jīradānū reto dadhāti oṣadhīṣu garbham //1/

vi vṛkṣān hanti uta hanti rakṣaso viśvaṁ bibhāya bhuvanaṁ mahāvadhāt /
utānāgā īṣate vṛṣṇyāvato yat parjanyaḥ stanayan hanti duṣkṛtaḥ //2//

rathīva kaśayāśvāṁ abhikṣipann āvir dūtān kṛṇute varṣyāṁ aha /
dūrāt siṁhasya stanathā ud īrate yat parjanyaḥ kṛṇute varṣyaṁ nabhaḥ //3//

pra vātā vānti patayanti vidyuta ud oṣadhīr jihate pinvate svaḥ /
irā viśvasmai bhuvanāya jāyate yat parjanyaḥ pṛthivīṁ retasāvati //4//

yasya vrate pṛthivī nannamīti yasya vrate śaphavaj jarbhurīti /
yasya vrata oṣadhīr viśvarūpāḥ sa naḥ parjanya mahi śarma yaccha //5//

divo no vṛṣṭiṁ maruto rarīdhvaṁ pra pinvata vṛṣṇo aśvasya dhārāḥ /
arvāṅ etena stanayitnunehi apo niṣiñcann asuraḥ pitā naḥ //6//

abhi kranda stanaya garbham ā dhā udanvatā pari dīyā rathena /
dṛtiṁ su karṣa viṣitaṁ nyañcaṁ samā bhavantu udvato nipādāḥ //7//

mahāntaṁ kośam ud acā ni ṣiñca syandantāṁ kulyā viṣitāḥ purastāt /
ghṛtena dyāvāpṛthivī vi undhi suprapāṇaṁ bhavatu aghnyābhyaḥ //8//

yat parjanya kanikradat stanayan haṁsi duṣkṛtaḥ /
pratīdaṁ viśvaṁ modate yat kiṁ ca pṛthivyām adhi //9//

avarṣīr varṣam ud u ṣū gṛbhāya akar dhanvāni atyetavā u /
ajījana oṣadhīr bhojanāya kam uta prajābhyo avido manīṣām //13//

Invoke the mighty one with these songs; praise Parjanya;

seek to win him with obeisance. Bellowing, the bull of quickening gifts places seed in the plants as germ.(1)

He shatters the trees and he smites the demons: the whole world fears him of the mighty weapon. Even the sinless man flees before the mighty one, when Parjanya thundering smites the evil-doers.(2)

Like a charioteer lashing his horses with a whip he makes manifest his messengers of rain. From afar arise the thunders of the lion, when Parjanya makes rainy the sky.(3)

The winds blow forth, the lightnings fall; the plants shoot up; heaven overflows. Nurture is born for the whole world when Parjanya quickens the earth with seed.(4)

In whose ordinance the earth bends low; in whose ordinance hoofed animals leap about; in whose ordinance plants are omniform, as such, O Parjanya, bestow mighty shelter on us.(5)

Give us, O Maruts, the rain of heaven; pour forth the streams of your stallion. Hither with this thunder come, pouring down the waters as the divine spirit our father.(6)

Bellow towards us; thunder; deposit the germ; fly around with thy water-bearing car. Draw well thy water-skin unfastened downward: let the heights and valleys be level.(7)

Draw up the great bucket, pour it down; let the streams released flow forward. Drench heaven and earth with ghee; let there be a good drinking place for the cows. (8)

When, O Parjanya, bellowing aloud, thundering, thou smitest the evil doers, this whole world exults, whatever is upon the earth.(9)

Thou hast shed rain: now wholly cease; thou hast made the deserts passable again. Thou hast made the plants to grow for the sake of food; and thou hast found a hymn of praise from (thy) creatures.(10)[1]

As we see, this hymn is basically an invocation and a prayer to Parjanya. The first, extra-literary aim of the poet here is to

1. Translation according to Macdonell, A.A. : *A Vedic Reader for Students*, Oxford University Press, 1917, p. 104 ff.

make Parjanya pour down his fertilizing rain, so as to obtain abundant crops, an aspect of primary importance. This power of the monsoon, here personified as Parjanya, to make the plants grow, is constantly stressed all along the passage: 'bellowing, the bull of quickening gifts places seed in the plants as germ" (1); "the plants shoot up...nurture is born for the whole world" (4); "deposit the germ" (7); "thou hast made the plants to grow for the sake of food" (10); Thus, a great stress is given to the fertilizing activity of the rain, which is of course very close to the every-day concerns of the people. This aspect of the monsoon, though not entirely lacking in the *Mahākāvya* rains descriptions, is nevertheless greatly side-tracked there.

Moreover, this hymn presents a very realistic picture of the violence of the monsoon, and the overall tone is resolutely epic: Parjanya is likened to a bellowing bull (1); he shatters the trees and smites the demons: the whole world fears him of the mighty weapon (2). Likewise, the image of Parjanya arriving on his chariot whipping his horses is an image of war, and the clouds roar like lions, ferocious animals par excellence. Moreover, the violence and intense activity of nature in this season is strikingly rendered by the very rapid succession of events in verse 4, and by the pressing repetition of imperatives in verses 6 to 8.[2]

In the monsoon descriptions of *Mahākāvyas*, though they sometimes also contain certain images rendering the violence of this season, as well as in the descriptions of other seasons, nature always appears much tamer and more domesticated, which in those days, it undoubtedly was. The Vedic people were closer to nature and knew it better. Natural phenomena were considered to be divine manifestations, and to avoid their excessive violence, the gods had to be propitiated. This is what happens in the Parjanya hymn: after asking the god to release his rain, the poet asks him to stop: "thou hast shed rain: now wholly cease" (10). Thus evocations of nature as they appear in the Ṛg-

2. See also Lienhard, Siegfried: "A history of classical poetry Sanskrit-Pali-Prakrit" in *A History of Indian Literature*, vol. 3, Wiesbaden, 1984, p. 56.

Veda can always be read at two levels: the descriptive or poetic level, and the religious level which is superimposed on it.[3]

Sometimes, though, certain passages describing a season in the Ṛg-Veda seem to be more purely descriptive, and thus closer to *Mahākāvya* season descriptions. This is the case for example for the frog-hymn (VII, 103) which describes the activity of the frogs at the onset of the monsoon:

saṁvatsaraṁ śaśayānā brāhmaṇā vratacāriṇaḥ /
vācaṁ parjanyajinvitāṁ pra maṇḍūkā avādiṣuḥ //1//

divyā āpo abhi yad enam āyan dṛtiṁ na śuṣkaṁ sarasī śayānam /
gavām aha na māyur vatsinīnāṁ maṇḍūkānāṁ vagnur atrā sam eti //2//

yad īm enāṁ uśato abhy avarṣīt tṛṣyāvataḥ prāvṛṣi āgatāyām /
akhkhalīkṛtyā pitaraṁ na putro anyo anyam upa vadantam eti //3//

anyo anyam anu gṛbhṇāti enor apāṁ prasarge yad amandiṣātām /
maṇḍūko yad abhivṛṣṭaḥ kaniṣkan pṛśniḥ saṁpṛṅkte haritena vācam //4//

yad eṣām anyo anyasya vācam śāktasyeva vadati śikṣamāṇaḥ /
sarvaṁ tad eṣāṁ samṛdheva parva yat suvāco vadathanādhi apsu //5//

gomāyur eko ajamāyur ekaḥ pṛśnir eko harita eka eṣām /
samānaṁ nāma bibhrato virūpāḥ purutrā vācaṁ pipiśur vadantaḥ //6//

brāhmaṇāso atirātre na some saro na pūrṇam abhito vadantaḥ /
saṁvatsarasya tad ahaḥ pari ṣṭha yan maṇḍūkāḥ prāvṛṣīṇaṁ babhūva //7//

...

The frogs having lain for a year, like Brāhmans practising a vow, have uttered forth their voice roused by Parjanya. (1)

3. See Gonda, Jan: "Vedic Literature" in *A History of Indian Literature*, vol. 1, Wiesbaden, 1975, p. 161 ff.

When the heavenly waters came upon him lying like a dry leather-bag in a lake, then the sound of the frogs unites like the lowing of cows accompanied by calves. (2)

When he has rained upon them the eager, the thirsty, the rainy season having come, one with a croak of joy approaches the other while he speaks, as a son (approaches) his father. (3)

One of the two greets the other when they have revelled in the discharge of the waters. When the frog, rained upon, leaps about, the speckled one mingles his voice with (that of) the yellow one. (4)

When one of them repeats the speech of the others, as the learner that of his teacher, all that of them is in unison like a lesson that eloquent ye repeat upon the waters. (5)

One lows like a cow, one bleats like a goat; one is speckled, one of them is yellow. Bearing a common name, they have different colours. In many ways they adorn their voice in speaking. (6)

Like Brahmins at the over-night Soma sacrifice speaking around as it were a full lake, ye celebrate that day of the year which, O Frogs, has begun the rains. (7)...[4]

But even here this appearance of pure descriptiveness is deceptive, for the aim of this hymn is not only the poetic description of one of the characteristics of the monsoon, the croaking frogs, although this passage, which denotes a close observation of nature and contains numerous comparisons, does in no way lack poetic qualities: the frogs are speckled or yellow (4), they low like cows or bleat like goats (6), one speaks with the other like a son with his father (3), or repeats the other's words like a pupil those of his teacher (5). But most importantly, the frogs are compared to brahmins performing *soma* oblations on the *saṁvatsara* day (7). Here, again, this description of the frogs finds its place in a religious context. This hymn to the frogs is a charm to obtain rain, and these animals, just like brahmins, have a role to play in the production of rain. It is thus a hymn of praise and of prayer, for

4. Translation according to Macdonell, A.A. : *op. cit.*, p. 141 ff.

brahmins and frogs to continue their beneficient activities.[5] Thus this passage too has fundamentally a religious aim and cannot be reduced to a poetic description of nature.

These two passages from the Ṛg-Veda, both describing the monsoon, show that there is a wide gulf between such Vedic "season descriptions" and the season descriptions which appear later in *Mahākāvyas*. As S. Lienhard remarks: "As comparison will show us, there is a clear break in tradition between Vedic and classical poetry. The difference between them is so great that any attempt to interpret the Vedic Samhitās (or isolated, particularly poetic parts of them) in the spirit of *kāvya* is doomed in advance to failure".[6] Thus it seems that we must rule out a direct influence and continuation in *Mahākāvya* literature of such Ṛg-Vedic season descriptions, and look elsewhere for the probable origin of this theme.

After the Vedic period, Indian poetry was divided into two main streams: the first, which was the literature of the courts, gave birth to the two great epics, the Mahābhārata and the Rāmāyaṇa. The second, lyrical poetry or *kāvya*, originated probably around 500 BC in the literary circles of towns, and was only later to find a gradual footing at the courts.[7] These compositions consisted of very short poems, mostly of one stanza only (*muktakas*) and they were not written in Sanskrit but in various Prākrits. About the use of Prākrit S. Lienhard remarks: "...it would be an error to deduce from the pre-eminent position enjoyed by Prākrit among these writers that their poetry was particularly popular in character, close to nature or rustic although certain connections with contemporary folk-poetry and now lost folksongs must have existed".[8] This seems to pinpoint with a great deal of probability the origin of our theme. Again, while discussing the *ṣaḍṛtuvarṇana* genre, to which the Ṛtus. belongs, S. Lienhard writes: "The latter (i.e.: season descriptions) which often have an erotic strain, present us with a wealth of subtle descriptions of nature and may

5. See Gonda, J. ; *op. cit.*, p. 143.
6. Lienhard, S. : *op. cit.*, p. 57.
7. See Lienhard, S. : *op. cit.*, pp. 57 and 62.
8. Lienhard, S. : *op. cit.*, p. 62.

contain elements taken over from Indian folksongs."[9] And indeed, the seasons are intimately connected with every-day life in the villages, and it seems highly plausible that the season descriptions were originally folksongs describing the activities of the people at various times of the year, and were maybe more intimately connected with the festivals taking place during each season.[10]

The most ancient layer of *kāvya* literature is now lost to us, its extremely short form having probably accelerated its disparition. But, somewhat surprisingly, we find traces of these early *muktakas* in the Buddhist canon, especially in the Thera- and Therīgāthās, the Songs of the monks and of the nuns. These are collections of stanzas composed by monks and nuns, disciples of the Buddha, probably around 500 to 100 BC.[11] Most of these verses are of course religious in content and speak of the life of renunciation adopted by these hermits, but quite a few of them show that their author had a good knowledge of profane poetry, and can in many respects be compared to *kāvya* verses. Among these, we find verses dedicated to the monsoon, the time of the year when the monks gave up their peregrinations and were therefore free, if so inclined, to dedicate some time to the writing of poetry. Here are two examples from the Theragāthā:

nīlā sugīvā sikhino morā kāraṁviyaṁ abhinandanti /
te sītavātakalitā suttaṁ jhāyaṁ nibodhenti //22// (Cittaka)

Blue, with beautiful necks, the crested peacocks call in Kāraviṁī; urged on by the cool breeze they awaken the sleeper to meditation.[12]

9. Lienhard, S. : *op. cit.*, p. 107.

10. Thus, the Bhaṭṭ. and Kir. autumn descriptions take place in a rural setting and describe the happy life of the cowherds. The Ragh. spring description takes place during the festival of this season.

11. See Warder, A.K. : *Indian Kāvya Literature*, Delhi 1974, para. 538 (vol. 2).

12. Translation according to Norman, K.R. : *The Elder's Verses I, Theragāthā*, London 1961, p. 3.

nīlabbhavaṇṇā rucirā sītavārī sucindharā /
indagopakasañchannā te selā ramayanti maṁ //13//
(Vanavaccha)

These rocks delight me, the colour of the blue clouds, beautiful, with cool waters and pure streams, covered with Indagopaka-mites.[13]

These two verses contain many themes which are typical of *kāvya* monsoon descriptions: the peacocks, the cool breeze, the blue clouds and the Indragopa-insects. Therefore, season descriptions must already have been firmly implanted in *kāvya* literature proper, at the date of the above-quoted verses, since their influence is felt even in religious writings which do not belongs to the *kāvya* genre but to the *āgamas.*

After its first appearance in the *muktaka* genre, the motif of the seasons must have evolved into short lyrical poems of several stanzas. Among such season descriptions, it seems that we must distinguish between two different genres: descriptions of an isolated season on the one hnnd, and cycles of seasons on the other. Descriptions of single seasons seem to occur only in *Mahākāvyas,* and no isolated description of this kind has come down to us.[14] This genre might well be the older of the two, for not only does it appear less sophisticated than the cycle genre, but it is also the first to appear in bigger poems: the R., Aśvaghoṣa's two *Mahākāvyas,* and indeed also the Kum. contain only descriptions of isolated seasons. It is only from the Ragh. onwards that we find cycles of seasons incorporated in *Mahākāvyas.*

The cycles of seasons are of course a genre of their own right and appear also as independent poems and not only in *Mahākāvyas.* The most famous and also the oldest poem of this kind is of course the Ṛtus. Although it is often attributed to Kālidāsa[15], it is probable that it was composed sometime between

13. Translation according to Norman, K.R. : *op. cit.*, p. 2.

14. See Lienhard, S. : *op. cit.*, p. 107.

15. An ardent defender of the theory that the Ṛtus. was composed by Kālidāsa is for instance V. Raghavan in his work *Ṛtu in Sanskrit Literature*, Delhi 1972, p. 38 ff.

Aśvaghoṣa's and Kālidāsa's time, that is, between the first and the fifth centuries A.D.[16] It is the oldest extant poem of its kind, but its quality is so high that it must have had now lost predecessors.[17] After the Ṛtus., several similar *ṣaḍṛtuvarṇanas* were composed.[18]

Still the question remains unanswered, how these season descriptions, which appear first as *muktakas*, and then as short lyrical poems, found their entrance in the *Mahākāvya* genre. As we mentioned at the beginning of this chapter, *Mahākāvya* are composite genre, resulting from a blending of the epic and of the lyrical, that is *kāvya*, traditions. From the point of view of their subject-matter as well as of their length, though they are of course much shorter than either the Mahābhārata or the R., the *Mahākāvyas* derive from the epics. But the influence of *kāvya* literature is felt in the minute elaboration of details, the care devoted to poetic expression, and in the numerous disgressions or deviations from the plot, which gain increasing imporlance in *Mahākāvyas* as we advance in time. Older *Mahākāvyas*, like for instance Aśvaghoṣa's, still carry the action forward relatively fast, whereas later ones, for which the Naiṣ. is the perfect example, seem to consist merely of a string of various digressions on all sorts of topics, which tend to drown the story to the utmost.

Thus, lyrical descriptions such as the seasons[19] found their way from short lyrical poems into the Mahākāvya genre. In earlier *Mahākāvyas*, this kind of descriptions was probably meant to function as an ornament on the basically epic body of the text, which might be one of the reasons why such descriptions appear very often to be easily detachable from the context, although the skill of the poet may of course greatly contribute to their natural insertion in the story. But their function as ornaments cannot apply to later *Mahākāvyas*, which, as we have

16. See Lienhard, S. : *op. cit.*, p. 108.

17. For instance, we already find a small *ṣaḍṛtuvarṇana* in the Taitt. Āt. I, 3-4.

18. See Lienhard, S. : *op. cit.*, p. 109.

19. The seasons are not the only lyrical theme which passed into Mahākāvyas : this is the case for other typically lyrical themes too (see in the next chapter Daṇḍin's definition of a Mahākāvya).

already mentioned, consist mostly of digressions like season descriptions and other similar themes, and in which there is hardly any epic plot left to be adorned.

The season descriptions must have found their way into *Mahākāvyas* at an early date; for although the Mahābhārata contains little on the seasons,[20] the R. has four major season descriptions. In this respect, we must remember that the R., though it is one of the two great epics, is already greatly influenced by *kāvya* literature. The vastly accepted view nowadays is that the R., although it is traditionally attributed to a single poet, Vālmīki, was in fact composed over many centuries, several layers of accretions being added to its basie core. According to J. Brockington, the season descriptions belong to the second stage of composition of the text, dating approximately from the third century BC.[21] The passages belonging to this stage are strongly influenced by *kāvya* literature. Their language is more elaborate, and a greater attention is dedicated to nature, which is described in a detailed way: most of the plant and animal names date from this stage of composition. Moreover, the tone is generally not epic but lyric, and most meters longer than the *śloka* date from this stage.[22] As we see, this fits very well for the R. season descriptions. Thus these season descriptions as they appear now in the R. may well have been originally independent season descriptions which were later incorporated in the text.

As far as season descriptions are concerned, we may assume that the R. had a great influence on later *Mahākāvyas*, for all the six major *Mahākāvyas* with which we are dealing here contain season descriptions. The R. may well have been a

20. We find a description of the monsoon and of autumn in Āraṇyakaparva 179, and the same two seasons are also described in the Harivaṁśa, 108, 15.

21. Brockington, J. : *Righteous Rāma* : *the Evolution of an Epic*, Delhi 1984, appendix, p. 329. Surprisingly, J. Brockington does not list the spring description among the passages dating from the second stage of composition. This must be an omission, for it does not seem that the spring description differs in any significant way from the other season descriptions.

22. See Brockington, J. : *op. cit.*, chapter II : Composition.

trend-setter in this respect. But the way of dealing with the theme of the seasons was never absolutely systematized in the *Mahākāvya* genre: the poets had the choice between cycles of seasons and descriptions of isolated seasons, and in the latter case they moreover had the choice of the season and the number of isolated season descriptions they wanted to incorporate in their text. And indeed, we see that the poets made ample use of this liberty, for we do not find any two texts among the *Mahākāvyas* which contain the same combination of season descriptions.

Thus, from their humble origins of folksongs, the season descriptions first found their way into the *muktaka* genre of early *kāvya* literature, and from there developed into short lyrical poems, either cycles or now lost descriptions of single seasons, which in turn found their way into the *Mahākāvya* genre. This is at least what we can infer from the sparse material which has come down to us.

CHAPTER III

POETICIANS ON ṚTU

In this section, we shall deal with three poeticians and what they have to say on the seasons: Bharata, Daṇḍin and Rājaśekhara. Interestingly, these three theoreticians deal with *ṛtu* from three different points of view: Bharata mentions the seasons with relation to *rasa*, Daṇḍin with relation to his definition of a *Mahākāvya*, and Rājaśekhara's main contribution on the seasons is with relation to the concept of *kavi-samaya* or poetic convention. We shall here expound their views on the seasons, hoping that they will shed some further light on the nature of these season descriptions.

Bharata

Bharata's Nāṭyaśāstra, which was probably composed around the beginning of our era, is of course basically a work of dramaturgy and not of poetics. But considering the later poeticians' appropriation in their definition of *kāvya* of certain elements of drama such as the *saṁdhis*, the *saṁdhyaṅgas*, the types of heroes, etc..., as well as the enormous influence of Bharata's *rasa*-theory on later poetics, we can safely conclude that the theory of drama functioned as a model for poetics, and that dramas, which are an earlier genre, were the source of inspiration for writing *kāvyas*.

In XXVI, 27-37, Bharata shows how the seasons should be represented in a drama, giving a short season description. But these seem to be purely stage directions, indicating how an actor should represent the seasons by means of *abhinaya* (representation by gestures) and as such do not apply to literary works other than dramas. More important for us is the view put forth by Bharata that the seasons contribute to the production of *rasa*: they are the *vibhāvas* or material causes of *rasa*. In VI, after verse 45, Bharata says: *tatra sambhogas…ṛtu …ādibhir vibhāvair utpadyate*: "the sentiment of love in union arises from causes such as the seasons, etc…". Similarly, in VII, after verse 8, while discussing the *bhāvas* or permanent states of mind whose manifestations are called *rasa*, Bharata remarks: *ratir…bhāvah ṛtu…ādibhiḥ vibhāvaiḥ samutpadyate*: "the *bhāva* of love arises from causes such as the seasons, etc…". In these two instances, Bharata makes use of the general term *vibhāva*, which covers both the *ālambana-vibhāvas* (objects of a given *rasa*) and the ***uddīpana-vibhāvas*** (instigatory causes of a given *rasa*). The seasons belong to the latter category.[1]

Thus we see that at a very early date, season descriptions were used with the specific aim of producing *rasa*. Bharata only mentions the *sambhoga-śṛṅgāra-rasa* or sentiment of love in union. As we shall see in a later chapter, the season descriptions in *Mahākāvyas* indeed mainly evoke this particular rasa, along with its counterpart the *vipralambha-śṛṅgāra-rasa* or sentiment of love in separation, but occasionally they are used to produce other *rasas* too.

Daṇḍin

In Daṇḍin's Kāvyādarśa (The Mirror of Poetry), probably composed in the seventh century AD, we find for the first time the motif of season descriptions specifically mentioned in connection with the *Mahākāvya*-genre.[2] In I, 14-19, Daṇḍin defines the *Mahākāvya*-genre as follows:

sargabando mahākāvyam ucyate tasya lakṣaṇam /
āśīr namaskriyā vastunirdeśo vāpi tanmukham //14//

1. For instance a later dramaturgist-poetician, Bhoja, in his Śṛṅgāra-Prakāśa, includes the seasons among the ***uddīpana-vibhāvas*** (chapter 16).

2. Bhāmaha, who lived at the same time as Daṇḍin, or even somewhat before him, gives a similar definition of *Mahākāvyas* in his Kāvyālaṁkāra, but does not mention the season descriptions.

itihāsakathodbhūtam itarad vā sadāśrayam /
caturvargaphalopetaṁ caturodāttanāyakam //15//

nagarārṇavaśailartucandrārkodayavarṇanaiḥ /
udyānasalilakrīḍāmadhupānaratotsavaiḥ //16//

vipralambhair vivāhaiś ca kumārodayavarṇanaiḥ /
mantradūtaprayāṇājināyakābhyudayair api //17//

alaṁkṛtam asaṁkṣiptaṁ rasabhāvanirantaram /
sargair anativistīrṇaiḥ śravyavṛttaiḥ susaṁdhibhiḥ //18//

sarvatra bhinnavṛttāntair upetaṁ lokarañjakam /
kavyaṁ kalpāntarasthāyi jāyeta sadalaṁkṛti //19//

They call *Mahākāvya* a composition in chapters whose characteristics are (as follows): it starts with a benediction, an homage or with thc mention of the topics. (14)

It originates from the legends of history, or from a different source based on reality. It is endowed with the fruit of the fourfold human aims and its hero is clever and noble. (15)

It is adorned with descriptions of towns, the ocean, mountains, the seasons, the moon- and sun-rise, and of parks, plays in the water, wine-drinking and of the pleasures of love. (16)

And with (descriptions of) separations, marriages, and the birth of a son, as well as with (descriptions of) politics, ambassadors, expeditions, war and the prosperity of the hero. (17)

It is elaborate, with uninterrupted *rasa* and *bhāva*, endowed with chapters which are not too long, which have meters which are nice to hear and good *saṁdhis* (junctures of plot construction), (18)

and which always have different meters at the end. A *kāvya* which entertains people and possesses good ornaments will remain until the next *kalpa*. (19)

Daṇḍin's definition of *Mahākāvyas* is important for our topic, for it shows that at his time descriptions of the seasons were considered as a 'must' for this genre. Of course, the Kāvyādarśa is descriptive as well as prescriptive, as Daṇḍin himself says in verse I, 2:

pūrvaśāstrāṇi saṁhṛtya prayogān upalakṣya ca /
yathāsāmarthyam asmābhiḥ kriyate kāvyalakṣaṇam //2//

After having synthesized the earlier disciplines and having examined the practices (of writing *kāvya*), we are making as per our capacity a treatise of poetics (lit. characteristics of *kāvya*). (2)

Daṇḍin's definition of *Mahākāvyas* is not only interesting from the point of view of the *ṛtu* descriptions, but for the other descriptive themes which he mentions, too. In the preceding section, we mentioned that *Mahākāvyas* are a blending of the epic and of the lyrical genres. This double origin is also very clearly reflected in Daṇḍin's definition. Thus, the descriptions which are mentioned in verse 16, such as towns, the ocean, mountains, the seasons, etc..., are typical of *kāvya* or lyrical poetry, whereas those enumerated in verse 17, more specially in the second line, such as politics, ambassadors, expeditions, wars etc..., are of course typical of the epic genre.

In later works of poetics, we find definitions of the *Mahākāvya* genre which are practically identical to Daṇḍin's. As we see, Daṇḍin does not further elaborate the topic of season descriptions. The first poetician to devote a greater place to this theme seems to be Rājaśekhara, with whom we shall presently deal.

Rājaśekhara

For our work on the seasons in *Mahākāvya* literature, it is extremely important both from the point of view of Indian poetics and from the point of view of the topic of season descriptions, to study a passage which exclusively deals with the seasons, namely, the 18th *adhyāya* entitled Kālavibhāga (Division of Time) of Rajaśekhara's Kāvyamīmāṁsā, or more precisely, of its first and only extant *adhikaraṇa*, the Kavirahasya or Secret of the poets.[3] This *adhyāya* deals with almost all the

3. The Kāvyamīmāṁsā of Rājaśekhara (about 880—920 A.D.) seems to have been composed in 18 *adhikaraṇas* (chapters) according to Rājaśekhara himself. But only the first one, entitled Kavirahasya (Secret of the poets) has come down to us, of which only 18 *adhyāyas* out of the 19 it contained have survived.

major themes and characteristics of season descriptions. For this reason, we shall give a complete translation of this *adhyāya* which, to our knowledge, has not been translated into English.

The 18th *adhyāya* on Time is inscribed in the larger context formed by *adhyāyas* 14 to 18. *Adhyāyas* 14 to 16 deal with a topic of utmost importance for us, namely the concept of *kavi-samaya*, and *adhyāyas* 17 and 18 deal with two major constituants or indeed determinants of *kavi-samayas*, that is Space and Time respectively.

What is a *kavi-samaya*? To answer this question we shall quote Rājaśekhara's own definition of the term:

> *pūrve hi vidvāṁsaḥ sahasraśākhaṁ sāṅgaṁ ca vedam avagāhya, śāstrāṇi cāvabudhya, deśāntarāṇi dvīpāntarāṇi ca paribhramya, yān arthān upalabhya praṇītavantas teṣām deśakālāntaravaśenānyathātve 'pi tathātvenopanibandho yaḥ sa kavisamayaḥ |*
>
> (p. 78, 11. 19-22)[4]

The ancient scholars, having studied the thousand branches of the Veda along with its limbs, having understood the sciences, and having travelled in different countries and continents, have represented things as they experienced them. A *kavi-samaya* is a description of those things in a certain way, although they are unlike that, due to belonging to a different place and time.

Thus we could render *kavi-samaya* as 'poetic convention'. As per Rājaśekhara's claim at the end of *adhyāya* 16, this topic of *kavi-samaya* was so to say lying asleep in oblivion, and he evoked it again.

Thus, typical images of Sanskrit poetry, such as the hare or deer in the moon, the whiteness of fame, the idea that the couples af *cakravāka*-birds are separated during the night and that the *cakora*-birds drink the moon-shine, and so on and so forth, all these are nothing but *kavi-samayas* or poetic conventions.

Rājaśekhara's justification of such fanciful but well established images is that these things were seen or experienced by

4. These page and line-numberings refer to B. Bhattacharya's edition of the Kāvyamīmāṁsā, Gaekwad's Oriental Series, vol. 1, Baroda 1934 (3rd ed.).

the ancient *kavis* either from the tradition or during their extensive travels. This may really account for the existence of certain *kavi-samayas*, but leaves us rather doubtful about others which seem to be mere superstitions and unfounded beliefs.

With reference to *jāti* (species), *dravya* (substance), *guṇa* (quality) and *kriyā* (activity), the *kavi-samayas* are divided into three main categories: 1) objects which do not exist in a given Time or Space but are described as existing. 2) Objects which exist in a given Time or Space but are not described. 3) Objects which are described as limited to a given Time or Space though they exist also beyond them.

What is the importance of *kavi-samayas* for our topic ? As we have seen above, Time, as well as Space, figure in the definition of *kavi-samayas*. That is why, after dealing with *kavi-samayas*, Rājaśekhara dedicates one *adhyāya* each to Space and Time. The importance of Time under which heading Rājaśekhara deals with the seasons, is made clear in the last verse of *adhyāya* 18:

> *iti kālavibhāgasya darśitā vṛttir īdṛśī* /
> *kaver iha mahān moha iha siddho mahākaviḥ* //102//
>
> The practice of a division of time is shown in this manner, for there is a great delusion here for the poet. The one who masters this is a great poet (*mahākavi*).

The topic of *kavi-samaya* and that of Time, or more precisely, of the seasons, are closely connected with each other in the sense that many themes of season descriptions are nothing but *kavi-samayas*. Thus, the idea that the cuckoo sings only in spring or that the peacock sings and dances only during the monsoon are *kavi-samayas* (see. p. 82, ll. 17-18). Similarly, the *vṛkṣa-dohadas* (trees' longings) according to which some trees will bloom in spring only after certain operations have been performed on them, are also *kavi-samayas*. Inversely, though they exist, the *mālatī*-creeper is never mentioned in spring descriptions, nor the flower and fruit of the sandal-wood tree, nor the fruit of the *aśoka* tree (see p. 80, ll. 1-2).

The seasonal winds, which are supposed to blow from various directions according to the season, are also *kavi-samayas*. Rājaśekhara deals with this topic in the 18th *adhyāya* itself. Since there is no real concensus on this subject between poets and scholars (*ācāryas*), Rājaśekhara remarks: *vastuvṛttir atantraṁ, kavisamayaḥ pramāṇam* (the nature of the object is '*atantra*', (i.e., not the object of the rule), the poetic convention is the criterion) (p. 99, l. 9). This simply means that a poet should not bother to know which wind really blows in a particular season, but follow the sanctioned poetic convention on this subject.

Again, towards the end of *adhyāya* 18, Rājaśekhara remarks:

> *deśeṣu padārthānāṁ vyatyāso dṛśyate svarūpasya* /
> *tan na tathā badhnīyāt kavibaddham iha pramāṇaṁ naḥ* //92//
>
> In various regions, there are differences in the nature of the objects. (In poetry) one must not compose as it is (in reality). For us, the criterion is how it was composed by the poets.

It would be an error to imagine that all the elements belonging to season descriptions fall into the category of *kavi-samayas*, but we would probably not err much by assuming that most of them do. Rājaśekhara lived of course after most of the poets whose season descriptions we are studying here, but it seems probable that the idea of the prescriptiveness of season descriptions must have been largely prevalent much before his time. Rājaśekhara's above-quoted verse (92) gives us a good idea of the prescribed and indeed stereotyped nature of season descriptions. This explains why all the poets, whatever their place of birth, describe the seasons so similarly, from the point of view of some of their characteristics, such as flowers, etc..., as well as from their climatic point of view. This is most conspicuous in the case of winter, which is always described with snow and frost, although the greatest part of the Indian subcontinent never experiences such cold. This might be a transposition of the Himalayan climatic conditions into other parts of India.[5]

5. A striking example for this is the R. winter description (III, 15), in which winter is described as a cold season endowed with snow and frost, although the scene is in South India, on the shores of the Godāvarī-river. Moreover, there is a reference to the Himalaya in verse 9 : *suvyaktaṁ himavān himavān giriḥ* (the mount Himavat is very obviously '*himavān*') (i.e. : endowed with snow), although it is thousands of miles away !

Similarly, spring, and what to say of *śiśira*, hardly exist as such in most parts of India which know only three basic seasons, a hot season, the monsoon, and a somewhat cooler season.

Thus we should consider these season descriptions to be governed by the rule of *kavi-samaya*, and not expect to find many realistic or naturalistic traits in them, denoting a close observation of nature, but accept them as a system of more or less codified images and topics, in whose context, of course, each poet tries to be as innovative as possible. This system does not only contain elements which result from a breaking of their proper boundaries of time and space, but also elements of pure belief, unfounded world views and superstitions.

The Kālavibhāga

The author of the Kāvyamīmāṁsā starts the 18th chapter on Time with an enumeration of the various units into which time is divided: *nimeṣas*, *kāṣṭhās*, *kalās*, *muhūrtas*, day and night, *pakṣas* (15 days), months, seasons, *ayanas* (half-years) and years. After this very formal introduction, Rājaśekhara describes the various winds which blow during the different seasons. He then launches into a full-fledged *ṣaḍṛtuvarṇana*, starting with the monsoon and dedicating an average of some ten verses to each seaon.[6] Then he develops at length the topic of the four stages of the seasons, ending with a classification of fruits and the duration of their ripening.

As we said, Rājaśekhara dedicates a separate discussion to the seasonal winds, before even starting his season description. There seem to be various different opinions about most of these winds, which Rājaśekhara duly enumerates, adding his own opinion here and there: thus, in the monsoon, there is either the eastern or the western wind. The autumn wind does not blow from any specific direction. In winter, there is either the west wind or the north wind, or both, and the same holds for *śiśira*. In spring, the southern wind blows, and in summer it is either

6. Surprisingly, the greatest number of verses (14) is dedicated to summer, whereas in other cycles, this season is usually quite side-tracked.

the south-western wind, or else its direction is not fixed. As we see, the only seasonal wind about which there is no controversy is the southern breeze of spring. Perhaps not surprisingly, this is also the only wind which is mentioned quite frequently in *Mahākāvyas*. Winds from other dirctions are hardly mentioned.[7]

In his *ṛtu-varṇana* which follows the discussion on the winds Rājaśekhara's treatment of the seasons is extremely exhaustive. His aim being purely prescriptive, that is, teaching the future poets how to deal with season descriptions, he enumerates very comprehensively all the characteristic themes and elements of each season. He gives particularly great stress to the plants, flowers and animals which are typical of certain seasons. In fact, we find a much greater number of these enumerated in Rājaśekhara's *ṛtu-varṇana* than in any of the *Mahākāvya* season descriptions.

Generally speaking, Rājaśekhara's season description seems to be somewhat more on the 'popular' side than any of the season descriptions which can be found in the R. or in the *Mahākāvyas*. Thus we find certain topics in Rājaśekhara's cycle of seasons which are as a rule never touched upon by the season descriptions which are the object of our study.

One such topic is food. Certain food-items being indeed seasonally determined, especially fruits and vegetables, we would expect to find some of these mentioned in season descriptions. But surprisingly, food is hardly ever mentioned in our season descriptions, may be because it was considered to be an 'unpoetic' subject. Fruits are of course often mentioned, but only rarely as being eaten. A striking example for this is the case of the mango. Whereas mango-flowers, though quite insignificant both in shape and in colour are frequently mentioned and praised in spring descriptions, the mango-fruit is hardly mentioned in summer descriptions. Rājaśekhara on the other hand does not shrink from describing various dishes, even such 'exotic' ones as boar, deer and mustard, which are eaten in

7. We find once in R. III, 15, 15 the mention of the west wind in winter. In other seasons, the winds are of course mentioned, especially in the monsoon and in winter, but not the direction they blow from.

winter (verse 33). Verse 69 also mentions various dishes which are used to rejuvenate languishing sexual desires in summer, such as mango-juice and other fruit-juices, rice, butter-milk, and more surprisingly the essence of deer and *lāva*-birds.

Rājaśekhara does not hesitate either to stress the disagreeable side of certain seasons. Thus verse 61 describes the terrible heat of summer, in which the rivers are dried up and the thirsty travellers converge around water-supplying places. Similarly, verses 66 to 68 as well as 71 evoke very realistically the distress of various creatures during the summer heat, reminding us of very similar verses of the Ṛtus.[8] In the *Mahākāvyas*, on the other hand, the disagreable aspects of certain seasons, especially of summer, are usually quite side-tracked. The same can be said of one more theme which is evoked by Rājaśekhara, namely the mention of base or poor people. Thus in verse 27, we read that the sun tortures intensely like a rogue who has recently become rich, and that the mud resorts to drying up (or wasting away) like a poverty-stricken lover. Verse 46 says: this is the terrible season of *śiśira*, which is cursed by the poor, and verse 47 compares the soft lustre of the sun to the order of one who has lost his fortune. In *Mahākāvya* season descricriptions on the other hand, the only misery which is ever alluded to is that of being separated from the beloved object.

The formulation of the four stages of the seasons, which follows the actual season description, seems to be Rājaśekhara's own contribution to the subject, and it was taken up by later poeticians, such as Bhoja in his Śṛṅgāraprakāśa. These four stages are as follows: *saṁdhi* (union of two seasons), *śaiśava* (infancy of a season), *prauḍhi* (maturity of a season) and *anuvṛtti* (transference or continuation of certain characteristics belonging to one season in the next).

As far as our texts are concerned, it seems that we find a clear *ṛtu-saṁdhi* only in Kir. X, 25, which describes characteristics of the rains and of autumn. Still in the same passage, we also find winter described as already strongly mixed with spring (verse X, 28). But this cannot be a *saṁdhi*, since a *saṁdhi* is the union of a season with the preceding one, nor an *anuvṛtti*, since

8. See *Ṛtus*. I, 11ff.

this term designates the continuation of a season in the next. Thus this could be one more stage, the premature appearance of a season during the previous one, which is not mentioned by Rājaśekhara. At the beginning of the Ragh. spring description, we find a verse which might evoke the infancy of spring:

> *kusumajanma tato navapallavās tadanu ṣaṭpadakokilakūjitam /*
> *iti yathākramam āvirabhūn madhur drumavatīm avatīrya vanasthalīm*
> //IX, 26//

The birth of the flowers, then the new sprouts, and after that the song of the bees and of the cuckoos: it is in this succession that spring manifested itself, after descending on these forest-regions filled with trees.

But generally speaking, while reading the season descriptions of the R. as well as of the six *Makākāvyas* which concern us here, we find that the poets did not go much into the subtleties of these stages and usually described the seasons in their developed stage.

We shall now proceed to give the translation of Rājaśekhara's Kālavibhāga. Whenever it is relevant, we shall give references in the form of notes to verses of the R. or the six *Mahākāvyas.*

ADHYĀYA 18: THE DIVISION OF TIME[9]

Time is separated by being divided into *kāsṭhās*, etc...Thus:

*A *kāṣṭhā* is of ten and five *nimeṣas*, and thirty *kāṣṭhās* are called a *kalā*. And thirty *kalās* become a *muhūrta*, and day and night together are of thirty of these (*muhūrtas*).(1)

Such days and nights take place during the months of Caitra

9. This translation follows B. Bhattacharya's edition of the Kāvyamīmāṁsā, to which we have already referred in note 4. This edition only contains line-numbers, but no verse-numbers. To facilitate the reading, we are giving verse-numbers in our translation, ignoring the line-numbers. In order to distinguish and highlight the theoretical *kārikās*, as opposed to the illustrative of 'poetic' verses, we shall keep an asterisk at their beginning.

and Āśvayuja. After Caitra, for three months, there is an increase of the day and a decrease of the night by one *muhūrta* per month; after that, there is an increase of the night and a decrease of the day by one *muhūrta*. After the month of Āśvayuja, the same is reversed. As per the solar calendar, a month is the passing of the sun from one constellation to the other, and the year is of two *ayanas* (half-years), the *dakṣiṇāyana*, starting with the monsoon, and the *uttarāyana*, starting with *śiśira*.[10] A *pakṣa* is of fifteen days and nights. The growing moon is the white *pakṣa*, and the growing darkness is the black *pakṣa*. This is the ancestral measure of the month. The entire practice of rituals prescribed in the Veda is also on this basis. The reversed moon-*pakṣa* is also related to the ancestors.

The *kavis* and the people of Āryāvartta resort to this calculation. And thus, two *pakṣas* are a month. Two month are a season. The rotation of six seasons is a year. And the astrologers say that it starts with Caitra, and those who know the nature of the world hold that it begins with Śravaṇa. Therein, (the months of) Nabhas and Nabhasya are the monsoon, Iṣa and Ūrja autumn, Sahas and Sahasya winter, Tapas and Tapasya *śiśira*, Madhu and Mādhava spring, and Śukra and Śuci summer. There, the poets say: "During the monsoon, there is the east wind." And the scholars say: "It is the west wind, whereas the east wind hinders the monsoon."

Thus they said: "The monsoon is hampered by the eastern wind, and autumn is hampered by the western wind."

Thus they said:

"In the monsoon, the sky is filled with the weight of clouds which carry water, and west winds blow which are fragrant with *kadamba*-flowers."(2)

And in the opinion of Yāyāvarīya (i.e.: Rājaśekhara): "The real nature of the object is *atantra* (i.e. : not the object of the rule), the poetic convention is the criterion."

10. The *dakṣiṇāyana*, or southern half-year, designates the six months that the sun spends south of the equator, and inversely, the *uttarāyana* are the six months which it spends north of the equator.

Thus they said:

"Let (Aruṇa) the joy of Vinatā, who is at the head of the sun's chariot, bestow happiness onto you, like the eastern wind of the monsoon, like the rising smoke of fire, like the first creation of the universe, like the highest auspicious OM of the collection of the Vedas, and like the cries of joy of Nandi[11], when the enemy of Madana desires to celebrate and dance at twilight."(3)

In autumn, the wind is not fixed to a particular region. For instance:

"At dawn, winds blew which were cool due to carrying along the frozen dew, and perfumed by the fragrant wealth of *śephāli*-buds."(4)

Some say that in winter there is the west wind. Others say that it is the north wind. And Yāyāvarīya thinks that there are both. Between these two, here is the example for the west wind:

"The west wind blows, cutting through the rows of birch-trees which are born on the summit of the Himalaya and have a bark (full of) gashes; scattering the agitated *cātaka*-birds which are frightened by the mass of the huge waves of the Revā-waters; raining heavily water-drops (coming from) ice-blocks melting due to its speed, and hastening with strength through the pine-trees which are dripping with a thick (sap) due to being crushed by elephants." (5)

Example for the north wind:

"The snowy north winds are blowing, disturbing the hair-dress of the Lampāka-women, pleasing the *rallaka*-deer, kissing the quiet waters of the Candrabhāgā-river. These

11. *nandināndīninādaḥ* can simply mean : the cries of joy of Nandi. But the *nāndī*, (this term actually derives from Nandi), also designates the benediction at the beginning of a performance, which is also the context here. Thus we could also translate this by 'the recitation of the benediction by Nandi'. The story goes that Nandi, as he was watching Śiva performing his dance for the creation of the universe, was as rapt in contemplation as if he was watching a theatrical performance. Hence, the name *nāndī* was given to the benedictions at the beginning of dramas.

are terrible for the branches of the birch-trees, have a fragrance as delicious as that of the musk-deer, are the lovers of the Bālhava-women and the makers of sports for the Kulūta-women."(6)

In *śiśira* too, just like in winter, there is either the north wind or the west wind. In spring it is the south wind. Thus it is said:

"Shaking the forest-rows in Laṅkā, repeatedly teaching dance to the creeper-like locks of the Kerala-women, instantly loosening the ties of the braided hair of Āndhra-women and agitating the *nāgavallī*-flower, here arrives the impetuous southern wind, mixed (*milita*) with (sandal wood) which grows on Mount Malaya, which is the charioteer of (Love) the fish-emblemed one, the friend of the spring-season, and the thief of the self-respect of women."(7)

Some say: "The wind in summer has no fixed direction". Others say: "It is the south-western wind." And according to Yāyāvarīya, it is both. Here is the example for the first opinion:

"Embracing heaven and earth due to the whirl-winds, thick pillars of dust are tying together the sky which creates the illusion of columns of the forth-coming multitude of clouds. And what is more, the river-beds, from which the streams have departed, indicate now, with the abundance of water from the mirages, the wealth (of water) which will come in the course of the day."(8)

The second opinion:

"The sun is torturing with its rays which seem to be full of fire, the entire earth seems to be filled with the spread of coals, the south-western wind seems to be raining fire made out of chaff, and Manmatha is hitting with his arrows which seem to be fiery."(9)

Moreover:

THE MONSOON

During the monsoon, the clouds steal away the expedition-effort of the kings, while placing the pregnancy in the *balākas*, producing the seeds of the bamboos with their thunder, and marking the dust (with rain-drops).(10)[12]

The time of the clouds, which is related to the delicious smell of the parched earth, is of high value, giving flowers to the *sallakī*-and *sāla*-trees, and to the plantain and jasmines, and making the *lāṅgalīkas* bloom.(11)

The woods are black-blue on account of the dark leaves, the mountains shine, washed by the rain-water, the rivers have multiplied shores due to the abundance of water, and the grass is thickly covered with *indragopa*-insects.(12)

This season which gives joy to the *cakoras*, is the thief of the movements of the renounced ones, has the husbands' paths watched by their wives who are separated from them, is the companion of the travellers who are heading towards their homes, and has a noisy sky due to the clouds.(13)[13]

This is the first hospitality offered by the season of clouds: playful activities with women[14], a luxurious bed on the top of a high palace, the *catuḥsama*-unguent containging musk.(14)

The coming of the clouds (i.e.: the monsoon), which releases on separated lovers water which is the poison of love, which has fluttering, sweet-voiced *cātakas*, and which produces the birth of love in the deer, marks the beginning of the frogs' noise, has snakes which are proud, for they are filled with intoxication, and (is filled) with the cries of *madgu*-birds and herons which are happy due to the dancing of troups of peacocks.(15)

12. The fact that the monsoon puts an end to the kings' war-expeditions is often mentioned in the R. monsoon description. See e.g. IV, 27, 15 and 33. 'The clouds placing the pregnancy in the *balākas*' explains R. IV, 27, 21 ; *meghābhikāmā balākapaṅktiḥ* and R. IV, 27, 22 : *hṛṣṭā balākā ghanam ahhyupaiti*. The same theme is also mentioned in the Meghadūta, I, 10.

13. 'This season is the thief of the movements of the renounced ones' : Hermits give up their peregrinations during the monsoon. The same theme is evoked in two R. verses, IV, 27, 10 and 34. During the same season, travellers return home. See R. IV, 27, 15 or Śiś. VI, 29.

14. In this verse, we are following the variant reading *kila kāminībhiḥ*.

Indeed, the departure of summer is charming, for it is endowed with the blooming buds of the *kuṭajas*, full of blossoming *nīpa*-flowers, kinsman to the birth of *dhava*-plants, it has *arjuna*-trees covered with clusters of blossoms, a sky stained by the *kadambas*, it is provided with the blossoming of the *ketakīs* and shakes the groups of *nicula*-trees.(16)[15]

End of the Monsoon

AUTUMN

There approaches autumn, quickly threatening (*tarjayanti*) the peacocks which have lost their intoxication, giving pride to the ospreys and to the bees, making the lotuses blossom and opening the *kumuda* and *utpala* lotuses.(17)[16]

Autumn shines, while keeping flowers in the *bandhūkus*, *bāṇus* (reeds), *asanas*, *kuṁkumas* (saffron), *śephālikās*, *saptapalāśas*, *kāśas*, *bhāṇḍīras*, *saugandhikas* and *mālatīs* (jasmine) (18)

Autmun, which has wagtails, is endowed with the clearness of the water and is followed by flocks of *kādambas* (geese), *kāraṇḍavas* (ducks), *cakravākas*, *sārasas* (cranes) and *krauñcas* (culews), whose heart does it not break?(19)

Autumn shines with wonderful deeds, bringing home the flocks of swans, cleansing the waters by the sight of the Agastya-constellation and carrying a brilliant foetus in the form of pearls.(20)[17]

15. Most of these flowers, especially *kuṭajas*, *nīpas*, *kadambas* and *ketakas* are extremely frequently mentioned in *Mahākāvya* monsoon descriptions.

16. Here, we have preferred the reading '*tarjayanti*', for it is well-known that the peacocks sing and dance, full of intoxication, during the rainy season, but that they stop singing in autumn. See for instance Kir. IV, 25 or Śiś. VI, 45. Lotuses are one of the most typical attributes of autumn. See below, in the section dedicated to this season.

17. In autumn, the swans come back from lake Mānasa in the Himalayas, where they are supposed to spend the monsoon. This is a *kavisamaya*. The constellation Agastya appears in autumn, when the waters lose their turbidness and mud. Thus it is a poetic fancy that it is this constellation itself which makes the water clear. The same image appears in the Ragh. autumn description (IV, 21).

Bulls digging the earth with the tips of their hoofs, elephants rending the banks with their tusks and ruru-deer leaving their worn-out horns, make the world curious to watch (them). (21)[18]

During this season, the moon-lit water has a clear lustre, all over the sky shines blue, the sky (lit. the path of Airāvata) appears like day, and the pieces of dry clouds are white.(22)

During this season, the following are to be performed by kings who are bent upon an expedition: on the day of Mahānavamī, worshipping of all the weapons and giving a *nīrājanā* (waving of lights) to the horses, soldiers and elephants. And during Diwali, various entertainments.(23)[19] During autumn, there is an abundance of stars shining with a greater lustre in the sky. The earth is fit for the movement of the chariots. The sun has a shining heat and Viṣṇu wakes up in the company of the gods.(24)[20]

The paddy-crops in the fields are bending due to their ripening. The old *āmalaka*-fruits become valuable as they are ripening to blackness. The *ervāruka*-fruit loses its inner smell when it breaks and the cucumbers become sour when they are over-ripe.(25)[21]

In the farmers' yards, which are beautiful due to the smell emanating from the falling new *śāli*-grains, the young women

18. The image of bulls digging up the earth in their autumnal intoxication appears in Ragh. IV, 22 and Kir. IV, 11.

19. Autumn is the season for military expeditions. This theme is especially prominent in the R. and Ragh. autumn descriptions. See R. IV, 29, 30 or Ragh. IV, 24.

20. 'The earth is fit for the movement of the chariots' : another theme which is typical of this season, in which the mud on the roads dries up, so that the traffic, which was hindered during the rains, can start again. See for instance Kir. IV, 18.

'Viṣṇu wakes up' : Viṣṇu is supposed to sleep during the monsoon and wake up in autumn. Thus in R. IV, 27, 22, in the context of the monsoon description, he is said to go to sleep.

21. The ripening rice is exremely typical of autumn descriptions (see below, in the section dedicated to *śarat*). *Āmalakas, ervārukas* and *trapussas* (cucumbers) are, on the other hand, never mentioned in the autumn descriptions we are studying.

are pleasing with their gestures wherein their bracelets glide from their hands which are shaken by the movement of the pestle.(26)[22]

The sun is intensely torturing like a rogue who has recently become rich. The ruru-deer abandons its horn, like an ungrateful one (abandons) a friend. The water becomes clear just like the virtuous reflection of a sage. The mud is resorting to drying up (or wasting away) just like a poverty-stricken lover.(27)

The rivers flow, having sleeping tortoises in the belly of the new sand-banks which have designs of lines of pearl-oysters placed in successive curves, (the rivers) in which takes place the tilling made by the gaping mouths of herons chasing the fishes which are on flight in the shallow water of the waves.(28)

During autumn, the quiet mass of the river-water is resting, having banian-trees on its shores which are free of mud, shining with the easy-going heaps of large fishes and with plenty of small fishes which are whirling due to their fear of the attacking ospreys, with their sand-banks wherein are rolling the tortoises and (endowed) with the chattering of the agitated cranes.(29)

End of Autumn

WINTER

Glory to the new entrance of the winter-season, which has, in succession, two-three buds on the *mucukundas*, three-four sprouts on the *lavalīs*, and five-six flowers on the *phalinīs*.(30)[23]

The beautiful women with their ornaments of *punnāga* and *rodhra* flowers, whose body is bent due to the upper garment, and who have designs of indigo and saffron (paste) shining

22. Similarly verses, describing not the threshing but the churning of the milk by young women, are found in Bhaṭṭ. II, 16 and Kir. IV, 14-17.

23. This verse probably illustrates the infancy (*śaiśava*) of winter, since this season is still endowed with flowers, which are quite uncommon for winter descriptions.

on their faces, are wearing tied hair perfumed with oil.(31)

As the winter season grows, with its wind scattering the heaps of pulverized snow, the breasts of the young women obtain a little heat.(32)

In this season, having eaten the flesh of boars, new rice, curds, prohibited juices and very delicious mustard and deer, people ridicule the medical science.(33)

Long life always to this season of cold, where hospitality is performed with lukewarm water, where any kind of food and drink is palatable, and where one sleeps tightly embracing a good or a bad woman.(34)[24]

There is glory to the following characteristics of winter: the peacocks which are bereft of pride, having lost their tail, the land which has well-grown wheat and barley, the delivery of the tigress and the misty waters.(35)[25]

In this season the fields shine with ripened *śamī*-grains, the nights are characterized by the Triṣaṅku-constellation and bones are cooking.(36)

During winter, the gardens are characterized by dumb cuckoos, and on the faces of the female bees, there is the seal of silence. The flying of the birds in the sky is characterised by slowness, and there is a decline in the pride of the snakes.(37)

There is an abundance of ripening for the jujube-fruits and the orange-fruits, and sugar-candy too is available. And an unprecedented splendour of sweetness is produced in the belly of the black sugar-cane and of the red sugar-cane.(38)

Those for whom there is the luxury of a bed in the interior of a house and a wife at their side, who has big youthful eyes, and who have a fire-place in which the fiery

24. *Sudurbhagā* also means 'a very unfortunate woman', but this does not seem to make any sense here. Our translation is substanciated by verse 42, in the *śiśira* description, which says that there is no difference between embracing a bad or a good woman in this season.

25. 'The misty waters' : *salilaṁ sabāṣpam.* Nearly the same terms are found in R. winter description (III, 15, 22).

smoke is hidden, they consider winter as a remainder of summer. (39)

End of winter. *Śiśira* has the characteristics of winter. But the peculiarities are :[26]

The night is long with its parts which are fit for various amorous activities. There blows a terrible wind which must be conquered by means of saffron-paste. The stay on the bed is characterised by a double cotton blanket. What else? The spreading smoke of incense is invaluable now. (40)

Embracing and filled with delight, the young people sleep during the long night, having conquered the cold by means of the lassitude caused by long love-pleasures, their cotton-quilts having glided down to their feet, their ties having come loose due to the repeated balancing of the thighs. (41)

During this season, the difference between drinking a tasty water and a non-tasty water, between snow and fire as per touching, between embracing a bad woman and a good woman, between the liking for the moon and for the sun, is not felt. (42)

During the cool season, there is the growth (lit. activity) of the flowers on the *marubaka*-tree, and the cursing of the plays in the water. Among all flowers, the *kundas* are prominent, the orb of the sun has the beauty (coming) from the deer-marked (moon) and the sandal (paste) burns. (43)[27]

The reddishness of the gradual ripening, which is an order of birth, is taking place in the white mustard plants, which have rows of thorns separated by gradually declining sprouts and wherein hardly two-three flowers are left. (44)

Now, one's looks do not go to the pleasure-tanks where the fishes are submerged deep in the water, which are hit by a

26. Rājaśekhara describes *śiśira* as a cold season, just like winter. This is not always the case for other poets (see section on *śiśira*).

27. The idea that during the cool season, the sun and the moon resemble each other, which appears already in the previous verse, can already be found in the R. winter description (III, 15, 13 & 18).

heavy north wind, and in which the lotuses and creepers have only their stems left. (45)

This is the terrible season of *śiśira*, which makes the elephants intoxicated and only makes the deer happy, which nurtures the boars and has quiet buffaloes, which is cursed by the poor and praised only by the rich. (46)

The fire of dry cow-dung is as beautiful as the sulkiness of a young wife. The cold wind is as disagreable as the embrace of an unfaithful one. Now the lustre of the sun is soft just like the order of one who has lost his fortune, and the moon bears similarity to the face of a love-longing woman. (47)

During this season, the women who are by nature bilious are allaying the misery (of thc fever) of *śiśira*, though it is so great, by means of smearing their buttocks, the region of their breasts, the roots of their arms and thighs, with stewed saffron, and the young women (allay it) by means of embraces during the whole night. (48)

End of Śiśira

SPRING

In the month of Caitra, there is an increase of intoxication for the parrots, the *sārika*-birds, the pigeons, the gallinules, the black bees and the male cuckoos. This is the only season of intoxication, which is the friend of the mango-tree. (49)[28]

During this season, the mind of beautiful women is excessively set on joyful dancing, on the balancing swings, on the song beautified by the story of Gaurī, and on the various forms of the worship of Kāma. (50)[29]

The male cuckoo coos on the fifth note, the young woman's charms are strikingly dazzling, and during spring, Smara joins his bow with new flowers. (51)[30]

28. Among all these birds, the most popular one for spring descriptions is of course the cuckoo, which is mentioned in numerous verses of *Mahākāvya* spring descriptions (see below in the section dedicated to spring).

29. Beautiful women swinging on *dolās* appear in Ragh. IX, 36 and XIX, 44, both spring descriptions.

30. i.e. : keeps his flower-arrow on his bow, ready to strike.

In spring, the special attire of the young women, who are full of devotion for their amorous lovers, is pleasing, with their knitted, golden embroidered clothes, and with red sandal-paste in the parting of their hair. (52)

This season has *karṇikāra*-trees filled with flowers, *kāñcanāra*-trees worshipped by the world of flowers, *kovidāra*-trees which are expert in blooming and *sinduvāra*-trees which are about to blossom. (53)

The *rohītaka*-tree, the hog-plum tree, the *kiṅkirāta*-tree, and the *madhūka*—and *moca*-trees, along with the *mādhavī*-creeper, and the *śobhāñjanaka*-tree and the *kesara* are glorious in spring with the weight of their flowers. (54)

The tying of the hair is by looking at the buds of the *mādhavī* creeper, speech is gotten from the melodious song of the cuckoo, and the way of worshipping Manmatha is with *damanaka*-flowers. In this season, the god Madhu is the teacher of the women. (55)

Strange that the *kurabaka* has not been embraced, the *tilaka* has not been seen, that the *aśoka* has not been hit by the feet of beautiful women and the *bakula* has not been sprinkled by wine from their mouth. But even then, during Caitra, they are covered with flowers. (56)[31]

During Caitra, the red and the black *aśokas* are multi-coloured. That third one, the golden *aśoka*, is yellowish. From within their flowers, the army of Manmatha is victorious in the three worlds. (57)

For the betel-nut trees and the cocoa-nut trees, for the date-trees and the *pāṭalī* and *kiṁśuka*-trees, for the *kharjūra*, *tāḍa* and *tāḍī*-trees, spring is the cause of bestowing crowns of flowers. (58)

End of Spring

31. These are the *vṛkṣa-dohadas* or longings of the trees. According to the *kavi-samaya*, these trees are supposed to bloom only after the operations mentioned in this verse have been performed on them. But here, on the other hand, they bloom even without them. Similarly, in Kum. III, 26, the *aśoka*-tree blooms although it has not been hit by the feet of beautiful women.

SUMMER

Summer is the maker of whiteness for the new jasmines, is beautiful with the blooming *śirīṣas*, is the bestower of flowers for the golden *ketakīs* and makes the *dhātakīkas* bloom. (59)

Having got rid of their miserable tiredness by means of *kharjūra-*, *jambū-* and bread-fruits, mangoes, *moca-*, *priyāla-* and *pūgī*-fruits and cocoa-nuts, the couples resort to sexual union. (60)[32]

The rivers are without water and with holes, the water-supplying places are filled with travellers during the terrible day. In the month of Śuci, when a drink made out of yeast is sought, the streets carry (people) early in the morning as well as in the evening. (61)

A sleep at noon in the huts, plays in the water at the end of the day, love-making at the end of the night, these are the handy combinations to eliminate the intense heat. (62)[33]

The moon-light which is as pleasant as sandal-wood paste, the garlands of gusts of winds coming from the waters, the dripping of water-drops from the palm-leaf-fans, these three offer a (funery) oblation to Śuci. (63)

This is the great secret of the production of coolness: the powder of camphor, a piece of mango, pan which is made out of a wet betel-nut, pearl-garlands, stars and a thin garment. (64)

The following is the incarnation of *śiśira* even during summer: necklaces of pearls which are smeared with sandal-wood paste and wet with water, stitched along with garlands of lotus-stems, and garlands of blooming *campakas* on the head. (65)

32. Similar aphrodisiac concoctions are mentioned in verse 69. Ragh. XVI, 52 and XIX, 46 attribute the same powers to mangoes and *pāṭalas* mixed with wine, also in the context of summer.

33. This verse, as well as verses 63, 64, 65, 70 and 72 mention diverse cooling devices to which people resort in order to alleviate the summer-heat. This theme is also very common in *Mahākāvya* summer descriptions, in which the favourite seem to be baths, sandal-wood paste, flowers, thin garments, gems and pearl-necklaces. (See below in the section dedicated to *grīṣma*).

During this season:

The creatures are as though being cooked, the sands are as though burning, the rivulets are as though boiling and the moon-rays are as though melting away. (66)

The deer are attracted by the mirages on the plain grounds, knots of watery hair are generated due to the thinning down of the rivers, due to the drying up of the water the lakes have suffocating fishes, and the pitchers on the wheels of the wells hit against each other while coming up (because they are empty). (67)

The young elephants, the deer and the donkeys get intoxicated and become agitated. One takes rest after climbing onto the plain-lands which are in bloom with *karaviras* and *karīras*. (68)

Rasālas (rice with sugar and spices) mixed with mango-juice, cooked rice mixed with water, fruit-juices, butter-milk, the essence of deer and *lāva*-birds (quails), and boiling milk, this is the medicine for the rejuvenation of love during summer. (69)

The young women who are beautiful with the cool sandal-paste and are wearing garlands of pearl necklaces wet with water, after sitting down on the structures of their bed made out of plantain-leaves, having called the god of Love, make him sit down next to them. (70)

In summer, the forest-regions are full of the noise of the crickets. The buffaloes, along with the elephants and hogs are bathed in mud, the troups of snakes and deer have their tongues lolling, and the birds have their wings (lit. shoulders) hanging from their base. (71)[34]

A beautiful castle having its terrace bathed in moon-light, wine mixed with water which has been tasted by women, garlands of *pāṭalas* and jasmines around the neck, indeed instantly transform summer into winter. (72)

End of Summer

34. Animals suffering from the intense heat are similarly described in Ṛtus. I, 11 ff. Especially in I, 20, the snakes are described in practically the same terms, *vilola-jihvadvaya*...(with lolling tongues).

A season should be described in its four stages, namely: *saṁdhi* (union), *śaiśava* (infancy), *prauḍhi* (maturity) and *anuvṛtti* (transference). The union is in between two seasons. The union of *śiśira* and spring is as follows:

> The flowers of the *kunda*-trees have fallen down, the (other) trees are heavy with the emergence of flowers, the cuckoos take their songs in their minds but do not spell them out, the sun's rays steal away the pleasure of coolness but do not assume the cruelty of giving rise to tiredness. (73)

The infancy of spring :

> There are flowers inside the knots of the creepers, and sprouts in the middle of the buds. The fifth note, which is in the throat of the female cuckoo, can be taken up by a mere wish. And what will happen if within two-three days the bow of the god of Love, which conquers the three worlds and has been renounced for a long time, comes under his control? (74)

The maturity of spring :

> Now, the jasmine-flower bears a similarity to six months-old pearls, the *kāñcanāra*-flower obtains lustre from a cloth washed in red colour, the *madhūka*-bud robs the Hūṇa-women of their beauty, and the *kesara*-flower falling from the top of its stalk shines, similar to the navel of the Lāṭi-women. (75)[35]

> *The characteristics of a by-gone season, such as flowers, etc..., when transferred, are called *liṅgānuvṛtti* (transference of characteristics), and that is to be known from the world of *kāvya*. (76)

During the monsoon, the transference of the blooming of lotuses, which is characteristic of summer, (is exemplified below):

> In the sky resides the blanket of the long rows of clouds, spotted like the throat of a sparrow. The crazy troups of

35. 'The *kāñcanāra*-flower obtains lustre from a cloth washed in red colour' : according to V. Raghavan, this might be a device to dye these flowers. See *Ṛtu in Sanskrit Literature*, p. 90.

frogs seem to be holding a discussion with a great uproar. The heated earth releases, due to the rain, a smell similar to that of sprinkled rice-grains. The sun (lit. lord of rays), though invisible, is inferred by the blooming of the black lotuses. (77)

Others are also like this. Thus:

*In the usage, that which is called a *dhūlīkadamba* blows during the summer-time. The same becomes a *dhārāka-damba* when the monsoon arrives. (78)

For instance:

Peacock, are you not getting excited for the monsoon-battle, whose face, the directions, is smeared with *dhūlīkadambas*, which is adorned with the red-rayed rain-bow, and which is releasing the shining weapon of the thunder-bolt? (79)[36]

*The *jāti*-flower which is generated during the monsoon and is called *kārddami* (muddy), the same one becomes highly glorious in autumn, endowed with fragrant bees. (80)

For instance:

Soaked in a strong perfume, the heap of jasmine-creepers endowed with great clusters of blooming buds shining with big dew-drops, has blossomed. At that moment, the moon rose from the western ocean, and the water, with its blanket made out of numerous swans, looked like a bed with the white moon-shine for its pillow and with designs of snakes' hoods. (81)

A little transference of the *ketakīs* is also desired by some people.

For instance:

The autumn-season is indicated by days which are grey with *ketakī*-pollen and reddened by lotuses, just like a newly-arrived person (is indicated) by his feet (which are dusty and red). (82)

*Here, on the face of winter, though the transference of characteristics of autumn, such as *bāṇas* and *asanas*, along

36. The monsoon phenomenon is also seen as a battle in R. IV, 27, 20 and 28.

with *kuruṇṭakas* is observed (in reality), there does not appear to be any custom in the composition of the poets. (83)

Where there is an identification of winter and *śiśira*, all the characteristics are of course transferred. Also it was said : the year is of twelve months, and with the synthesis of winter and *śiśira*, there are five seasons.

*Spring, with its variegated wealth, should be portrayed with the transference of the characteristics of the flowers of the *marubaka*, the *damanaka*, the *puṁnāga*, and also with a little transference of the *kundas*. (84)

For instance :

In the house of the young Vāhīkas, the *damanaka* is wearing an ear-ornament (which is nothing but) a cluster of blossoms. The intoxication of low women is becoming apparent in the wind which is fragrant with *marubakas*. The mango-fruit is dripping with a fragrant juice coming as soon as it is cut, and juice spread in a vessel full of water creates (designs of) shining moons. (85)

Or for instance :

Slowing down for the *kundas*, distressed at the budding *tamālas*, afraid of the *kiṅkirātas*, sorrowful at the red *aśokas*, squinting for a long time at the *campakas* which are in full bloom, the traveller, though tired with grief, is anxiously approaching while scattering with his tattered garments the circle of bees which are making a noise which is harsh to the ear, and which are greedy for the heaps of new honey. (86)

Or for instance :

The slow wind, having agitated the sandal-wood trees in the vicinity of the Kāverī-river, while spreading the honey of the multitudes of *kundas*, shakes the Lāṭi-women's locks of hair which have fallen on their brows and which are straight from the root, and from which the flowers have fallen due to being pulled out while playing with their lovers. (87)

Other transferences are also in the same way :

*During summer, there is the transference of flowers such as the *pāṭalis* and the *campakas*, the *kesaras* and the *vicakilas*.

There, some people also want the *marubaka*, which is born in winter. (88)

For instance :

Glory to this summer-attire of the deer-eyed ones, which has blooming *śirīṣas* on the ear, *pāṭali*-flowers with garlands of jasmines on the head, a lotus-fiber-necklace around the neck, stems of the black lotus encircling the fore-arms, fragrant sandal-wood water on the region of the breasts, eyes which are red on the surface due to the bath, and a body wet with dripping water. (89)

And also :

A *śirīṣa*-flower on the ear, which competes with the sharpness of *kuśa*-grass, a bunch of *marubakas* shining with *pāṭalas* on the neck, such a beautiful attire of the charming women, which takes place at the peak of the day, shines forth when it is revealed by the wetness of fresh water. (90)[37]

Likewise, other examples too (have to be known) :

*The characteristics belonging to the seasons and their transference are indicated here in brief. Wise people must see the rest with their own intelligence. How far can we name (each and every thing ?) (91)

*In various regions, there are differences in the nature of the objects. (In poetry) one must not compose as it is (in reality). For us, the criterion is how it was constructed by by the poets. (92)

*The flower is useful thanks to its beauty, its food, its smell, its juice, its fruits and for worship. In six ways it is shown. The seventh one is not useful. (93).[38]

For instance :

*A flower which is mentioned in the first month should be rendered as a growing (young) fruit in the second month, and in the next month, it should be rendered more ripe, and after that, as having achieved perfection in the ripeness. (94)

37. This verse, as well as the preceding one, describes the womens' summer attire. This is also the subject-matter of verses XVI, 43 and XIX, 45 of the Ragh.

38. i.e. : when it decays naturally on the tree.

*This procedure is seen in the case of flowers born on trees, and it cannot at all be compared to the fruits of the creepers. There, the duration should be of two months of time only, for the flower, the fruit and the process of ripening. (95)

*Fruits can be distinguished on the basis of redundancy inside, outside, inside and outside, all over, numerous, and devoid of redundancy. (96)[39]

*The *lakucas* (kind of bread-fruit), etc....have inside redundancy, the *mocas* (bananas), etc....have outside redundancy. The mangoes, etc....have both and the *kakubhas*, etc....have it all over. (97)

*The bread-fruits, etc...have numerous redundancies, and the black *kapitthas*, etc....are devoid of redundancy. These six varieties of all fruits have to be known by the poets. (98)

*One must describe the seasons in the texts, either separately, one, or two, or three, or in a compact way (cycle), in their own order or in disorder. (99)

*There is no blemish in distorting the order in the case of a poet who is adept at meaning (lit. touches the path of meaning). When the distortion of the order becomes an ornament, then some beauty is achieved. (100)

*The ornament made by one who lacks genius becomes a blemish. The blemish of a genius-poet becomes an ornament. (101)

*The practice of a division of time is shown in this manner, for there is a great delusion here for the poet. The one who masters this is a great poet. (102)

This is the end of the 18th *adhyāya* (section) entitled Division of Time, of the first *adhikaraṇa* (chapter) called Secret of the Poets of the Kāvyamīmāṁsā (Exegesis of Kāvya) composed by Rājaśekhara.

39. The term *vyāja* literally means 'pretence' or 'deceit', but this meaning does not seem to make any sense here. What is meant by *vyāja* seems to be the uneatable parts of the fruits, such as the rind, the seeds or the kernel. Hence, we translate *vyāja* by 'redundancy'.

Part II

CHAPTER I

THE TEXTS AND THE CONTEXTS OF THE SEASON DESCRIPTIONS

In this chapter, we will try to see the importance of the theme of season descriptions in all our texts separately. The importance of this theme should be examined from three points of view :

— the importance of the season descriptions with reference to the plot or story of a *kāvya*, that is, with reference to the text as a whole.

— with reference to the formal peculiarities that each season description displays, such as the meter, the narratological aspect, as well as the poetic characteristics.

— with reference to the accepted theory of *rasa*, namely the accomplishment of various sentiments and emotions through the theme of the seasons, independently and also with relation to the whole text.

As we see, these three problems have a direct bearing on the importance of the role of these season descriptions in the text or in the story told by the text. As we mentioned above in the section dedicated to the history of this theme, season descriptions originate from short lyrical poems and can also be found as independent poems. This genre was incorporated into *Mahākāvya* literature. Thus, one of the problems that the authors of *Mahākāvyas* faced, since they were practically obliged by the law of the genre (see above Daṇḍin's definition of a *Mahākāvya*) to incorporate season descriptions in their texts, was to make these descriptions relevant and important to the story, a constraint which is of course lacking in independent season descriptions of the Ṛtusaṁhāra type.

In our opinion, a season description can be made relevant to the text as a whole according to the three parameters we listed above : if it has an importance or plays a role in the plot itself, if the hero figures in the description or even makes it, that is, if he is the narrator of the description, and finally, if it evokes a given *rasa* which is relevant to the story or at least to the passage itself. Thus, from the point of view of *Mahākāvyas*, a 'successful' season description would be the one which fulfills all these three requirements, independently of its intrinsic poetic qualities.

The Rāmāyaṇa

In the R. there are four major season descriptions, each occupying one full *sarga*[1] : winter (III, 15), spring (IV, 1), the rains (IV, 27) and autumn (IV, 29).[2] As we can see, these seasons follow each other in the natural order, and they occur quite grouped together in the work : spring, the rains and autumn are all described in *kāṇḍa* IV; winter, the first description, is somewhat more detached from the others, since it appears towards the beginning of *kāṇḍa* III. Many things happen between the winter description and the spring description : Rāma and his brother sustain numerous fights against the Rākṣasas, Sītā is abducted, the two brothers travel a long way to find her and have many adventures on the way. But still, we

1. There is moreover one short description of the rainy season in II, 57, 10-14, before Daśaratha starts for his hunting expedition during which he will kill by mistake a young ascetic. We shall not deal with this passage here, for it is greatly superseded by the main monsoon description in IV, 27.

2. The references are to the critical edition of the R. : ed. Bhatt, G.H., *The Vālmīki-Rāmāyaṇa*, Baroda, 1960-1975.

can assume that these four seasons mark the evolution of a year in the R.[3]

The winter description occurs in the Araṇyakāṇḍa (III, 15), when Rāma, Lakṣmaṇa and Sītā are sojourning in the wilderness of the Pañcavatī forest, on the shore of the Godāvarī river, a long way from Ayodhyā. At dawn, they go to the shore of the river in order to perform their ritual ablutions. On the way, Lakṣmaṇa, addressing his brother, makes a description of the winter-season which has just set in.

The actual winter description is from verse 4 to verse 24. After that, Lakṣmaṇa evokes the fate of their brother Bharata who, though delicate and used to luxury (28) is also living the life of a hermit in Ayodhyā itself, out of devotion to Rāma. He then goes on to criticize Kaikeyī, Bharata's mother, for being responsible for all their misfortunes, for which Rāma rebukes him from verse 35 onwards, telling him that he must not talk ill of his mother. At the end of the *sarga* (37), they reach the river and perform their ablutions.

This description does not seem to have a great importance in the plot of the R.[4] At the most, its function is to stress the sad fate of the three exiles. Although Lakṣmaṇa does not deplore their own misfortune, but only Bharata's, out of compassion for him, it is nevertheless clear that their own fate is as little if not less enviable than Bharata's. For indeed, although the scene is on the shore of the Godāvarī river, winter, though termed '*ṛtur iṣṭaḥ*', the desired season, (1), is nevertheless described as harsh and cold, endowed with snow and frost, and as such designed to make the life of the three exiles even harder. Thus, although this theme is but indirectly evoked, the function of this winter description is probably to accentuate the picture of the life full of hardships led by the three main protagonists of the story.

The actual description of winter, as we have seen, occupies

3. This gives us an indication of the time Sītā spends in Rāvaṇa's captivity, namely approximately one year, since she is abducted shortly after the winter description, and since Rāma and the monkey-army leave for Laṅkā to rescue her in the course of the following autumn.

4. This is indirectly shown by the fact that it is the only R. season description which Bhaṭṭi does not preserve in the Bhaṭṭ.

only some twenty verses of this *sarga.* Though it is entirely narrated in a direct speech by Lakṣmaṇa, it is very impersonal in nature, and nothing, or next to nothing in it refers to the characters of the story or to their situation. Lakṣmaṇa addresses Rāma only once in the whole passage, in verse 4, and there is once an allusion to Sītā, in 14, but only in the context of an *upamā* (comparison) : the orb of the moon is likened to her face. From verse 25 onwards, there is of course a shift in the topic, and Lakṣmaṇa evokes their own personal concerns, but this is no longer part of the actual winter description.

The whole winter description is composed in *ślokas,* excepting the last verse (39), which is an *upajāti,* and it is quite homogeneous, both style-and content-wise, visibly forming one piece. The style of this description is simple, the most frequent *alaṁkāras* being the *svabhāvokti* (description of the own nature of an object) and the *upamā* (comparison).

According to the theory, it is difficult to distinguish any particular *rasa* in this passage, for the tone is very impersonal. But there is a definite 'mood' of melancholy pervading these verses, provoked by the description of the general emptiness, somnolence, absence of movement and of sight, due to the fog, which are so typical of winter and create the impression that time is suspended.

The next season description, spring, appears at the beginning of tke Kiṣkindhākāṇḍa (IV, 1). The two brothers, from whom Rāvaṇa has in the meantime ravished Sītā, arrive on the shore of the Pampā river, following the instructions of Kabandha who had told them to go to this river in order to meet Sugrīva, the monkey-king.

The first three verses are dedicated to the description of the beauty of this river. The spring season itself is mentioned for the first time only in verse 4. If we keep in mind the theory of the stages of composition of this text, we could think that on the basis of a simple geographical indication (the two brothers arriving on the shore of the Pampā), a poetic description of this river was developed, to which was in turn added a description of spring, which, as the most charming season, could only enhance both the beauty of the Pampā and Rāma's love-longing. But this remains of course a simple conjecture.

Like the winter description, this spring description is entirely composed in *ślokas*, except the last two verses (48 and 49), which are *upajātis*. In this passage, Rāma himself speaks, describing the season to his brother, from verse 3 onwards. Unlike the winter description, this spring description is not at all impersonal or detached. The style of the whole passage is quite homogeneous : Rāma addresses his brother very often, so that the formula *paśya saumitre* recurs frequently, and all along the description, he gives vent to his grief at being separated from Sītā, which is aggravated by the beauty of the Pampā and of spring, the season of love. Curiously, Rāma's touching complaints do not elicit any consolatory response on the part of Lakṣmaṇa, and at the end of the *sarga* the two heroes go on their way, bound to meet Sugrīva and his handful of faithful followers at the beginning of the next *sarga*.

Needless to say, the dominant *rasa* of this passage is the *vipralambha-śṛṅgāra-rasa*, or the sentiment of love-in-separation. Of course, not all the verses of his passage contain references to Rāma's situation or state of mind, but in his direct speech (3-46) not less than 16 verses mention either his remembrances of Sītā, or his laments at being separated from her. Mostly, the construction of these verses is very similar : Rāma describes the beauty of certain characteristics of spring, and then says that they cause him only suffering due to his wife's absence. Each and every thing increases his grief : the season itself, the Pampā, the songs of the birds, the spring-breeze, and the couples of peacocks and deer. Thus spring acts here as the *uddīpana-vibhāva* of the *vipralambha-śṛṅgāra-rasa*.[5]

This spring description does not have any vital importance for the plot of the R. Its main function is of course to stress Rāma's acute despair which is contrasted with the pleasantness of the season. Moreover, the description of spring and of the Pampā, which is made by Rāma in an introspective mood, provides a diversion between the preceeding and the following *sargas*, which are dedicated to action.

5. According to Raghavan (see p. 11), Rāma occasionally overcomes his grief, carried away by the beauty of spring, whenever he does not mix his laments in the description.

The description of the rainy season appears in IV, 27. Rāma and Lakṣmaṇa, after helping Sugrīva to regain his throne in Kiṣkindhā, retire on mount Mālyavat when the monsoon arrives. Sugrīva has promised them his help to find Sītā, but due to the rains, their expedition comes to a forced halt, and they have to await autumn to resume it.

Thus, as they are residing on the mountain, Rāma makes to Lakṣmaṇa a description of the monsoon. His discourse starts in verse 2. Up to verse 34, we have the description of the rainy season, and then, from verse 35 onwards, up to verse 44, Rāma evokes his own concerns and sorrows: he thinks of his brother Bharata, and of Sugrīva who is happily spending the monsoon, having regained both wife and kingdom, whereas he himself is deprived of both, and hopes that the monkey-king will not forget him and will keep the promise he gave him. Lakṣmaṇa in turn answers him in the last verse of the *sarga* (46), consoling him and assuring him that all will be well, according to his wishes.

Unlike the winter and the spring descriptions, this monsoon description is not quite homogeneous in style and in content. The meter is the *śloka*, excepting verses 15 to 32 and the last two verses, 45 to 46, which are *upajātis* (21, 23 and 31 being *indravajrās* and 28, 45 and 46 *upendravajrās*). Thus nearly half of the verses are composed in a longer meter than the *śloka*. A change of meter at the end of a *sarga* is normal, but when it occurs in the middle of a *sarga*, it seems necessarily to indicate an interpolation. And indeed, if we examine these verses written in *upajātis*, we find that they differ in a significant way from the *ślokas*: they never make any allusions to the personal situation of Rāma, nor do they contain any addresses to Lakṣmaṇa, unlike verses 2 to 14, composed in the *śloka* meter. Thus these verses in *upajāti* meter contain an absolutely impersonal description of the season.

From the point of view of *rasa*, the first part of the description clearly reflects the *vipralambha-śṛṅgāra-rasa*. Unlike in the spring description, Rāma does not so much complain about the torture that the season inflicts upon him. Only one verse (14) contains the expression which is so typical of the spring description. Speaking of the blooming *kuṭaja*-trees, Rāma says:

mama śokābhibhūtasya kāmasaṁdīpanān......(they increase my love-longing, overcome with grief as I am). But Rāma's love-longing is indirectly brought about by a host of images: in 6, the sky is likened to a love-sick person, in 7, the earth releasing vapour is compared to Sītā shedding tears, in 12, the lightning on the black background of the clouds is likened to Sītā struggling in Rāvaṇa's lap, etc....The impossibility of obtaining the object of love finally results in a state of frustration, for Rāma is obliged to wait for the rains to stop and for the good will of Sugrīva before he can resume his quest for his beloved.

From the point of view of style, this passage contains more difficult *alaṁkāras* than the preceeding winter and spring descriptions, which are largely based on *svabhāvokti.* Here on the other hand, apart from the numerous *upamās* (5, 6, 7, 9, 10, 11, 12, etc...) and *rūpakas* (11, 20, 28), we find for instance a *yathāsāṁkhya* in verse 24, *atiśayoktis* in 4 and 8, etc....[6] As we can see, this passage contains figures of speech which are typical of later *kāvya* poetry. We must note that the longer meters are not always an indication of better poetry, for some of the most extraordinary images can be found in the *śloka*-verses of the beginning of the description.

This monsoon description is a typical example of a season description which is indispensably interwoven with the plot, displaying contextual and sentimental elements together. The rains play a role in the story, for they force the two brothers to give up temporarily their quest for Sītā. And like the spring description, they also serve to underline Rāma's unhappiness. Moreover, a description of the monsoon is of course welcome at this point of the story, for it shows the passing of time, and serves to fill a moment of waiting.

The autumn description occurs two *sargas* later, in IV, 29. This passage is clearly divided into several different parts. The beginning of the description shows us Rāma wandering alone

6. A *rūpaka* is a metaphor, and an *atiśayokti* is what is called a poetic fancy. A *yathāsāṁkhya* is a figure of speech consisting of ordered sequences of terms, such as nouns and adjectives, or subjects and objects of comparison, so arranged that item 1 of the first sequence matches item 1 of the second, item 2 of the first matches item 2 of the second, and so on. (see Gerow, *A Glossary of Indian Figures of Speech*).

on the summit of a mountain, observing the onset of autumn with its clear skies, thinking of his dear Sītā and swooning due to grief. Then he speaks, from verse 7 to 12, wondering how his beloved, who used to enjoy this season in his company, will now bear to spend it without him. This is a real monologue, since Rāma does not have any interlocutor.

Then his brother arrives on the scene, and seeing Rāma thus afflicted with sorrow he addresses him in verse 16, exhorting him not to let himself go and to find courage. In 22, Rāma speaks again, this time to Lakṣmaṇa, and makes a description of autumn. This time, he does not mix any laments about his own fate in it, and thus this passage is quite impersonal, except for a few addresses in the vocative to Lakṣmaṇa. In verse 30, he mentions the fact that autumn is the time for military expeditions, and this reminds him of his own circumstances. He then launches into angry invectives against Sugrīva, who is seemingly fully devoted to pleasure and is not keeping his promise to him, although autumn has now arrived. This passage reaches its climax in the threatening ultimatum Rāma dictates to his brother before sending him as a messenger to the monkey-king. Thus, as we can see, the actual autumn description is very short, covering only verses 22 to 30. This is not very surprising, for now Rāma is eager to act and to resume his search for Sītā.

Like in the monsoon description, we again find in this passage a series of verses which are composed in *upajātis*: the last two verses (51 and 52) as well as verses 15 to 20 (verses 16 to 19 being *upendravajrās*). Here again, verses 15 to 20, which contain Lakṣmaṇa's admonitions to Rāma, are visibly interpolated. The tone is highly moralizing, Lakṣmaṇa extolling the virtues of yoga and of action, not at all in keeping with the rest of the description. The whole passage could be skipped without any inconvenience, for when Rāma speaks again in 22, he never alludes to what his brother has just said. Moreover, we see that there is a logical link between verse 14, before Lakṣmaṇa's speech, and verse 21: in 14, Lakṣmaṇa comes along, in search of fruits, and sees Rāma, and in 21, Rāma addresses him, and starts making a description of autumn.

In this passage, the *vipralambha-śṛṅgāra-rasa* is again predominant. But this *rasa* appears only in the prologue to the description, and in Rāma's monologue at the beginning of the passage. Thus, in verse 3, he swoons, thinking of Sītā. Unconsciousness (*apasmara*) can be one of the *vyabhicāri-bhāvas* (mental states) of the *vipralambha-śṛṅgāra-rasa.* In Rāma's monologue, this *rasa* is also very prominent : Rāma worries about Sītā, wondering how she can bear without him the sight of the *sārasa*-birds, of the blooming *asana*-trees or of the *kalahaṁsa*-swans. He also evokes his own unhappiness in verse 11 : *tāṁ vinā mṛgaśāvākṣīṁ caran nādya sukhaṁ labhe* : living without this fawn-eyed one, I do not get any happiness now.

But at the end of the description, his grief turns into anger (*roṣa*) and even rage, when he thinks of Sugrīva's faulty conduct. Thus the autumnal season itself causes a change of attitude in Rāma : previously, he was dejected and lamenting, whereas now all his martial spirits are roused.

Like the description of the rainy season, this autum description plays of course a great role in the story, from the point of view of the various emotions it provokes in Rāma, and also because it announces that the search for Sītā can be started, for now the rivers have calmed down, and the paths are practicable again.

If we take a global view at all these R. season descriptions, the following characteristics become obvious : all these descriptions are direct speeches, made by one of the characters of the story addressing another one. Except in the case of the spring description, this kind of discourse usually elicits a response from the listener at the end of the passage. In the autumn description, as we have seen, we even have a dialogue : first Rāma speaks, then Lakṣmaṇa and then again Rāma.

The use of the direct speech in these R. season descriptions should not surprise us, for it is a typical trait of the ancient epic. This is of course even more prominent in the Mahābharata, where, at the beginning of each *sarga*, we find similar formulas like, for instance '*janamejaya uvāca*'. In the R., this kind of formulas are usually integrated in the verse, but we still find in this text many direct discourses. Moreover, the whole R. is supposed to be told to Rāma by his two sons, Kuśa and Lava, according to the first *kāṇḍa*. The type of speech which contains a poetic description, like the season descriptions, could be called a 'lyrical discourse'.[7]

From the point of view of *rasa*, we see that all these descriptions, excepting winter, which does not have any particular *rasa*, are *vipralambha-śṛṅgāra-rasa*. This is of course due to Rāma's situation, and also to the fact that he himself makes these descriptions. Thus we see that these three season descriptions are skilfully used to depict the hero's emotional state.

The general remark which can be made about these R. season descriptions is that all of them, even winter which is perhaps the least relevant to the plot, are attached in some way or other to main story. They are all relevant to the emotional context, and, in the case of the monsoon and autum descriptions, to the emotional context as well as to the furtherance of the plot.

The Kumārasaṁbhava

The Kum. contains only one season description, namely that of spring, in III, 23 to 40. *Sarga* II describes how the gods, afraid of the *asura* Tāraka, whose power is increasing day by day, go together to see Brahmā, to ask for his help. Brahmā himself cannot do anything againt Tāraka, since it is thanks to his own boon that the *asura* has become so powerful. But he promises the gods that the future son of Śiva and Pārvatī will kill him. But Śiva, after the death of his previous wife Satī lives retired in the mountains, solely dedicated to penance, and has no intention to remarry.

But the gods have a solution to this problem. At the begining of *sarga* III, Indra invites Kāma, the god of Love, to come, and asks him to see to it that Śiva falls in love with Pārvatī, who is attending on him in his own *āśrama*. Thus Kāma, filled with apprehension, sets out for Śiva's hermitage, in the company of his wife Rati and of his best friend, Spring (23).

In verse 24, Spring displays his magic in the wood of Śiva's hermitage. Due to his premature arrival, the sun returns before the proper time to the Northern region (25), and the *aśoka*-tree

7. See Soehnen, Renate : *Untersuchungen zur Komposition von Reden und Gespraechen im Rāmāyaṇa*, p. 44, Reinbeck, 1979.

blooms without being touched by the feet of lovely women (26). Flowers are born, the cuckoos sing, and the ascetics of the hermitage can hardly keep control over themselves (34). A number of different creatures succumb to love (36 to 39) and only Śiva remains unperturbed in this meditation (40). Thus a general feeling of intoxication and joyousness pervade the whole hermitage, until Nandi, noticing someting unusual, appears, and intimates silence. After this, all activity stops, and the whole forest stands still, looking like a picture (42) : the calm before the tempest.

This spring description is composed in the *upajāti* meter, verse 31 being an *upendravajrā*. Since it appears in the middle of a *sarga*, there is no change of meter at the end. This passage is entirely written in the narrative style, without any direct speech, unlike in the R. season descriptions.

Among all the *Mahākāvya* season descriptions, this Kum. spring description can undoubtedly be said to be one of the most relevant and important from the point of view of the plot: it sets the scene for Kāma's action, and by its very sweetness and pleasantness, it forms a very striking contrast with the tragic events which follow. As we know, just at the moment when Kāma is aiming his arrow at him, Śiva comes out of his meditation and sees him (but not without seeing Pārvatī's beauty first), and, in his terrible anger, reduces him to ashes. The unfortunate Rati swoons, seeing her husband's plight, and then gives vent to pathetic laments in *sarga* IV. Pārvatī, deeply dejected, returns to her parents.

Thus, the whole scene of the spring description is slowly and carefully built up a veritable crescendo of *rasa*, the *śṛṅgāra-rasa* of course, for which spring acts as the *uddīpana-vibhāva*. This *rasa* finds its climax in verses 36 to 39, which describe in an incomparably charming and touching way the amorous behaviour of various denizens of the wild, ranging from the very trees to to the *kiṁpuruṣas*, who all come under the sway of love. These amorous gestures are the *anubhāvas* of the *śṛṅgāra-rasa* : the male bee drinks out of the same flower-bowl as the female and the male antelope scratches the female with his horn (36) ; the she elephant gives to the male a cheek-full of water fragrant with lotuses and the *cakrāvaka*-bird offers to his beloved a half eaten stem (37); the *kiṁpuruṣa* kisses his mistress (38) and even the trees are embraced by the creepers (39). Thus these amorous gestures increase in intimacy and intensity, but find a sudden anti-climax in verse 40, which says that Śiva, for whom all these efforts are made, remains master of himself. Thus the *śṛṅgāra-rasa* does not reach its ultimate fulfilment, which would be Śiva falling in love with Pārvatī, but since Kāma is unsuccessful, there is an anti-climax, which forms a great contrast with the charming scene preceeding it.

Thus this spring description is important for its masterful evocation of the *śṛṅgāra-rasa.* This description is also indirectly an homage to Śiva, for it shows the greatness of his power of concentration, since he also does not yield to love, although of course he feels attracted towards Pārvatī for a second, before he sees Kāma and destroys him.

Before turning to the Ragh., we shall briefly say a few words about a Kum. passage which is often treated as a season description[8], namely V, 20 to 26. The seasons are mentioned in these verses with relation to Pārvatī's penance, to which she resorts as a means of winning Śiva, since other methods have failed.

In this passage, we find of course certain elements of description which are typical of season descriptions, but it can by no means be called a season description, for the aim of the poet here is not primarily to describe the seasons, but the terrible *tapas* Pārvatī is practising : keeping her eyes fixed on the sun in summer, seated between four fires; exposed to the lashing rains of the monsoon without a roof to protect her; and plunged in icy-cold rivers during winter. Such *tapas* descriptions are often found in epic literature, and they must be considered as a poetic motif by themselves, which is in no way comparable to season descriptions.[9]

Thus, we see that only the seasons which can be disagreeable for an ascetic are mentioned here : summer with its sweltering heat, the monsoon with its unceasing downpour of rain, and the cold winter. Autumn and spring on the other hand,

8. Both Renou and Raghavan consider this passage as a season description.

9. For instance in the R. I, 62, 22-24, the *tapas* of Viśvāmitra is described in pretty similar terms.

which have an agreeable and moderate temperature, are not mentioned. Moreover, these seasons are here described very realistically as hard to endure, whereas in season descriptions usually only their positive aspects are stressed. Thus in these verses, the glare of the summer-sun hurts the eyes : *netrapraghātinīṁ prabhām* (20); during the monsoon, the rain is uninterrupted and mixed with wind : *nirantarāsv antaravātavṛṣṭiṣu* (25); in winter, the wind accumulates heaps of snow : *atyantahimotkirānilāh* (26). As we see, the aim of this passage is not to describe the seasons, but to praise the endurance of the goddess, who bears the vicissitudes of the climate without flinching.

The Raghuvaṁśa

In the Ragh., we find in total four season descriptions : autumn (IV, 14-24), spring (IX, 24-48), summer (XVI, 43-53) and a cycle (XIX, 37-47). These season descriptions are distributed in the work in a fairly regular way. If we omit the very quick enumeration of kings in *sarga* XVIII, we see that one king out of two is given with a season description. These kings are Raghu, Daśaratha, Kuśa and Agnivarṇa, Dilīpa, Aja, Rāma and Atithi do not have this priviledge.

The first season description of this work is that of autumn, which appears in *sarga* IV, just after Raghu has succeeded his father Dilīpa on the throne. This description is entirely composed in *ślokas*, and in the narrative style, without any discourses in direct speech.

This passage portrays at the same time the king Raghu and the autumnal season. The style is definitely epic, sustained by the use of the *śloka*, the epic meter par excellence. Here, no trace of *śṛṅgāra*: the *vīra-rasa* dominates the whole passage. Raghu is the founder of the dynasty, the greatest of all these kings, the conqueror of the whole earth. Autumn, which is the season for military expeditions, comes to him as soon as he has ascended the throne of Ayodhyā, filling him with martial ardour, as the last verse of this description shows : *yātrāyai codayāmāsa taṁ śakteḥ prathamaṁ śarat* (24) : autumn incited him to undertake an expedition, before even his own energy (did so). As we see, autumn acts as a real *uddīpana-vibhāva* of the *vīra-rasa*, or heroic sentiment.

Raghu's heroism pervades the whole description : he raises his victorious bow, alternating with Indra for the protection of the people (16), his power is likened to that of the sun (15), his fame is spread in the whiteness of the swans, the stars and the lotuses(19),[10] or more concretely, spread by the guardians of the paddy-fields who sing his glory (20). The picture is completed by the description of bulls tearing up the shores of the rivers, imitating him (22), and of his intoxicated elephants emitting fragrant ichor as if out of jealousy towards him (23).

All these elements of description contribute towards the production of *vīra-rasa.* Thus, the overall picture which is drawn of Raghu, along with, and often in comparison with certain autumnal characteristics, is that of great h.ro who seems to fill the whole earth and even space, with his power and his fame. In this sense, this description symbolizes Raghu's future exploits, which will indeed make him the master of the universe.

The spring description, which is entirely composed in the *drutavilambita* meter, occurs in IX, 24-48, during the reign of Daśaratha, Rāma's father. It is immediately preceeded by the description of Daśaratha's conquests of numerous countries, and followed by the tragic hunting expedition during which the king unvoluntarily kills a young ascetic. Thus, this spring description, which abounds in *śṛṅgāra-rasa*, forms a contrast to the epic scene which preceeds it, and to the tragic accident which follows. The description of spring in this context is Kālidāsa's own invention, for in the R., from which Kālidāsa draw his inspiration here, we find a short evocation of the rainy season in the same place (II, 57, 10-14).

Although the first verse of the passage (24) says that spring arrives as if to serve king the with new flowers, and the last verse (48) says that Daśaratha is enjoying the festival of spring in the company of his women, the king is never mentioned in the rest of the passage. Instead, other people are described, who could of course belong to Daśaratha's court, but this is never explicitely mentioned. While reading this passage, we rather get the impression that it describes in a very general way the activities of various people. Thus, this whole description is

10. Fame is always portrayed as white : this is a *kavi-samaya.*

attached to the context only by the first and the last verse. In this respect, this description does not play an important role in the plot, unlike the autumn description.

The dominant sentiment of this description is the *śṛṅgāra-rasa*, like in the Kum. spring description. But here, this *rasa* is brought about by different means. There are of course a few erotic images which appear in both passages, like that of the red *palāśa*-flowers which are likened to nail-marks left by spring on the trees (Kum. III, 29 and Ragh. IX, 31) or that of the cuckoos which dispell by their songs the anger of sulking women who then yield to love (Kum. III, 32 and Ragh. IX, 47). whereas in Kum., the *śṛṅgāra-rasa* is mainly brought about by the description of the amorous behaviour of a series of animals, in harmony with the context, since the scene is in the wilderness of the Himalaya. In the Ragh. spring description on the other hand, which does not seem to be linked with any specific context, or may with the spring-festival context, according to verse this *rasa* is achieved mainly by portraying women, their behaviour 48, in spring, their ornaments, their beauty and their amorous activities.

The summer description, composed in *upajātis*, takes place during the reign of Kuśa, the son of Rāma (XVI, 43-53). Kuśa has returned to Ayodhyā, which had been abandoned after Rāma's death. He restores the city to its pristine glory, and then summer arrives. This summer description is immediately followed in a very natural way by the description of Kuśa's plays in the water of the Sarayū river, in the company of the women of his harem.[11] It is during this bath in the river that Kuśa loses a precious ornament which falls to the bottom of the water. Kumudvatī, the sister of the Nāga king Kumuda, who resides at the bottom of the river, finds it. Kuśa, outraged, is about to fight with the Nāga king, thinking that he has stolen the ornament, but Kumuda explains the situation to him and offers him his sister in marriage to conciliate him.

Thus, the summer description plays a certain role here, for it is due to the summer heat that Kuśa is prompted to take bath

11. This description is no longer part of the summer description, for descriptions of plays in the water (*salila-krīḍā*) form a poetic motif by themselves (see above Daṇḍin's definition of *Mahākāvyas*).

in the river, which will in turn lead to his marriage to the Nāga-princess. This marriage has a symbolic significance, for it unites two clans which have always been sworn enemies, the Nāga clan and the clan of Garuḍa, the eagle who is Viṣṇu's vehicle, and who is thus also associated with Rāma, Viṣṇu's *avatāra*, and his son Kuśa. This is mentioned in the last verse of the *sarga*.

Excepting the first and the last verse of the description, this passage does not contain any reference to the king Kuśa. Otherwise, only undefined personages are mentioned: women in 48 and 50, or rich people in 49. Thus, like the spring description, this summer description is not greatly relevant to the context, nor does it add anything to the delineation of Kuśa's character. From the point of view of *rasa*, this passage cannot be classified very distincly. There are of course a few erotic allusions here and there, but this season cannot be said to be the *uddīpana-vibhāva* of the *śṛṅgāra-rasa*: on the other hand, the fact that summer kills all love-desire is constantly stressed.

The cycle of seasons, the first of its kind which we find in a *Mahākāvya*, appears in the last *sarga*, XIX, 37 to 47, during the reign of the last king of Kālidasa's, description Agnivarṇa.[12] This description of all the seasons follows the elaborate depiction of the love-pleasures this king is addicted to.

In this cycle, which starts with the monsoon, Kālidāsa impartially dedicates two verses to each season, *hemanta* and *śiśira* being seemingly considered as one and the same season, since only one verse is dedicated to each. This cycle is entirely composed in *rathoddhatās*. We must note that this cycle contains many images which appear already in the spring and summer descriptions of the same work: in XIX, 44, there is a description of the women swinging on *dolās* (swings), like in the spring description (IX, 46); the summer-attire of the king's mistresses is depicted in XIX, 45, in a similar way as in the summer description (XVI, 43), and the aphrodisiac drink made out of wine,

12. According to the Purāṇas, especially the Viṣṇupurāṇa, there are least four more kings after Agnivarṇa, who are not mentioned in the Ragh. The generally accepted idea is that the Ragh. is either an uncompleted work, or else that the last pages of the manuscript have been destroyed. See Jacobi, Hermann, 'Die Epen Kalidasas', in *Kleine Schriften* I, p. 424-427, Wiesbaden, 1970.

mango and *pāṭala*-flowers, which was already mentioned in XVI, 52, is again described in XIX, 46.

This entire cycle of seasons is centred around the activities of the king during the various seasons, and as such, serves to draw the portrait of Agnivarṇa. This debauched king is entirely dedicated to pleasure, and his sole activity is love-making, as the last verse of the cycle says: *indriyasukhāni nirviśann anyakārya-vimukhaḥ...*(devoted to the pleasures of the senses and averted from any other activities). Thus all the seasons are for Agnivarṇa a pretext for love-making, and act as the *uddīpana-vibhāvas* of the *śṛṅgāra-rasa*. This cycle of seasons is therefore of a great importance in this context, for it shows that throughout the year, this dissolute ruler had no other occupation than dallying with his mistresses. The change of seasons only brings about changes in this same activity: for Agnivarṇa, no hunting expedition in spring like for Daśaratha, no war in autumn like for Raghu, and not even plays in the water in summer, like for Kuśa. In the comfortable and luxurious world of his palace, he is content with passing from the artificial pleasure-hills to the terrace on the roof of his palace, and from his inner apartments to the swings.

Thus, this portrait of Agnivarṇa as it appears in this cycle of seasons can be compared with and contrasted to the portrait of Raghu in the autumn description. Whereas Raghu, the founder of the line, the most glorious of all these kings, was depicted as filling the universe with his power and fame, Agnivarṇa, the last sovereign described, the degenerate king whose vices are enough to disgrace all his glorious ancestors, is represented as secluded in the nut-shell of his palace, which he never seems to leave. Thus, in XIX, 40, he looks at the Sarayū river through the holes of the palace-windows. There is of course an erotic allusion in this, but it also shows that this king remains cloistered in his mansion. Similarly, verse XIX, 7, before the actual cycle, says that Agnivarṇa was never available to his ministers, but only showed them his foot once in a while through a hole in the wall. As we see, Agnivarṇa is really the opposite of his ancestors, all glorious kings who conquered the world.

Thus, this cycle of seasons as well as the autumn description play a great role in the story, for they are used in order to make a portrait of the two kings Agnivarṇa and Raghu, and tos tress their main qualities or faults. The spring and summer descriptions on the other hand, are only very loosely attached to the context, and hardly contain any references to the main protagonists of the *sarga* to which they belong.

We must note that Kālidāsa's evocation of Rāma's adventures in *sarga* XII does not contain any of the season descriptions which appear in the R. This is because the Ragh. version of Rāma's story is extremely condensed. This *sarga*, of 104 verses, describes all the events which happen between Rāma's departure into exile and the moment when he kills Rāvaṇa. Thus, it carries the action forward very fast, and does not contain any descriptive themes. But in the next *sarga* (XIII), during which Rāma and Sītā fly back to Ayodhyā in the chariot Puṣpaka, Rāma shows to Sītā from their aerial position all the places where he sojourned during his quest for her. Thus, in verses 26 he shows her mount Mālyavat on which he and his brother spent the monsoon, and verses 26 to 28 contain a brief evocation of the rainy season with its rain, thunder and dancing peacocks, and of the difficulty he had to bear this season without her. Verses 30 to 32 describe the Pampā river, on whose shores spring is described in the R. These three verses also contain a spring description, although the word spring is never mentioned. Thus, we find here such typical Kālidāsean images as the *cakravāka*-birds feeding each other lotus-stems (31) an image already appers in the Kum. spring description (III, 37). In verse 32, Rāma remembers how he mistook for Sītā a young creeper whose flowers were similar to Breasts. The image of the creeper-woman, as we shall see in a later chapter, is also very typical of spring descriptions from Kālidāsa onwards.

It is of course not surprising that some of the R. season descriptions should be evoked here. *Sarga* XII is wholly dedicated to action, whereas *sarga* XIII is of a lyrical and descriptive nature, reminding us of the Meghadūta.

The Bhaṭṭikāvya

As we know, the Bhaṭṭ, tells the story of Rāma, following

pretty faithfully its model, the R. Thus in the Bhaṭṭ. we find the spring description (VI, 73 to 86), the monsoon description (VII, 1 to 13) and the autumn description (VII, 14 to 17) at the same place where they occur in the R. The R. winter description on the other hand is not preserved, and instead, we find one more autumn description in II, 1—20, in a context where there is no season description in the R.: the young Rāma is leaving Ayodhyā for the first time with his brother Lakṣmaṇa and the sage Viśvāmitra, who has asked them to come to his hermitage in order to protect it from the incessant attacks of the Rākṣasas. At the moment when they are leaving the city, autumn appears.

Why did Bhaṭṭi insert an autumn description here? One explanation which is often given for this is that Bhatti must have copied Bhāravi's autumn description which occurs in *sarga* IV of his Kir. This is of course hard to affirm with certainty, for Bhaṭṭ. seems to have lived at approximately the same time as Bhāravi. In any case, there is no doubt that one of them must have copied the other, for these two autumn descriptions are strikingly similar, both from the point of view of the images they contain and from the point of view of the general atmosphere they evoke.

Unlike the R. season descriptions, and indeed the remaining season descriptions of the Bhaṭṭ., this autumn description is not written in the form of a discourse made by one of the characters, but in the narrative style. It is nevertheless intimately linked with the emotions Rāma feels due to this season, especially the second part of the description (10-20). Rāma observes everything and is delighted by most things he sees. Thus we often find the expressions *tutoṣa paśyan* (13): he was delighted to see, *mumude vilokya* (15): he rejoiced, having seen, *anandayat tam* (16): pleased him, *kutūhalaṁ...tatāna tasya* (17): stretched his curiosity, etc... This second part of the description which stresses Rāma's emotions is mainly characterized by *svabhāvokti*. Verse 11 is best suited to show Rāma's feelings and behaviour:

latānupātaṁ kusumāny agṛhṇāt sa nadyavaskandam upāspṛśac ca/
kutūhalāc cāruśilopaveśaṁ kākutstha īṣat smayamāna āsta//11//

Bending over every creeper, he plucked their flowers, and leaping up to every river, he drank their water. Out of curiosity, the descendent of Kakutstha sat down on every charming stone-slab, smiling slightly.

This verse renders particularly well the exuberant behaviour of a young boy who is going on a journey for the first time. Thus, there is a specific mood of joyousness and festivity which pervades the whole passage. Nature in autumn is beautiful, and men gift its fruits to Rāma (20). Everything announces that Rāma's expedition will be successful, and indeed he will defeat the Rākṣasas and bring back Sītā for his wife. There is no specific *rasa* which can apply to this passage or to this atmosphere.

Spring, like in the R., is described at the moment when the two brothers reach the Pampā river (VI, 73-86). It is remarkable that the word spring is not even mentioned once in the whole passage. But the readers must have been so conversant with the R. story that they could not miss this description, which moreover contains many typical characteristics of spring, such as flowers, bees and singing birds.

Like in the R., Rāma is talking, describing the season to his brother, and the *vipralambha-śṛṅgāra-rasa* is very prominent, for spring causes him nothing but torment, since he is separated from Sītā. His love-longing and grief are systematically stressed all along the passage.

The same remarks are valid for the description of the rainy season (VII, 1-13): excepting the first three verses which are written in the narrative style and describe 'objectively' the onset of the monsoon, the rest of the description is made by Rāma, and every verse contains his laments about his pitiful state. Thus, as compared to the R. monsoon description, we see that Bhaṭṭi, by systematically producing *rasa*, brings the feeling of love-in-separation to greater heights.

The second autumn description, which immediately follows the description of the monsoon is very short (VII, 14-17). Again Rāma speaks, from verse 15 onwards, but the actual autumn description is very short, for, from verse 17 onwards, he starts recriminating against Sugrīva, like in the R., autumn rousing his aggressive feelings. Thus this autumn description is really reduced to its deictic function as an indicator of time. This is partly due to the fact that autumn has already been described in *sarga* II, and partly because now Rāma is eager to act, and has no time or mood to describe the season.

Thus we see that in the three season descriptions which follow the R. Bhaṭṭi keeps the main characteristics of these R. descriptions: the direct speech, the use of the *śloka*, and the rendering of the sentiment of love-in-separation. The first autumn description on the other hand is written in the narrative style, and not in the form of a discourse, and in *upajātis*, excepting verses 6 and 19 which are *vaṁśasthas*. This is the only time in these *Mahākāvya*-season descriptions that we find a sudden change of meter in the middle of a *sarga*. This first autumn description also allowed Bhaṭṭi to introduce a different mood than the *vipralambha-śṛṅgāra-rasa* to which he was tied in the other three descriptions. And indeed, there is a striking contrast between the elated and happy young Rāma who goes on his expedition full of enthusiasm and the older Rāma who is deprived of his beloved, and filled with grief and even at times with bitterness.

The Kirātārjunīya

The Kir. contains two season descriptions : autumn (*sarga* IV) and a cycle of seasons (X, 18-38). As we know, the Kir. tells a story from the Mahābhārata (III, 27-41). The Pāṇḍavas are in exile in the forest. Draupadī advises them to rebell and attack their enemies. After some discussion on the topic, Yudhiṣṭhira asks Arjuna, who is Indra's son, to procure for them celestial weapons in order to ensure their victory. Arjuna agrees and sets out for the Himalaya.

It is at this point, in *sarga* IV of the Kir., that autumn sets in. This *sarga* is the first of a series of eight sargas (IV to XI) which are of Bhāravi's own invention, and contain purely descriptive or lyrical themes. Thus we find in them the description of autumn, then of the mountain Himalaya, and of the beginning of Arjuna's *tapas*, which is so terrible that the *ṛṣis* go and complain about it to Indra. They latter decides to send the Gandharvas and Apsarases in order to disturb his *tapas*. Thus, the celestial musicians and nymphs go to mount Indrakīla, where Arjuna is seated in deep meditation. There, they enjoy themselves, plucking flowers, taking bath, admiring the sun-set and moon-rise, and drinking and making love till morning. Then, in sarga X, the Apsarases, with the help of the six seasons, try to disturb Arjuna's *tapas*, but fail in their attempt, for he remains unperturbed. After that, Indra declares himself satisfied with his son, and advises him to seek Śiva's favour for the obtainment of his aim. In the following *sargas*, while describing Arjuna's fight with Śiva disguised as a Kirāta, Bhāravi again follows his model pretty faithfully.

Thus we see that in these eight *sargas*, Bhāravi treats practically all the lyrical themes which Daṇḍin prescribes for a *Mahākāvya*. And indeed, with Bhāravi appears a decisive change in the way of writing a *Mahākāvya* : much less emphasis is given to the smooth advance of action, and more is given to descriptive digressions.

As we have seen, autumn appears at the moment when Arjuna leaves his brothers and goes on his expedition. This description is composed in the *vaṁśastha*-meter, exepiting the last two verses which are *puṣpitāgrā* (37) and a *mālinī* (38). This autumn description gives us an idea of Arjuna's travels : we see the roads, the fields, the rivers, the villages, the farmers and their herds go by under his eyes, till, in the last verse of the *sarga*, his destination, the Himalaya, is described as it appears in the distance.

As we mentioned above, this autumn description and the first Bhaṭṭ. autumn description bear many similarities to each other. Like Rāma, Arjuna is filled with delight and curiosity by what he sees. The expressions *dadarśa sa* (11, etc. ...) : he saw, *nananda paśyan* (2, etc. ...) : he rejoiced seeing or *tasya ... kutūhalam...ādadhe* (12) : he was filled with curiosity, recur frequently in this passage. Thus we really see autumn through the eyes of Arjuna. But here again, like in the Bhaṭṭ autumn description, no particular *rasa* can be observed.

The beginning of this description is made in the narrative style, but from verse 20 onwards, the Yakṣa who is guiding Arjuna on the way, seeing the hero's delight, starts speaking and describes to him the beauty of autumn. Thus from verse 20 to 36 we find the form of the discourse. But this passage does not have many characteristics which are typical of a discourse : we do not find in it any imperatives of vocatives, except in verse 21, where the Yakṣa addresses Arjuna in order to pay him homage. Moreover, the Yakṣa describes the season in a perfectly impersonal way, never mentioning his own emotional response to it, unlike in the R. season descriptions. But the Yakṣa's relation with Arjuna is of course not the same as that of Rāma towards his brother, for the Yakṣa simply wants to please his master by making a poetic description of the season.

The cycle of seasons, which occurs in the circumstances which we described above, and is entirely composed in the *puṣpitāgrā* meter, starts with the rainy season, just like the Ragh. cycle. Thus, at first the rains are described (19-23), then autumn, (24-27), winter (28-29), *śiśira* (30), spring (31-35) and summer (36).

But in this cycle, the seasons are not very clearly delimited. Thus, autumn is depicted in a *ṛtu-saṁdhi* with the monsoon (verses 24, 25 and even to some extent 26). Winter is represented as already strongly mixed with vernal characteristics, in 28 and 29, and *śiśira* anyway seems to be mixture of winter and spring. Therefore, two seasons strongly dominate this passage, namely the monsoon, which extends also into autumn, and spring, which already starts in winter. Summer is greatly side-tracked, since it appears only in one verse (36), just long enough to make some mocking comments about spring, the only direct speech of the whole passage. The two prominent seasons, the rains and spring, are also the seasons which are usually describcd as the most erotic and romantic. It is therefore not surprising that these two seasons should be given a great importance here, for the aim of the seasons is to disturb Arjuna's penance and make him yield to the charms of the Apsarases.

This passage is of course full of *śṛṅgāra-rasa*. Under the influence of the seasons, which clearly act as the *uddīpana-vibhavas* of this *rasa*, the whole world is filled with feelings of love, from the bee, in verse 34, which amorously kisses a flower, to the Apsarases themselves, who, although they are supposed to kindle love in Arjuna, ironically fall prey to it themselves.

Arjuna on the other hand remains unperturbably fixed in his *tapas*, and his powers of concentration are stressed all along the passage and opposed to the way in which the rest of the world succumbs to love : *na dhṛteś cacāla jiṣṇuḥ* (23) : Jiṣṇu did not vacillate in his resolution. *Vikṛtim upayayau na pāṇḍusūnuḥ* (29): the son of Pāṇḍu did not undergo any transformation. *Lebhe sitaturage vijayaṁ na puṣpamāsaḥ* (35) : the month of flowers did not obtain a victory over the possessor of white horses. *Bhuvanaparibhavī na yat tadānīṁ taṁ ṛtuganaḥ kṣaṇam unmanīcakāra* (37) : that is why, then, the troup of the seasons which makes the world suffer, did not disturb him (even) for a moment. And finally verse 38 :

śrutisukham upavīṇitaṁ sahāyair aviralalāñcchanahāriṇaś ca kālāḥ /
avihitaharisūnuvikriyāṇi tridaśavadhūṣu manobhavaṁ vitenuḥ // 38 //

(The Apsarases') song, which was agreeable to hear and accompanied on the *vīṇā* by their companions, (the Gandharvas), and the seasons which were charming due to their numerous characteristics, did not provoke any perturbation in Hari's son, but caused love in the wives of the gods.

Thus we see that this cycle of seasons serves to glorify the greatness of Arjuna and of his *tapas*, just like the Kum. spring description serves to glorify Śiva, since, just like Śiva, Arjuna does not yield to the temptations of the seasons.

The Śiśupālavadha

The Śiś. contains only one cycle of seasons in sarga VI. Just like the Kir., the Śiś. retells a Mahābhārata story (II, 41-45). The scene takes place during Yudhiṣṭhira's consecration as king. Gifts are distributed to all the kings, and the gift of honour goes to Kṛṣṇa. This thoroughly infuriates Śiśupāla, the Cedi king, his life-long enemy. After an angry exchange of words, Kṛṣṇa finally beheads Śiśupāla by means of his discuss in front of the whole assembly. This is how the Mahābārata story goes.

The Śiś. basically keeps the same story, but with many additions and some changes. The most significant change is that

Kṛṣṇa does not straight away kill his opponent, which would considerably have reduced the size of the poem, but Śiśupāla leaves the assembly, declaring war on him. Then both parties go and mobilize their troups, and Kṛṣṇa sets out for the expedition. After this starts a series of digressions, from *sarga* IV to XI, just like in the Kir. Thus *sarga* IV describes mount Raivataka on which Kṛṣṇa is encamped, V describes his camp, VI the seasons, VII a pleasure—walk in the forest, VIII the bath of the Yâdava-women, IX the evening, X banquets and the pleasures of love and XI the sun-rise. After these various descriptive themes, the thread of the narrative is resumed, and after a tremendous battle, Kṛṣṇa finally beheads Śiśupāla with his discus.

Thus, the season description occupies the whole of the sixth *sarga*. It takes place after Kṛṣṇa has set his camp on mount Raivataka, and, according to the first verse of the passage, the seasons arrive all together in order to pay homage to Kṛṣṇa and allow him to enjoy himself. This cycle is very long one, containing a total 79 verses. It is not actually one cycle, but two following each other, the second being much shorter than the first. Unlike the Ragh. and Kir. cycles, it does not start with the monsoon, but with spring. Thus we first have the description of spring (2-21), then of summer (22-24), of the monsoon (25-40), of autumn (41-54), of winter (55-61) and of *śiśira* (62-66). Then again we have spring (67-70), summer (71), the monsoon (72-73), autumn (74-76), winter (77) and *śiśira* (78).

Just like Bhāravi, and unlike Kālidāsa, Māgha does not dedicate an equal number of verses to each season. He dwells longer on spring, the monsoon and autumn. In the first cycle, an extremely short place is given to summer as compared to the other seasons : only three verses. Māgha has recourse to a stratagem in order to leave the description of this season : verse 25 says that 'a row of clouds approached the mountain *without waiting for its turn* (*apratipālitasvasamayā*), as if the intempestive arrival of the monsoon had prevented the poet from further dwelling on summer ! The real reason, as we shall see in a later chapter, is probably that summer, due to its rather disagreable nature, is usually not greatly liked by the poets.

The second cycle is distinguished from the first by two characteristics : from the point of view of the style, it contains in all the verses the difficult *yamaka* which consists in having the second and fourth *padas* identical in sound but with different meanings.[13] This second cycle is also distinguished from the first by the use of the meter : whereas the first cycle, up to verse 66 is entirely composed in *drutavilambitās*, the second cycle, from verse 67 onwards, is composed in a variety of different meters : 67 is a *prabhā*, 68 a *svāgatā*, 69 an *upajāti*, 70 an *aupacchandasika*, 71 a *toṭaka*, 72 an *aupacchandasikā*, 73 a *kalahaṁsa*, 74 an *upajāti*, 75 an *aupacchandasikā*, 76 a *mattamayūrī*, 77 a *vasantatilakā*, 78 a *drutavilambita* and 79 a *vasantatilaka*. As we see, Māgha uses this second cycle as a real 'show-piece' to exhibit his skill in the composition of *yamakas* and in the use of the most diverse meters. This is of course typical of Māgha's time, in which such a display of purely technical mastery was very much in fashion. By this display of virtuosity, as well as by the very length of this double cycle, Māgha has characteristically tried to do more and better than his model and rival Bhāravi.[14]

Although, as we have seen, the first verse of the *sarga* states that all the seasons have come exclusively for Kṛṣṇa's sake, the hero of the Śiś. is remarkably absent from this description. In the whole *sarga*, though it is very long, only a few verses mention Kṛṣṇa (1, 2, 41, 42, 53, 54, 79), and out of these, only three verses reflect his thoughts, feelings or actions : *madhuripor ...mudaṁ...vitatāna śukāvalih* (53) : the row of parrots caused joy to the enemy of Madhu. *Akalayan muditām iva sarvataḥ... śaradam* (54) : he found that on all parts autumn seemed to be joyful. *Śrīmān...acodi sa mayūragirā vihartum* (79) : the Glorious one was prompted to enjoy himself by the song of the peacocks. In this respect, this cycle of seasons is not very contextual, nor is it relevant to the plot, since the main protagonist of the story hardly figures in it.

Instead of describing Kṛṣṇa's reactions to the seasons, Māgha prefers to dwell on the mostly amorous, activities, of a

13. According to Mallirātha, it is out of desire to write these *yamakas* that Māgha added this second cycle.

14. The whole plan of the Śiś. is visibly inspired from the Kir. See to this effect Jacobi, Herman, 'On Bhāravi and Māgha', in *Kleine Schriften I*, pp. 447-471, Wiesbaden, 1970.

great number of unidentified people, who have for the most part nothing to do with the story as such. The main *rasa* of this passage is undoubtedly the *śṛṅgāra-rasa*, for it contains a great number of erotic verses. But quite a few verses, which describe the lonely travellers or else their languishing wives waiting for them at home, evoke the *vipralambha-śṛṅgara-rasa.* Thus this cycle is the only one among these season descriptions which evokes at the same time these two opposite aspects. But Māgha could of course easily achieve this, since his cycle is not restricted to a given situation or character, but rather describes the seasons in general, in the same way as, for instance, the Ṛtusaṁhāra.

This *sarga* is written in the narrative style, but we must note that Māgha introduces far more often than his predecessors single verses, or occasionally several consecutive verses, in the direct speech. We find this trait before Māgha only once in the Ragh. spring description (IX, 47) where the cuckoos speaks, and once in the Kir. cycle (X, 36) where the summer-season speaks. In the Śiś., a great number of creatures are made to speak, which are as varied as a lover (*praṇayin*) (11-12), an unidentified personage (17-19), the bees (*ali*) (39), the swans (*haṁsa*) (44), the mistresses (*priyāḥ*) (65), the jasmine-creeper (*kundalatā*) (66) and the beauty of spring (*madhuśrīḥ*) (69).

The Naiṣadhacarita

As we know, the Naiṣ. retells the story of Nala and Damayantī as it appears in the Mahābhārata (III, 50-55), but only the first part of it, up to their wedding, omitting the tragic events which follow.

The season description appears in I, 76-106. Nala, though he has never seen Damayantī, has heard so much of her beauty and qualities that he is madly in love with her. In order to allay the burning fever of love-longing, he goes to a pleasure-park near his palace, hoping to find some relief. It is in this park or forest that the seasons are described. In the Mahābhārata, there is nothing which corresponds to this description, but it was probably suggested to Śrīharṣa by one verse (III, 50, 17) which says that Nala, unable to bear his love-longing, used to spend his time retired in a park near his palace. This indirectly gives us an idea of the amplification the story underwent in the Naiṣ. : from one Mahābhārata verse we reach some thirty verses in the Naiṣ.

This season description is a very unusual one, for the seasons are never mentioned in it, except in verse 105, which says that the wood Nala is visiting is 'filled with all the seasons'. We shall subsequently dedicate a full chapter to proving that this passage, despite its peculiar nature, is indeed a season description. Here, we shall merely examine some of its general characteristics.

This description is entirely written in *vaṁśasthas* and in the narrative style. At the beginning of the passage (76), it is said that a gardener shows to Nala the beauties of the park by point ing them out with his fingres. But although he is thus in the same situation as Rāma describing the seasons to Lakṣmaṇa, or as the Yakṣa describing autumn to Arjuna, this gardener never actually speaks, his role being limited to gestures. On the other hand, like in the Śiś., we find a few verses in the direct discourse : in I, 79-81, Nala speaks to a *ketaka*-tree, and in I, 90, the cuckoo speaks in order to curse unfortunate wayfarers.

The main function of this passage is to portray the state of mind of the king, who is full of intense love-longing for Damayantī. The whole park in which he is walking is seen through his eyes. Some things fill him with curiosity, others with delight and yet others with fear. In this respect, this description is quite similar to the autumn descriptions of the Bhaṭṭ. and Kir., in which, as we have seen, the season is also described as it is seen by the two heroes. This Naiṣ. passage is highly evocative of the *vipralambha-śṛṅgāra-rasa*, and all the things Nala observes serve as the *uddīpana-vibhāvas* of this *rasa*, for everything reminds him Damayantī and increases his love-longing. Thus, this passage describes the climax of Nala's desire and despair at being away from her. Fortunately for him, for his love seems at times to verge on distraction, he shortly afterwards meets in the some park the celestial *haṁsa* who will help solving his problem by acting as a messenger between him and Damayantī.

We shall now try to draw some general conclusions about the various aspects of these season descriptions with which we have been dealing here. From the point of view of tbe meters used in these passages, we see that there is nothing like a prescribed or 'favourite' meter for this topic. When the season descriptions appear in the middle of a *sarga*, they are composed in the same meter as the rest of the *sarga* to which they belong. The poets did not try to 'underline' these descriptions, or to make them more conspicuous by a change of meter. But this would probably be against the rule of *Mahākāvyas*. When these descriptions occupy a whole *sarga*, usually only the last few verses are in a different meter.[15] Whereas Bhāravi follows this rule with moderation (in the Kir. autumn description only the last two verses are composed in different meters), Māgha, in the last 13 verses of the season description uses not less than 9 different meters. Thus, about the use of the meter in these descriptions, we can only make remarks which would be valid for the works in general, namely that as we advance in time, the poets have been making use of more and more complex meters, and this trait, as far as the season descriptions are concerned, is specially conspicuous in Māgha's cycle.

From the point of view of narrative devices, we see that the R., with its use of the direct speech in the season descriptions, did not exert any influence on later season descriptions. As we have seen, from Kālidāsa onwards, these descriptions are always written in the narrative style, with the exception of Bhaṭṭi in the passages he copied from the R. and of the second part of the Kir. autumn description, in which the Yakṣa speaks. But this direct speech as we have seen, does not have much in common with the R. type of discourses. On the other hand, we increasingly find isolated verses in direct speech. There are already traces of this in Kālidāsa and Bhāravi, but this trait reaches its culminating point in Māgha.

But the R. surely exercised an influence on later season descriptions by using the seasons as the *uddīpana-vibhāvas* of certain *rasas*. As we have seen, the *rasa* produced by the spring, monsoon and autumn descriptions of the R. is always the *vipralambha-śṛṅgāra-rasa*, due to Rāma's situation. The same *rasa* also appears in the corresponding Bhaṭṭ descriptions, in the

15. As we have seen in the case of the R., the verses in *upajati* which occur in the middle of the *sarga* in the monsoon and autumn descriptions are probably later interpolations.

Naiṣ. season description and at times in the Śiś. cycle. Its counterpart, the *śṛṅgāra-rasa* is also very common, appearing in the Kum. and Ragh. spring descriptions, and in the Ragh., Kir. and Śiś. cycles of seasons. The Ragh. autumn description is an exceptional case, for it is the only one which illustrates the *vīra-rasa*, or heroic sentiment. On the other hand, there are of course a few season descriptions which do not seem to evoke any definite *rasa*. This is the case for the R. winter description itself, as well as for the Ragh. summer description and the Bhaṭṭ. and Kir. autumn descriptions.

Another point in which the influence of the R. season descriptions is visible, is the way in which they describe the reactions and feelings of the hero in connection with a given season. This point is of course ultimately connected with the *rasa* problem. As we have seen, the reaction of the hero to the seasons is given great prominence in all the Bhaṭṭ. season descriptions, as well as in the autumn description of the Kir. and in the season description of the Naiṣ. This aspect is much less stressed in the Śiś. cycle, wherein Kṛṣṇa is hardly mentioned. It is of course totally lacking in the Kum. spring description and in the Kir. cycle, but this is due to the situation of the two heroes, Śiva and Arjuna, who are in deep meditation and thus do not respond to the seasons. This aspect is also neligible in the Ragh. season descriptions. In the case of the autumn description and of the cycle, the two kings Raghu and Agnivarṇa are of course present, but they seem to form a part of the picture, and are not detached from it and looking at the seasons like spectators. In the spring summer descriptions, the king Daśaratha and Kuśa are hardly mentioned at all, and thus these two descriptions can be said to be less successful, for their contextuality is lost.

CHAPTER II

PERSONIFICATIONS OF THE SEASONS

In this section, we shall examine in which texts and in what way the seasons appear in a personified form. The idea itself that the seasons are persons, or perhaps should we rather say deities, is a very old one since it appears already in the Veda where it is said that although they are male by name (*ṛtu*, m), they are in reality women (I, 164, 16). Their worship as deities seem to have been well-spread in Vedic times.[1]

As for the texts with which we are concerned here, we can note that neither in the R., nor in the Bhaṭṭ., the seasons appear as personifications. In the Kum., spring appears of course in his personified form of Kāma's friend, and in the Ragh. too, except in the cycle of seasons of *sarga* XIX, the seasons, that is spring, summer and autumn, are personified to various extents. In the Kir. autumn description of *sarga* IV, there are no personified seasons, except in one single verse, but in both the Kir. and Śiś. cycles, the seasons are personified. In Kir. X, 18, the seasons appear in a group (*ṛtugaṇa*) which evokes a group of people. The same term is also used to designate them in Śiś. VI, 1, wherein they are moreover said to "set their foot on the earth" (*ādadhe bhuvi padam*), which still further accentuates their resemblance with human figures. As for the Naiṣ., it does not represent the seasons in a personified form, except in verse I, 105, which makes an allusion to "Spring, the friend of Love".

1. See Renou p. 146 and Raghavan p. 4.

We must note first that all the seasons are not personified to the same extent and in the same manner. In fact, only two seasons have the privilege of being personified in a systematic and well-defined way : spring, either in its probably original male personification of Madhu, the friend of Kāma, or from Kālidāsa onwards, personified as a female, and autumn, which is always represented as a woman.[2] All the remaining seasons are only sporadically and mostly vaguely personified, and thus never reach the status of full-fledged personifications.

Spring

The first one among our texts which represents this season in its personified fo m is the Kum., in which spring appears as the dear friend of Kāma (*mādhavena abhimatena sakhyā*) in III, 23. These two divinities (for Mādhava undoubtedly has the status of a god in this text), are traditionally associated in mythology, due to the fact that spring is the season of love.[3] In the Kum., spring is much more than a mere personification : he is a real character in the story. He accompanies Kāma to Śiva's retreat, spreads his magic in the woods of the god's hermitage and finally consoles Rati at the loss of her dear spouse.

The chief task of Spring in this text is to help his friend Love to achieve his aim, which he does very concretely by preparing arrows for him. It is well-known that Kāma's arrows are made out of flowers, and spring, being the season of flowers, is thus the ideal provider of these 'weapons' :

> *sadyaḥ pravālodgamacārupattre nite samāptiṁ navacūtabāṇe /*
> *niveśayāmāsa madhur dvirephān nāmākṣarāṇīva manobhavasya*
> *//27//*

> Then, when he had brought to completion an arrow (made out) of a fresh mango (-shoot), which was endowed with charming feathers due to the growth of the leaves, Spring

2. We might discern in this an influence of the Ṛtus., for in this text too, only autumn and spring are personified.

3. They appear for instance together in the Śivapurāṇa (Pārvatīkāṇḍa) which also describes the onset of spring and the burning of Kāma's body.

fixed bees on it, as if they were the syllables of the name of Manobhava (i.e. : Love).

Thus, Spring is closely associated with Kāma in the latter's "war-like" activities. This is also already revealed by the opening verse of the Ṛtus. spring description :

praphullacūtāṅkuratīkṣṇasāyako dvirephamālāṁ vidadhad dhanurguṇām /
manāṁsi bhettuṁ surataprasaṅgināṁ vasantayodhaḥ samupāgataḥ priye //VI, 1//

With its blossoming mango-shoots for sharp arrows, carrying a garland of bees which is the string of his bow, this warrior, spring, has arrived, my dear, in order to break the hearts of lovers.

As we can see in this verse, the image of Spring has become absolutely similar to that of Kāma himself, for usually it is the latter god who has flower-arrows, a bow-string made out of bees, and who breaks the hearts of lovers. May be due to the fact that they are often represented together, the image of Spring has finally merged with that of the god of Love himself.

In the Ragh. spring description, spring is also occasionally depicted as a male personification. Thus, in IX, 32, he is represented as an artist who "decorates" the forests with *kurabakas*, like one would decorate the body of a woman with leaf-like designs :

viracitā madhunopavanaśriyām abhinavā iva pattraviśeṣakāḥ /
madhulihāṁ madhudānaviśāradāḥ kurabakā ravakāreṇatāṁ yayuḥ //32//

Placed by Spring on the beauty of the forests like very fresh leaf-designs, the red amaranths which are expert in (the art of) giving honey to the bees, became the cause of their buzzings.

Although the representation of Spring as a male personification seems to be an old and well-established one, Kālidāsa introduces a new way of depicting this season, namely as a woman. This trait already appears in one verse of the Kum. spring description, in which *madhu-śrī* (Beauty of Spring) decorates herself with the help of typical spring-elements (III, 30). But it is mainly in the Ragh. spring description that this new way of personifying the season is developed.

One of the main reasons for this change of "iconography" seems to be the desire on the part of the poet to respect the consistency of certain images. This can be understood by examining two very similar, but so to say "inverted" verses, which appear in the Kum. and Ragh. spring descriptions :

> *bālenduvakrāṇy avikāsabhāvād babhuḥ palāśāny atilohitāni /*
> *sadyo vasantena samāgatānāṁ nakhakṣatānīva vanasthalīnām*
> //Kum. III, 29//

> Since they were not open, the very red *palāśa*-flowers were curved like the young moon, and (looked) like nail-marks on the rows of forests which had recently been united with spring.

> *upahitaṁ śiśirāpagamaśriyā mukulajālam aśobhata kiṁśuke /*
> *praṇayinīva nakhakṣatamaṇḍanaṁ pramadayā madayāpitalaj-*
> *jayā* //Ragh. IX, 31//

> The multitude of buds placed on the *kiṁśuka*-tree by Beauty of the departure of *śiśira* (i.e. Beauty of spring), looked like nail-mark decorations (made) on her lover by a young woman whose shame has vanished due to her passion.

In the Kum. verse, *vasanta*, the lover, is a masculine, and the forest-rows, his mistresses, a feminine (*vanasthalī*). In the Ragh. verse on the other hand, it is the *kiṁśuka*-tree, a masculine, who is the lover. Spring in order to be his beloved, must therefore necessarily be a feminine. But since there does not exist any feminine name of spring in Sanskrit, the poet solved the problem by adding the substantive *śrī* to the masculine name, in order to feminize it. Thus, the term *śrī* which can translated by "beauty" or "splendour" does not seem to be much more than a feminizing device.[4] The use of this device does not seen to be restricted to the names of spring, for we

4. Some, like L. Renou, in his translation *Le Raghuvamsa*, translated this term by "goddess" (deesse), but *śrī* does not mean "goddess" in general, it is only one of the names of Lakṣmī.

also find it for instance in Ragh. IX, 32, quoted above, where we have *upavana-śriyām* (on the beauty of the forests). *Vana*, the forest, is a neuter, but in this context it has to be a feminine in order to evoke the image of a woman who is decorated with ornaments. Thus here too, the term *śrī* is used in order to feminize a neuter substantive.

The spring-woman appears again in another verse of the same passage, IX, 45, where she uses the pollen of the flowers for face-powder.

This way of representing spring as a female personification, which seems to be Kālidāsa's own invention, is again taken up by both Bhāravi and Māgha in their cycles of seasons. Thus, in Kir. X, 31, we find *vasantalakṣmīḥ*. She is clearly personified, since she is wearing anklets (*nūpura*) in the form of buzzing swarms of bees, and she moreover "sets her foot in the forests of lotuses" (*nirāse nalinavaneṣu padam*) :

> *kusumanagavanāny upaitukāmā kisalayinīm avalambya cūta-yaṣṭim /*
> *kvaṇadalikulanūpurā nirāse nalinavaneṣu padaṁ vasanta-lakṣmīḥ //31//*

> Desiring to enter into the forests of blooming trees, holding a mango-branch covered with young shoots, having swarms of buzzing bees for anklets. Beauty of spring set her foot among the forests of lotuses.

Here, Bhāravi does not use the term *śrī* in order to feminize spring, but its synonym, *lakṣmī*. The word *lakṣmī* is so to say Bhāravi's poetic signature, for it appears in the last verse of each *sarga* of his Kir. This might also be the reason why he uses it here rather than *śrī*.

In the Śiś. cycle on the other hand, like in Kālidāsa's poems, spring is again personified by means of the term *śrī* (here we have *madhu-śrī*), in VI, 69, that is, in the second shorter cycle. Again, we must remember that Māgha, in a differenciated imitation of Bhāravi uses *śrī* in the last verse of each *sarga*.

> *jagad vaśīkartum imāḥ smarasya prabhāv anīke tanavai jayantīḥ /*
> *ity asya tene kadalīr madhuśrīḥ prabhāvanī ketanavaijayantīḥ //69//*

"Let me spread them as a sign of victory in Love's army, which is capable of conquering the word", thinking thus, the creating Beauty of spring produced for him plantains, as garlands of banners.

Here *madhu-śrī* is personified only due to the fact that she speaks or thinks, and her physical aspect is not described. Moreover, she is called *prabhāvanī* (creating) which gives rise to the idea of an abstract principle. As it was the case in the Kum. spring description, where Spring makes arrows for Kāma, Beauty of spring here, although she is a female, is also at the service of the god of Love, making for him banners of victory.

Thus we see that the personification of spring has undergone a remarkable transformation from male to female, and this in spite of the fact that spring's names are all masculine, and that as a male personification this season is well-established in mythological stories. As we have seen in the case of Ragh. IX, 31, the poetic context could give rise to the need of having a female spring. But there is undoubtedly a deeper underlying reason for this change of sex of the season, as we shall see in the next chapter, in the section dedicated to *vasanta*.

Autumn

Unlike spring, autumn is consistently described as a female personification in the Ragh. autumn description, as well as in the Kir. and Śiś. cycles of seasons. This is probably due to its Sanskrit name, *śarat*, a feminine. In the Ragh. autumn description, autumn is only very vaguely personified. Thus in verse IV, 14, this season goes to the king Raghu, similar to a second royal fortune: *enaṁ samupasthitā pārthivaśrīr dvitīyeva śarat*. And in verse 17, it tries to imitate the splendour of the king:

puṇḍarīkātapatras taṁ vikasatkāśacāmaraḥ|
ṛtur viḍambayāmāsa na punaḥ prāpa tacchriyam //17//

With its umbrella of white lotuses and its fan of shining *kāśa*-grass, the season imitated him, but could not obtain his splendour.

Thus the autumnal season here is personified only by some of its actions, like going to the king and imitating him, but it is not really described in its person. In the Kir. cycle of seasons on the other hand, autumn reaches the state of a fully developed female personification:

> *dhṛtabisavalayāvalir vahantī kumudavanaikadukūlam āttabāṇā/*
> *śarad amalatale sarojapāṇau ghanasamayena vadhūr ivālalambe*
> //24//
>
> Wearing a row of bracelets made out of lotus-stems, clothed in a single very fine raiment[5] made out of *kumuda*-forests, and having obtained reeds (or: holding an arrow), autumn was taken by the rainy reason, like a bride, by her lotus-hand whose palm was spotless.

The image which is evoked here is of course that of a marriage between autumn, which is the bride, and the rainy season (*ghanasamaya*, m) her bridegroom[6]. The term *āttabāṇā* can be interpreted in two different ways: as far as the natural season is concerned, it means "which has obtained reeds", but for the personified autumn-bride, it signifies "holding an arrow". This is to be explained by the fact that in case of inter-caste marriages, a *kṣatriya*-girl marrying a man from a higher caste was made to hold an arrow during the ceremony.[7] Here we should probably not stretch the point too far by imagining that autumn must be a *kṣatriya* and the monsoon a *brahmin*, for the qualificative *āttabāṇā* is probably mainly used here for the sake of the pun it allows on reeds and arrows, but it is nevertheless noteworthy that autumn, as we shall see in the next chapter, is the season for military expeditions, and as such, personifying it as a *kṣatriya*-girl has some meaning.

This way of personifying the season as a woman, more

5. A *dukūla* is a very fine cloth made out of inner bark of the *dukūla* plant.

6. Technically speaking, this is a *ṛtu-saṁdhi* (union of two seasons), which, thus announced by this symbolic marriage between autumn and the rainy season, continues during the whole autumn description.

7. See *Manusmṛti* III, 44 : *śaraḥ kṣatriyayā grāhyaḥ...utkṛṣṭavedane*. In literature, this trait appears for instance in Kum. VII, 7, where Pārvatī is made to hold an arrow during the wedding-ceremony, for she is marrying Śiva the supreme god, whereas she is just the daughter of the Himālaya.

precisely as a bride, is not novel since it appears already in Ṛtus. III, 1, in a very similar description, although here the season's husband is not mentioned:

kāśāṁśukā vikacapadmamanojñavaktrā sonmādahaṁsarutanūpuranādaramyā /
āpakvaśālilalitānatagātrayaṣṭiḥ prāptā śaran navavadhūr iva ramyarūpā //1//

Autumn has arrived like a new bride whose form is beautiful, having for garment the *kāśa*-grass and for charming face the blooming lotus, beautiful due to the sound of her anklets (which is nothing but) the songs of the intoxicated swans, and having for lovely, bent and slender body the rice which is nearly ripe.

The autumn-woman appears once again in the Śiś. cycle of seasons, in not less than three verses. Verse VI, 42 again contains the image of autumn as a bride, or here rather as a mistress, but her lover is not the rainy season like in the above-quoted Kir. verse, but a mountain:

sa vikacotpalacakṣuṣām aikṣata kṣitibhṛto 'ṅkagatāṁ dayitām iva /
śaradam acchagaladvasanopamākṣamaghanām aghanāśanakīrtanaḥ //42//

The one whose name destroys sin saw autumn which had for eyes blooming lotuses, as though she was a mistress seated on the lap of (her lover) the mountain, and whose clouds could be likened to a transparent and gliding dress.

As we can see, there is a clear continuity in the way in which autumn is represented in these three verses from Ṛtus., Kir., and Śiś.[8] Verse VI, 52 of Śiś., on the other hand, introduces some originality in the description of the autumn-woman:

8. In Śiś. VI, 54, autumn is also personified to a certain extent since it has for eyes the lotuses in the ponds, for laughter the swans in the sky and for teeth the reeds.

vilulitām anilaiḥ śaradaṅganā navasaroruhakeśarasaṁbhavām|
vikarituṁ parihāsavidhitsayā harivadhūr iva dhūlim udakṣipat
||52||

The autumn-woman tossed into the air the pollen coming from the stamina of the fresh lotuses, which was falling down due to the wind, as if to spread it on the wives of Hari, out of desire to joke.

In this verse, unlike in the preceding ones, the season is not personified by a description of its physical aspect, but by its behaviour, which is absolutely human.

As we can see, there is a fundamental difference in the ways in which spring and autumn are personified. Spring seems to be a more "active" personification, making arrows or banners for the god of Love, decorating the forests, leaving nail-marks on the forests or on the trees, as their lover or mistress, making up her face with typical spring characteristics, etc... The personified spring, whichever its sex, makes use of the natural spring season, and even produces spring in nature.

Autumn, on the other hand, except in the last above-quoted verse (Śiś. VI, 52), appears as a more static and passive personification, so much so that these verses could be paintings of the season. The personified autumn is moreover never quite dissociable from the season as it appears in nature, and the two often seem to be superposed on each other. This is so, undoubtedly due to the abundant use of *rūpakas* in the three verses which represent the autumn-bride (Ṛtus. III, 1, Kir. X, 24 and Śiś. VI, 42)[9]: the lotuses are her face (Ṛtus.), or her hand (Kir.) or her eyes (Śiś.). Her clothes are the *kāśa*-grass (Ṛtus.), or the *kumuda*-forests (Kir.) or the clouds (Śiś.). In Ṛtus., the cackling swans are her anklets, and in Kir., the lotus-stems are her bracelets, etc... Thus, the personified autumn is mostly reducible to the natural autumn-season, unlike the personified spring which transcends its own natural manifestation.

The other seasons

We shall now turn to the remaining seasons, which are here

9. The same can nevertheless also be said of spring in Kir. X, 31.

treated together, since they are only rarely personified. Summer, in the Ragh. summer description is personified only once in verse XVI, 43, and in a vague manner: *athāsya...ājagāma gharmaḥ priyāveṣam ivopadeṣṭum* (then summer arrived, as if to recommend to him a dress for his mistresses...). Thus the season appears as a personal advisor or councellor in the service of the king, but it is not otherwise personified. In the Kir. cycle of seasons, summer (here *nidāghakāla*, the time of heat), is also personified, for, due to its white blooming jasmines, it seems to laugh at spring which has been as unsuccessful as the other seasons in its attempts at disturbing Arjuna's *tapas* (*smayata iva sma madhum*). But here also, its personification is not further developed.

The monsoon is somewhat more clearly personified, as a male figure, more precisely as a husband, in Kir. IV, 24 and X, 24. In Kir. X, 24, which is quoted above, the rainy season (*ghanasamaya*) is the bridegroom of autumn. It also appears in the quality of a husband, this time an absent one, in the only verse from the Kir. autumn description which contains the personification of a season, IV, 24. Here its wives are the directions of the sky, which are now, since it is autumn, deserted by their husband the rainy season. The term used here to designate the monsoon is *kadambānila*, which, in the sense it has here of "(season wherein blows) the wind (perfumed by) *kadambas*", seems to be a single occurrence in Sanskrit poetry, its usual meaning being simply that of "wind (perfumed by) *kadambas*".

vipāṇḍubhir mlānatayā payodharaiś cyutācirābhāguṇahemadāmabhiḥ /
iyaṁ kadambānilabhartur atyaye na digvadhūnāṁ kṛśatā na rājate//IV, 24//

With their clouds (or: breasts) which are pale due to their dried state (or: due to their melancholy), from which the golden threads which have the quality of the lightnings have fallen at the departure of their husband (the season wherein blows) the wind (perfumed by) *kadambas*, the thinness of the directions which are like wives cannot but shine.

As we see, in both verses in which it is personified (Kir. IV,

24 and X, 24), the only element which personifies the monsoon is the fact that it is a husband, but its personification is not further stressed, for in both cases the emphasis lies with its wives, autumn and the directions respectively. In both these verses, the rainy season bears a masculine name: *ghanasamaya* and *kadambānila*. These are of course not the monsoon's basic names, but metaphorical names. We can wonder why the poets have not chosen to depict this season as a woman, like they did with spring and autumn, since its most common names, *varṣāḥ* or *prāvṛṣ* are feminine. This might be due to the fact that in the poets' imagination, or according to the usual *clichés*, the rainy season with its violent downpour of rain, and with its thunder and lightning, does not possess the feminine characteristics with which the soft, peaceful and luminous Indian autumn is endowed. Moreover, autumn is the time of crops, fruits and fertility of the earth in general, with which women have always been associated. The monsoon on the other hand is the season which fertilizes the soil with its rain, a decidedly male type of activity. All these considerations may have prompted the poet to depict the rains as a male personification.

Winter (*hemanta*) is never personified in any of the texts we are studying here, and *śiśira* has this privilege only once, in Kir. X, 30, where it is somewhat surprisingly called *smaraikabandhu*: the only friend of Love. We know that usually it is Spring who bears this title. But spring in this cycle is only personified as a woman, and this might be the reason why *śiśira* replaces it here in the quality of Kāma's friend.

Thus it becomes apparent that all the seasons are not personified to the same degree and with the same precision, even in the cycles where they are announced together as *ṛtugana*[10]. *Hemanta*, *śiśira* and *grīsma* are either not personified at all (*hemanta*), or else extremely vaguely by the sole means of a descriptive epithet (*śiśira* is called *smaraikabandhu*) or by means of some actions in the case of summer. The names of these three seasons are of course all masculine, but their sex and exterior appearance are not clearly determined. The monsoon

10. Bhāravi is still the most systematic, for in his cycle, all the seasons, excepting *hemanta*, are personified to a certain extent. Māgha on the other hand personifies only autumn and spring.

fares a little better in this respect, for although it is only personified in two verses of Kir., it is at least clearly described as a male figure. As for spring and autumn, their personifications are well-established, as we have seen above.

Thus, the seasons which are personified most precisely, that is, spring, autumn and the monsoon, are also those which are most often and most abundantly described. Since winter, *śiśira* and summer are not given much scope in the season descriptions, it follows naturally that their personifications are also underdeveloped.

But in most cases, even when the seasons are very clearly personified, the poets take some verbal precautions while personifying them, by using *alaṁkāras* such as *upamās*, *rūpakas* and *utprekṣās*. Thus, verse III, 29 from Kum. and IX, 31 from Ragh. which contain similar images of nail-markes left by spring on nature, introduce this image by means of an *upamā* (*iva*). Summer, in Ragh. XVI, 43 is personified by means of an *utprekṣā* : *ivopadeṣṭum* (*as if* to recommend...), and in Kir. X, 36, we also find an *utprekṣā* : *smayata iva* (as though it was laughing...). The rainy season, which appears as the husband of the directions in Kir. IV, 24 is made so by means of a *rūpaka* : *kadambānilabhartur* (the monsoon which is a husband). Autumn, in Kir. X, 24 is likened to a bride by means of an *upamā* : *vadhūr iva*. In Śiś. VI, 42, this season is likened to the mistress of the mountain by an *utprekṣā* (*dayitām iva*), and in Śiś. VI, 52, it is personified by means of a *rūpaka* (*śaradaṅganā*), which can be rendered as "autumn which is a woman", and its personified behaviour is rendered by an *utprekṣā*. It seems therefore that the poets felt some reluctance to describe the seasons directly like human figures, and do so only in the context of certain images based on comparison : the seasons *look like* a wife or a husband, they *seem* to do certain things.

Let us now try to define in what circumstances the seasons appear in their personified form. Generally speaking, the seasons are personified, as if to offer an explanation for their independent or unnatural behaviour, when they appear, sometimes even before their proper time, with a precise aim or task to fulfill. Inversely, when they are not personified, it is because they arrive according to their proper time and natural order.

Thus the seasons are not personified in any of the R. season descriptions, where they appear one after the other, in their natural order, nor in the Bhaṭṭ. season descriptions which correspond to the R. They are not personified either in the autumn descriptions of *sarga* II of the Bhaṭṭ. and *sarga* IV of the Kir. where, although the autumnal season seems to come just at the right moment to allow the two heroes to depart, it is nevertheless never mentioned that it arrives with the explicit aim of allowing them to do so. An interesting case in this respect is the Ragh. cycle of seasons in *sarga* XIX, where, unlike in the other cycles, the seasons are not personified. And indeed, in this passage they do not arrive all at the same time in an artificial way, like in the Kir. and Śiś. cycles, but one after the other, spread on the duration of a whole year, in order to show how the king Agnivarṇa spends his time at different epochs of the year. The case of the Naiṣ. season description is an exception to this rule, for although verse I, 105 says that the wood in which Nala is enjoying himself is "filled with all the seasons", which probably means that they are all present there in order to contribute to the king's pleasures, they are not personified, excepting Madhu.

The case of the single season descriptions of the Ragh. is somewhat marginal. In these passages, the seasons are of course personified to various extents, especially spring, and they are announced by very similar formulas which give rise to the thought that they have come with the sole purpose of serving the respective kings :

—*athainaṁ samupasthitā pārthivaśrīr dvitīyeva śarat* .. (IV, 14)
(then autumn came to him, similar to a second royal fortune)

—*atha samāvavṛtte kusumair navais tam iva sevitum...madhur* (IX, 24)
(then spring arrived, as if to honour him with fresh flowers)

—*athāsya...ājagāma gharmaḥ priyāveṣam ivopadeṣṭum* (XVI, 43)
(then summer arrived, as if to recommend to him a dress for his mistresses...)

But in each case, especially as far as spring and summer are concerned, the poet does not say directly that they come in order to serve the king, but "as if" to honour him "as if" to recommend to him, using an *utprekṣā* both times.

On the other hand, in the other three passages in which the seasons appear as personifications, namely the Kum. spring description and the Kir. and Śiś. cycles of seasons, no such verbal precaution is taken, and it is very clear that the seasons arrive with a special purpose in mind, and of their own accord. In the Kum., as we know, Spring arrives in order to help Kāma, and the season clearly comes ahead of its time, as is revealed by several indices, in verses III, 25 and 26 :

> *kuberaguptāṁ diśam uṣṇaraśmau gantuṁ pravṛtte* samayaṁ vilaṅghya /...//25//
>
> As the hot-rayed (sun), *ahead of its time* was starting to go towards the region governed by Kubera...
>
> *asūta sadyaḥ kusumāny aśokaḥ skandhāt prabhṛty eva sapalla-vāni* /
> *pādena* nāpaikṣata *sundarīṇāṁ saṁparkam āsiñjitanūpureṇa* //26//
>
> Immediately, the *aśoka*-tree produced flowers along with sprouts, starting from the trunk itself. *It did not require* the touch of beautiful women's feet which are (adorned) with tinkling anklets.[11]

In the cycles of the Kir. and Śiś., the seasons come all together, with a definite aim : in the Kir., they come along with the *apsarases* and *gandharvas*, to help them disturb Arjuna's meditation. In the Śiś. they come together in order to contribute to Kṛṣṇa's enjoyment :

> *atha riraṁsum amuṁ yugapad girau kṛtayathāsvataruprasava-śriyā* /
> *ṛtugaṇeṇa niṣevitum ādadhe bhuvi padaṁ vipadantakṛtaṁ satām* //Śiś. VI, 1//

11. It is a topos of Sanskrit poetry that the *aśoka*-tree will bloom in spring only after a young woman's feet have been applied to it. See for instance Kālidāsa's *Mālavikāgnimitra*, act III.

Then the troup of the seasons simultaneously set their foot on the earth, creating a profusion of flowers on the trees which belonged to each one of them, in order to honour him who brings about the end of honest people's misfortunes, and who desired to enjoy himself on the mountain.

As we can see, the personified seasons do not appear for the sake of any insignificant personages. They only come to honour kings, divine heroes and gods. Even if they come with the rather detrimental purpose of destroying the hero's *tapas*, like in the Kum. spring description or in the Kir. cycle, the very fact that they are required as additional "weapons" is an indirect homage to the hero's power of concentration, for it is well-known that the seasons are apt at provoking feelings of love. It is therefore to be considered as a special favour when the personified seasons come to a certain personage, especially if they all come at the same time. Thus in Kum. II, 36, when the gods describe to Brahmā the extraordinary power of the demon Tāraka, it is said that all the seasons are attending upon him together throughout the year, and the same is also said of Rāvaṇa in Śiś. I, 66. It is thus a way of glorifying a personage and of exalting his power to say that the seasons attend upon him, and it is certainly one of the functions that the personified seasons fulfill in these descriptions.

In conclusion, we can say that only those cases are to be considered as pure personifications in which a gender, a particular action, or certain human characteristics are attributed to the seasons, like for instance in the case of spring. Marginal cases are often rendered through *upamās* or *rūpakas*, like *kadambānilabhartuḥ*. Highly fanciful personifications are those which are brought about by *utprekṣas*. For on the basis of an *utprekṣā*, we cannot actually say that an object is personified 'in toto' by its fanciful act.

Part III

CHAPTER I

ANALYSIS OF THE SEASON DESCRIPTIONS

In a former chapter, entitled 'The Texts and the contexts of the season descriptions', we have shown how the given season descriptions fit into their respective texts, and also how they contribute to the overall narration problem and sentiment (*rasa*) of the various texts.

In the present chapter, we shall deal with each season independently, irrespective of the texts in which it occurs, and see what are the characteristics and main features of the six seasons. While doing so, we shall apply various parameters and different methods to discern what the meaning of a given season is, that is, what it stands for or what it symbolizes.

Thus in this chapter, we shall not proceed passage-wise but season-wise, starting with *vasanta*. The choice of spring as the starting point is purely arbitrary, but indeed, there did not seem to exist any fixed convention among poets as to the season with which to start a cycle. According to Rajaśekhara, as we have seen above, the year starts either with spring or with the monsoon, and this is indeed what we find in our texts: both the Ragh. and Kir. cycles start with the rainy reason, and the Śiś. cycle starts with spring. But on the other hand, to mention just one example, the Ṛtusaṁhāra begins with summer.

In this chapter, we shall not deal with the Naiṣ., to which we shall subsequently dedicate a separate chapter, on account of the somewhat unusual and special nature of its season description.

Vasanta (Spring)

Spring is the season of love par excellence, as we have already noted above while discussing *rasa*. In Sanskrit poetry, as well as in world literature in general, it is the most erotic of all seasons,[1] under whose influence all creatures, animals as well as men, fall as it were prey to love.

How is this erotic influence of spring brought about in the texts we are studying here ? We shall try to answer this question by arguing that it is mainly due to the fact that spring is represented as a woman, indeed because it becomes Woman personified, that it exercises this influence. For we must keep in mind that Sanskrit poetry is largely male-written. Moreover, the seasons in our texts always appear with reference to a male hero and are often described by him and/or seen through his eyes. It is therefore but natural that spring should appear in the guise of a woman.

This probably accounts for the fact that although spring's names are mostly masculine in Sanskrit, and it often appears as a male divinity, the friend of Kāma, it is nevertheless often made into a female personification, from Kālidāsa onwards, by adding the suffix *śrī* or *lakṣmī* to its basic name. This stylistic device of personifying the season has abundantly been exemplified in our section on the personifications of the seasons, we shall therefore not return to it here.

But, excepting the instances when it is expressly personified as a woman, how is spring revealed to be a woman in the texts we are studying here ? First of all, without being explicitly compared to a woman but by itself, by its mere presence and appearance, it has on the hero the same effect as a beautiful woman, creating intense love-longing and passion in him. This is very well exemplified in Rāma's situation for instance.

1. In T.S. Eliot's *The Wasteland*, we find for instance the following verses which, under somewhat different geographical circumstances, could have been pronounced by Rāma himself :

> April is the cruellest month
> Breeding lilacs out of the dead land
> Mixing memory and desire
> Stirring dull roots with spring rain.

In this case, spring the temptress can "make use" of the sight of various creatures in their mating or love-making mood, in order to provoke erotic feelings in the heroes of the texts. This trait is to be seen in the R. and course to a much greater extent in the Kum. spring-descriptions.

This season can also "make use" of another device, namely the sight of the women themselves and their amorous behaviour, as can be seen mostly in the Ragh. and Śiś. spring-descriptions. In this case, women become an essential aspect of the spring description. Indeed, they are reduced to the rank of other typical spring characteristics, and their main function is to arouse erotic feelings in their male spectators or lovers in the texts, as well as in the male readers.

Secondly, certain natural characteristics of nature in spring, like for instance blooming creepers, etc...., can be likened to women or to parts of the bodies of women, and as such arouse sensual interest in their male beholders. In this case, more or less explicit comparisons are made between spring and a woman.

As we have seen above, this appearance of the spring-woman is oriented towards male heroes. In the texts we are dealing with here, spring appears in three different kinds of situations, which are linked with three different types of heroes.

The first is the type of the love-lorn hero who is separated from his beloved one and in whom spring causes nothing but suffering. Rāma, in the R. as well as in Bhaṭṭ., and also certain characters of the Śiś., represent this type.

The second type is the hero who is practising penance, as we find him in the Kum. and Kir. spring-descriptions. In this situation, spring tries to seduce the ascetic and make him forsake his *tapas*, but in vain.

Finally, the third type of hero is the one who desires to enjoy himself and relish to the full all the pleasures of the vernal season. This is the case for the king Daśaratha and Agnivarṇa in the Ragh., as well as for Kṛṣṇa in the Śiś.

We shall now see in a more detailed way and with the help of examples how spring the temptress appears with relation to each one of these three types of heroes: the most perfect representative of the first type of hero is of course Rāma. All the beauties of the vernal season only increase the suffering and love-longing caused by Sītā's absence. The sight of certain animals in their mating season in one of the most tormenting things for him :[2]

paśya sānuṣu citreṣu mṛgībhiḥ sahitān mṛgān /
māṁ punar mṛgaśāvākṣyā vaidehyā virahīkṛtam //IV, 1, 46//

Look, on the motley highlands the deer are accompanied by their females, but I am deprived of the fawn-eyed Vaidehī.

Most of the natural characteristics of spring torture our love-lorn hero. We find thus a great number of verses in this passage which contain Rāma's laments and his painful remembrances of Sītā :

ayaṁ vasantaḥ saumitre nānāvihaganāditaḥ /
sītayā viprahīṇasya śokasaṁdīpano mama //12//

This spring, resounding with the songs of various birds, kindles my sorrow Saumitri, (for) I am deprived of Sītā.

Or also :

eṣa puṣpavaho vāyuḥ sukhasparśo himāvahaḥ /
tāṁ vicintayataḥ kāntāṁ pāvakapratimo mama //23//

This wind which carries flowers, which is agreeable to the touch and carries snow, seems like a fire to me who am thinking of my wife.[3]

The Bhaṭṭ. spring-description (VI, 74-86) is obviously largely inspired from the R. but it is shorter and also more condensed, for all the verses without exception contain allusions to the sad plight of Rāma himself or of separated lovers in general. Verse 80 for instance reminds us of verse 23 of the R. description :

dadair duḥkhasya mādṛgbhyo dhāyair āmodam uttamam /
limpair iva tanor vātaiś cetayaḥ syāj jvalo na kaḥ //80//

2. See also verses 15 and 17-19 of the same passage.

3. For similar expressions of grief, see also verses 4, 13, 14, 16, 21, 22, 45, etc... in the same passage.

Which sentient being would not become a flame due to the winds which bring sorrow to the likes of me, spread the most delicious perfume and as it were anoint the body ?

Likewise, the bees produce a similar effect on Rāma :

dahyo 'haṁ madhuno lehair dāvair ugrair yathā giriḥ |
nāyaḥ ko 'tra sa yena syāṁ batā 'haṁ vigatajvaraḥ ||83||

I am burnt by the honey-lickers (i.e. : the bees) like a mountain by terrible fires. Alas, which is the means here whereby I shall be cured of my fever ?

This type of lover also appears in the Śiś. spring description (VI, 2-21; 67-70) which, as usual, depicts various kinds of people in different amorous situations. Among them, we also occasionally find women whose husbands are away on some journey and in whom the arrival of spring naturally provokes intense love-longing and grief :

kusumakārmukakārmukasaṁhitadrutaśilīmukhakhaṇḍita-
vigrahāḥ |
maraṇam apy aparāḥ pratipedire kiu muhur mumuhur gatabha-
rtṛkāḥ ||16||

Other women whose husbands were away, their bodies wounded by the swift arrows sent by the bow of the flowery-bowed one (i.e., Kāma) even found death (and) how many more continuously swooned ![4]

The fact that the influence of spring is depicted, even if only occasionally, also on women seems at first sight to contradict the theory that this season appears as a woman in order to tempt and seduce the male heroes of our texts. We call this season "temptress" in the feminine because its influence is more often mentioned in connection with the heroes than with the heroines, but we must note that this seducing influence is a more general one, which neither men, nor women, nor even animals, as we shall see, can resist. What is involved here therefore is an extension of the significance of "temptress" given to this season originally with reference to the heroes.

4. See also verses 17-19 of the same passage.

Still in the Śiś. spring description, we find several mentions of lovers or husbands engaged in travels and therefore separated from their beloved ones :

aruṇitākhilaśailavanā muhur vidadhatī pathikān paritāpinaḥ /
vikacakiṁśukasaṁhatir uccakair udavahad davahavyavaha-śriyam //21//

The multitude of open *kiṁśuka*-flowers was endowed with the intense brilliance of a forest conflagration, for it entirely reddened the mountain-forests and made the travellers burn (with love).[5]

This verse reminds us of verse 34 of the R. spring description :

giriprasthās tu saumitre sarvataḥ saṁprapuṣpitaiḥ /
niṣpatraiḥ sarvato ramyaiḥ pradīptā iva kiṁśukaiḥ //34//

Saumitri, everywhere the mountain-highlands seem to be in flames because of the charming *kiṁśuka*-trees which are richly covered with flowers but entirely devoid of leaves.

In both verses, the image is the same : the mountains seem to be burning because they are covered with blooming red *kiṁśuka*-trees. Strangely enough, the R. verse does not mention Rāma's burning grief in connection with the fire-like *kiṁśukas*, although this image would be a very fitting one. It seems as if Māgha had repaired this omission by this verse of the Śiś.

As we can see, the metaphor of burning is a very common one in the above-quoted type of verses. Love-longing is likened to a fire or a fever (Bhaṭṭ. VI, 83) which internally consumes the unhappy lover. Even things as fresh and cool as the spring-breeze (R. IV, 1, 23; Bhaṭṭ. VI, 80), or at least neutral like bees (Bhaṭṭ. VI, 83) or *kiṁśuka*-trees (Śiś. VI, 21) are described as producing a burning effect on the lover.

We shall now turn to the second type of hero, the one practising *tapas*, who is represented by Śiva in the Kum. and Arjuna in the Kir. Towards this type of heroes, spring very literally acts as a seductress, trying to disturb them in their *tapas* and make them yield to love.

5. See also verses 5, 6 and 9 of the same passage.

In the Kum. spring description (III, 24-40), spring, in order to disturb Śiva's penance, deliberately provokes and then makes use of the sight of a great number of creatures in an amorous mood, ranging from even inanimate beings such as trees and creepers up to *kiṁpuruṣas*, who all take example from Kāma and Rati, the love-pair par excellence :

taṁ deśam āropitapuṣpacāpe ratidvitīye madane prapanne /
kāṣṭhāgatasneharasānuviddhaṁ dvaṁdvāni bhāvaṁ kriyayā vivavruḥ //35//

madhu dvirephaḥ kusumaikapātre papau priyāṁ svām anuvartamānaḥ /
śṛṅgeṇa ca sparśanimīlitākṣīṁ mṛgīm akaṇḍūyata kṛṣṇasāraḥ //36//

dadau rasāt paṅkajareṇugandhi gajāya gaṇḍūṣajalaṁ kareṇuḥ /
ardhopabhuktena bisena jāyāṁ saṁbhāvayāmāsa rathāṅganāmā //37//

gītāntareṣu śramavārileśaiḥ kiṁcitsamucchvāsitapatralekham /
puṣpāsavāghūrṇitanetraśobhi priyāmukhaṁ kiṁpuruṣaś cucumba //38//

paryāptapuṣpastabakastanābhyaḥ sphuratpravālosṭhamanoharābhyaḥ /
latāvadhūbhyas taravo 'py avāpur vinamraśākhābhujabandhanāni //39//

When Madana, with his flowery bow strung, reached that place in the company of Rati, the couples exhibited by their behaviour amorous feelings mixed with the emotion of love which had reached its peak. (35)

Following his beloved one, the male bee drank honey out of the same flower-bowl, and the black deer scratched with his horn the female deer whose eyes were closed due to the pleasure of the touch. (36)

Out of love, the female elephant gave to the male a cheek-full of water fragrant with lotus-pollen; the *cakravāka*-bird paid homage to his wife with a half-eaten lotus-stem. (37)

In the intervals of the songs, the *kiṁpuruṣa* kissed the face of his beloved, whose leaf-drawings were slightly blurred by drops of perspiration and which was beautiful with its eyes reddened by the flower-wine. (38)

Even the trees received embraces by the arms in the form of bent branches of their creeper-bride who had large clusters of flowers for their breasts, and who were beautiful on account of the trembling sprouts which were their lower lips. (39)

But all these efforts of spring are useless since, as is well-known, Śiva does not yield to its seducing influence :

śrutāpsarogītir api kṣaṇe 'smin haraḥ prasaṁkhyānaparo babhūva /
ātmeśvarāṇāṁ na hi jātu vighnāḥ samādhibhedaprabhavo bhavanti //40//

Although he heard the song of the *apsarases*, Śiva at that moment remained in the highest state of yoga; for indeed, no obstacles are capable of disturbing the *samādhi* of the self-possessed ones.

In a very similar context, spring also appears as the temptress in the Kir. cycle of seasons (X, 31-35). Of course here it is not only spring, but all the seasons which appear together along with the *apsarases* in order to make Arjuna forsake his *tapas* and arouse love-sensations in him, in which, needless to say, they do not succeed. Nevertheless, spring plays a prominent role in this cycle, for on the one hand the characteristics of many other seasons appear mixed with vernal ones, and on the other hand it is the only season which is described as erotic to a certain extent. Moreover, it becomes clear that it was spring which was expected to a produce a definite effect on Arjuna if we read the mocking comment made by the summer season which appears in turn after spring :

katham iva tava saṁmatir bhavitrī samam ṛtubhir munināvadhīritasya /
iti ...// 36 //

How will people feel any respect for you, since you have been despised by the sage like the (other) seasons ?

Thus we see that in both situations spring is miserably defeated in its attempts at seducing the powerful ascetics, and has to retreat. Moveover, we can note that in both texts the season is finally vanquished by the same means, namely, heat : in the Kum., all spring's efforts are definitely reduced to naught by the burning of Kāma by Śiva, and in the Kir. cycle it has to give up its place to summer, the hot season, which is, as we shall see, the enemy of love par excellence. Thus, the fact that the Kir. cycle of seasons ends with summer is a sure indication of the defeat of spring and love.

In the third kind of context, that in which the hero is enjoying a particular season or all the seasons, spring becomes, like a woman, an object of enjoyment. This is the case in the Ragh. spring description (IX, 24-48) and cycle (XIX, 43-44) as well as in the Śiś. cycle (VI, 2-21; 67-70), where Daśaratha, Agnivarṇa and Kṛṣṇa respectively have for sole aim to enjoy themselves : Daśaratha during the spring-festival, an occasion for general licentiousness, and Kṛṣṇa in the company of all the seasons. Thus it is said of Daśaratha :

atha yathāsukham ārtavam utsavaṁ samanubhūya vilāsavatī-sakhaḥ |
narapatiś cakame mṛgayāratiṁ sa madhumanmadhumanmatha-saṁnibhaḥ ||48||

Then, *having enjoyed to his heart's content* the festival of the (spring)-season in the company of wanton women, the king, who resembled the destroyer of Madhu (i.e. : Viṣṇu), Spring and the god of Love, longed for the pleasure of hunting.

Likewise it is said about Kṛṣṇa in the opening verse of the Śiś. cycle of seasons (quoted above) that he desired to enjoy himself on the mountain.

It is only in the cycle of seasons of the Ragh. that spring is not described more erotically than the other seasons, for there the libidinous king Agnivarṇa takes all the seasons as a pretext for various love-games. Moreover, this cycle itself follows a long description of the love-sports of the king, and does not markedly differ from it by its subject-matter. Thus, spring is divested of its specially erotic function in this passage.

In these enjoyment-of-the-season contexts, the women themselves become one of the most striking characteristics of the vernal season.[6] Indeed, they seem to be personifications of spring and become, with their various ornaments, the most alluring and love-provoking thing for their lovers in this season. This is very well illustrated by verse IX, 43 of the Ragh. spring description, where spring, with the help of various attributes, veritably seduces the lovers:[7]

> *aruṇarāganiṣedhibhir aṁśukaiḥ śravaṇalabdhapadaiś ca yavāṅkuraiḥ* /
> *parabhṛtāvirutaiś ca vilāsinaḥ smarabalair abalaikarasāḥ kṛtāḥ* //43//

> With the help of garments which defeat the redness of Aruṇa, shoots of *yava*-grass which occupy the ear and the songs of the female cuckoos, (all) troups of the god of Love, the lovers were made to be completely under the spell of love for women.

Women are usually mentioned in connection with some erotic element. Verse IX, 28 of the Ragh. description mentions for instance their lips which are sore due to the wounds left by their lovers' teeth. In the same passage, verse 36 depicts the

6. In the Ragh. spring description for instance, more than half of the verses describe or at least allude to women. This does not mean of course that women cannot also appear in other contexts : in the Kum. spring description for example, the *kiṁpuruṣa*-ladies are described in III, 33. But it is the case far less frequently. In the Ragh. description, it is as a matter of fact but natural that women should be mentioned so often for it is clearly mentioned in verse IX, 48, (quoted above), that the king is spending the spring-festival in the company of wanton women. In the Kum. spring description on the other hand, the scene is in an absolutely secluded and wild spot. Therefore spring makes use of the love-acts of various wild animals (the *kipuruṣas* themselves are not entirely human) and not of women, who are of course absent, in order to tempt Śiva.

7. See also verse IX, 31 for the same subject.

ladies as they are drinking wine, which is supposed to enhance their passion:

> *lalitavibhramabandhavicakṣaṇaṁ surabhigandhaparājita-*
> *kesaram /*
> *patiṣu nirviviśur madhum aṅganāḥ smarasakhaṁ rasakhaṇḍa-*
> *navarjitam //36//*

The women enjoyed the drink of wine, this friend of the god of Love, which hightens their skill in making graceful gestures, surpasses the *bakula*-flower by its sweet fragrance and is devoid of interruption in love towards their husbands (or: devoid of denial of love to their husbands).

Kālidāsa seems to have been particularly fond of describing the ladies' play on the swings, a pastime typical of spring and more precisely of the spring-festival, for he dedicates two verses to this theme. One in the spring description and another one in the cycle of seasons. Here again, the context is of gallant courtship since the women are sitting on their lovers' laps while swinging:

> *anubhavan navadolam ṛtūtsavaṁ paṭur api priyakaṇṭhaji-*
> *ghṛkṣayā /*
> *anayad āsanarajjuparigrahe bhujalatāṁ jalatām abalājanaḥ*
> //Ragh. IX, 46//

Enjoying the festival of the (spring)-season with its new (game of the) swing, the women, although experts, let their creeper-like arms become apathetic while twining them around the rope of the seat, out of desire to embrace the neck of their lovers.

Verse XIX, 44 of the cycle of seasons contains the same image, so to say in its next stage, for here the women actually let the rope go in order to embrace king Agnivarṇa's neck:

> *tāḥ svam aṅkam adhiropya dolayā preṅkhayan parijanāpavid-*
> *dhayā /*
> *muktarajju nibiḍaṁ bhayacchalāt kaṇṭhabandhanam avāpa*
> *bāhubhiḥ* // XIX, 44//

Having made them climb on his lap and swinging them on a swing operated by the servants, he obtained a tight embrace around his neck by their arms, when, out of feigned fear, they let the rope go.

In the Śiś. spring description likewise we find verses depicting women and some of their activities. The following verse for instance describes the agitated behaviour of a lady who is pestered by a bee:

vadanasaurabhalobhaparibhramadbhramarasaṁbhramasaṁbhṛta-
śobhayā /
calitayā vidadhe kalamekhalākalakalo 'lakaloladṛśānyayā //14//[8]

Another lady produced a *kalakala*-noise with her girdle, her glances flickering due to the locks (falling on her forehead), continuously moving and obtaining beauty due to the agitation provoked by the bee which was hovering (around her), eager for the fragrance of her face.

This woman's agitation is of course provoked by her fear of the bee. But the description is contrived in such a way that it becomes highly erotic, for the movements she makes are very similar to the movements of a woman during love-sports: the sound of the girdle, flickering glances and disorderly hair, continous movements and agitation are typical elements of descriptions of love-scenes. Of course, the erotic image only appears as an evocation behind the actual description, but the hint is nevertheless a very direct and obvious one.[9]

Thus, as we have seen in the above verses, women become a part of spring-nature, one more erotic component of spring,

8. The effects of alliteration in this verse are quite remarkable: whereas the first two *padas*, with the sound *bhra-* or *bhṛ-* repeated four times, obviously imitate the buzzing sound of a bee, the third and fourth *padas*, with *kalamekhalakalakalo 'lakalola...* render the sound of the girdle. The latter onomatopy reminds us of Ragh. IX, 37, in which the same sound is rendered by *madakalodakalola...*

9. For a similar scene and description, see for instance Kālidāsa's *Abhijñānaśākuntalam*, act I, verse 21, where the agitated behaviour of Śakuntalā, who is frightened by a bee, is likened to coquettish gestures.

so to say. Nevertheless, we must note here that women are not limited to the role of passive instruments which the spring season uses in order to highten the passion of men. For especially in the Ragh. and Śiś. spring-descriptions there are a great number of verses describing the intense amorous feelings which the arrival of spring arouses in the woman-folk too. So once again, it would be adopting too narrow a point of view to say that spring exerts its tempting influence only on men, and that this season appears only for the benefit of the heroes of our texts.

Nevertheless, we must note that all the verses which describe spring's influence on women contain the same basic theme, which is indeed a common-place theme of Sanskrit poetry: the women are angry and sulking, presumably because their lovers have been unfaithful to them, but, when spring arrives and torments them with love-longing, they are unable to sustain their angry pride and get reconciled with their lovers. So we can say that such verses are still viewed from a male perspective, for ultimately everything happens for the benefit of the lovers, with whom the angry women forcibly have to get reconciled, as we shall now see with the help of examples.[10] The first one is taken from the Śiś. description:

ajagaṇan gaṇaśaḥ priyam agrataḥ praṇatam apy abhimānitayā na yāḥ /
sati madhāv abhavan madanavyathā vidhuritā dhuri tāḥ kukura-striyaḥ //15//

The Yādava women who, due to their proud self-respect, neglected their lovers even whey they were prostrate at their feet, when spring arrived, tortured by desire, sought their presence in flocks.

The cuckoo, one of the most typical elements of spring, is also instrumental in provoking the ladies' reconciliation with

10. Such verses are of course not limited to the context of spring descriptions. They are also quite common in monsoon descriptions for instance.

their lovers, as is shown by a whole series of verses found in different texts:

cūtāṅkurāsvādakaṣāyakaṇṭhaḥ puṁskokilo yan madhuraṁ cukūja /
manasvinīmānavighātadakṣaṁ tad eva jātaṁ vacanaṁ smarasya //Kum. III, 32//

The male cuckoo, with his throat rendered astringent by eating mango-shoots, was melodiously singing (things) capable of destroying the anger of virtuous women, and which were the manifest order of the god of Love.

Once again, the same idea is found in the Ragh. spring description:

tyajata mānam alaṁ bata vigrahair na punar eti gataṁ caturaṁ vayaḥ /
parabhṛtābhir itīva nivedite smaramate ramate sma vadhūjanaḥ //Ragh. IX, 47//

"Abandon your sulkiness, enough of separations! Once gone, that charming age, youth, never returns", said the female cuckoos. Having thus so to say learnt the opinion of Love, the wives gave themselves up to pleasure.

The second verse from the Ragh. description, is obviously a continuation and elaboration of the Kum. one. Whereas the Kum. verse did not give the actual words of the cuckoo, simply saying the it sang "(things) capable of destroying the anger of virtuous women", the Ragh. verse, in a poetic fancy, actually quotes the words of these birds.

Exactly the same image is found for a third time in the Śiś. spring description. In this verse considerations other than those of metrics have made this cuckoo a female, for it is here compared to a dear friend and adviser of the women :

priyasakhīsadṛśaṁ pratibodhitāḥ kim api kāmyagirā parapuṣṭayā /

priyatamāya vapur gurumatsaracchidurayā 'duranācitam
aṅganāḥ // 8 //

Chided like by a dear friend by the female cuckoo whose voice was absolutely lovely and managed to extinguish their heavy anger, the women spontaneously offered their bodies to their lovers.[11]

Not only the cuckoos, but other spring characteristics too, provoke inordinate passion in the ladies. This is for example, the case of the mango-flower in the Ragh. cycle in XIX, 43 :[12]

dakṣiṇena pavanena saṁbhṛtaṁ prekṣya cūtakusumaṁ sapal-
lavam /
anvanaiṣur avadhūtavigrahās taṁ durutsahaviyogam aṅganāḥ
// 43 //

Having seen the mango-flower along with the young leaves sprouting due to the southern breeze, the women shook off their anger and went in search of the (king) from whom separation was unbearable.

Or the bees, in Śiś. VI, 7 :

ratipatiprahiteva kṛtakrudhaḥ priyatameṣu vadhūr anunāyikā /
bakulapuṣparasāsavapeśaladhvanir agān niragān madhupāvaliḥ
// 7 //

A line of honey-drinkers (i.e. : bees) came out of a tree, buzzing in a charming way (because they had drunk) the liquor of the juice of *bakula*-flowers, and which Rati's husband seemed to have sent in order to humble the wives who were angry with their dearest ones.[13]

The number of quotations of similar verses could be indefinitely prolonged, but as we see, they are mostly variations on the same theme.

11. The same theme is again mentioned in Śiś. VI, 70.

12. In Śiś. VI, 68 the mango-tree, which is described as "the most beautiful thing of the spring-days" (*madhu-vāsara -sāram*) is also said to be "skilled in removing the anger of young women" (*yuvati-māna-nirāse dakṣam*).

13. In Śiś. VI, 13 and 68, the bees also have the same function.

To sum up our whole discussion, we can say that the temptress-spring is successful only with the first and third types of heroes : the love-lorn ones, whose mental and physical suffering at being separated from their beloved ones it increases up to the point of madness, and the ones who just desire to enjoy themselves and whose passion naturally grows even more in this season. On the other hand, spring is highly unsuccessful with the second type of heroes, the ascetics, for at least in these texts, their concentration on their penance is invariably too deep to allow any perturbation.

We shall now turn to the second situation in which spring is likened to a woman, that is, when certain natural characteristics of the season are compared to a woman or to parts of a woman's body. This trait is to be found in all our descriptions, irrespective of the types of heroes and situations in which they find themselves.

In this case, the woman/spring identification takes the form of analogies, similes, metaphors, etc..., which imply a one to one correspondence between a given natural phenomenon and a woman and/or parts of her body. In such cases, as per our understanding, the contextual subject of comparison (*upameya*) is the woman or the part of her body. However, from the point of view of the established rhetorical analysis, what is contextual is of course the natural phenomenon.

In this discussion, we shall first examine a somewhat marginal case, namely the one of the Pampā river in the R. spring-description. We refer to this case as marginal because the river here is not explicitly personified or compared to a woman. This passage (IV, 1) opens with a three-verse description of the river (1-3) and throughout the passage, the river continues to be mentioned (in verses 27, 28, 29, 32, 35, 44, 47).

Thus this entire spring-description is inserted and intermingled with a description of the Pampā. The name of the Pampā, like nearly all river-names in Sanskrit, is of course a feminine, and as such naturally evokes a female character. Moreover, her woman-like apparance is enhanced by such terms of descrition as *śobhate* (it shines, it is beautiful) (29; 44), *śivā* (auspicious) and *śubhā* (pure) (47). But it is in verse 2 that her woman-like appearance is most clearly stressed :

tasya dṛṣṭvaiva tāṁ harṣād indriyāṇi cakampire /
sa kāmavaśam āpannaḥ saumitrim idam abravīt // 2 //

Having seen her, his (i.e. : Rāma's) senses trembled with joy and, having fallen under love's sway, he said this to Saumitri.

We see that the sight of the Pampā, like the sight of a beautiful woman, creates intense love-longing in our hero. But the feminisation of the Pampā-river in this passage is much more than just an anecdotal element of description. For the Pampā here veritably comes to embody the "spirit" of spring, which is, as a consequence, definitely feminine in its nature. We can even go a step further and say that this female figure of the Pampā whose personification is here but sketched, might well prefigure the female personifications of spring itself, as they appear in the later texts.

We shall now turn to a whole series of spring phenomena which are this time explicitely compared with a woman, by the means of comparisons or metaphors. One of the most common spring characteristics to be likened to a woman is certainly the creeper (*latā*, f.). In our texts we find this image in Kum. III, 39; Ragh. IX, 29, 35, 42; Kir. X, 32 (here not actually a creeper, but a row of red amaranths : *kurabaka-rāji-*) and 34. In all these verses, the creeper (or plant) is likened to a woman and certain parts of it are compared to some parts of a woman's body. Thus we can find the equivalence established between :

—branches (*śakhā*) and arms.[14]

—the young sprouts (*pallava, kisalaya, pravāla*) can be compared to two different parts of a woman body :

(1) to the hands;[15]

(3) to the lips[16] or lower lips.[17]

14. In Kum. III, 39, we find *śākhā-bhuja*

15. In Ragh. IX, 29, the equivalence is not explicitly mentioned, but Mallinātha in his commentary, explains the term *pallava*, which appears in the compound *malaya-māruta-kampita-pallavā*, by the term *hasta* (hand).

In Ragh. IX, 35, we find : *kisalayaiḥ...iva pāṇibhiḥ*.

16. In Kum. III, 39, we find : *pravāloṣṭha...*

17. In Ragh. IX, 42 we find : *kisalayādhara...*, and in Kir. X, 34 : *pallavādharoṣṭhe.*

The comparison with hands arises when the sprouts are shaken by the wind and thus likened to hands making dance-gestures. The comparisons with the lips might be due to the fact that young shoots are usually considered to be of a red colour, but this is not explicitely mentioned in any of our verses here. In the Kum. and Kir. verses, the shoots are also described as trembling (due to the wind) and thus likened to trembling lips

—flowers (*puṣpa, kusuma*) can be likened to different things according to their colour or shape: (1) when they are white, they become the shine of the teeth[18] or a smile.[19]

(2) Presumably when they are red, they are compared to the lower lip[20] or to the mouth.[21]

(3) Lastly, due to their shape, or when they are assembled in clusters they are likened to breasts.[22]

—the creeper's smell of honey (*madhu-gandha* or *madhu-surabhi*) is likened to the (smell of) wine.[23]

—the humming of the bees (*bhramara-svana*) around the creeper is compared to the song of the dancer.[24]

—the breeze *śvasana* which shakes the creeper's bud is likened to a sigh which causes the lower lip to tremble.[25]

18. In Ragh. IX, 35 we find : *kusumakomaladantarucaḥ,*

19. In Ragh. IX, 42 we find : *smita-rucā*. Here *smita* means both "smiling" and "blossoming" at the same time.

20. In Kir. X, 32 we find : *vikasitakusumādharam.*

21. In Kir. X, 34 we find : *puṣpe mukha iva.*

22. In Kum. III, 39 we find : *puṣpastabakastanābhyaḥ* and in Ragh. IX, 35 : *kusumabhāranatā* : here the comparison is not explicitly rendered, but as far as the woman is concerned, *kusuma* can only refer to her breasts, for it is a common-place of Sanskrit poetry that women walk bent under the heavy weight of their breasts, just as the creeper is here bent under the mass of its flowers.

23. Both in Ragh. IX, 42 (*madhugandha*) and Kir. X, 34 (*madhusurabhi*) the equivalence is established by a *śleṣa*, for there is only one term, *madhu*, which designates at the same time honey and wine.

24. In Ragh. IX, 35 we find : *bramarasvanagītayaḥ.*

25. In Kir. X, 34 we find : *śvasanacalitapallavādharoṣṭhe.* Here, by *śleṣa*, *śvasana* can both mean "wind" or "sigh".

We see that the fully developed and detailed picture of a woman thus appears behind these creeper-descriptions. We must note that the creeper-woman appears in different kinds of situations which give rise to different images. The most simple one is when it is just compared with a woman, like for instance in Kir. X, 32. Of course, here the row of *kurabakas* (red amaranths) is called *vadhū* (bride), but no husband of this bride is mentioned in the verse :

> *vikasitakusumādharaṁ hasantīṁ kurabakarājivadhūm...* /
>
> The bride (who is) the row of red amaranths, laughing with its lower lip (in the guise of) a blooming flower...

More often, the creepers appear described as the consorts of the trees, for the obvious reason that they encircle them. This theme appears in its fully developed form in Kum. III, 39, which we quoted above, and is also alluded to in Ragh IX, 42 :

> *amadayan madhugandhasanāthayā kisalayādharasaṁtatayā manaḥ* /
> *kusumabhāranatā*[26] *navamallikā smitarucā tarucāruvilāsinī* //42//
>
> The jasmine creeper, who is the pretty bride of the tree, bent under the weight of its flowers, intoxicated the mind with its blooming (or : smiling) beauty accompanied by the perfume of honey (or : of wine) and spread over the sprout which is its lower lip.

Verse X, 34 of the Kir. spring-description also takes up the idea of the creeper-beloved, but this time her lover is not a tree but a bee which "kisses" her flower, thus producing a more erotic effect than the passive tree-lover :

26. We prefer this reading (given by MS Ct) to the more generally accepted one given by MS ct : *kusumasaṁbhṛtaya* (caused by the flowers). For *kusumabhāranatā* (bent under the weight of the flowers) add one more element of description. Whereas *kusumasaṁbhṛtayā*, which goes with *smitarucā*, does not virtually add anything for the term *smita*, a *śleṣa*, can already mean both "smiling" and blossoming".

śvasanacalitapallavādharoṣṭhe navanihiterṣyam ivāvadhūnayantī /
madhusurabhiṇi ṣaḍpadena puṣpe mukha iva śālalatāvadhūś
cucumbe //34//

The *śāla*-creeper, similar to a bride, who seemed to be shaking off a newly-born jealously, was kissed by the bee on her mouth-like flower which was fragrant with honey (or : with wine), and whose lower lip (in the form of) a sprout was trembling due to the breeze (or due to sighs).[27]

This very skilfully contrived verse manages to describe at the same time a creeper shaken by the wind and from whose honey-smelling flower a bee comes to drink honey, and a woman who is shaking off her jealousy (the bee goes to many flowers) and whom the unfaithful lover kisses on her mouth smelling of wine in order to be pardoned. This double description is rendered possible by the use of numerous *śleṣas.* Thus the verb *ava-DHŪ*—, whose primary meaning is "to get rid of something by shaking it off" can apply as well to a creeper agitated by the wind, and to a woman who is shaking off her jealousy. *Śvasana* means "breeze" if applied to the creeper, but "sigh" if to the woman, and *madhu* can both mean "honey" for the creeper and "wine" for the woman.

The creeper-woman appears in one more context, namely when it is likened to a dancer due to its sprouts which are agitated by the wind. This image is found twice in the Ragh. spring-description (IX, 29 and 35). We shall here quote verse 35 in which the image is found in a more complete and developed form:

śrutisukhabhramarasvanagītayaḥ kusumakomaladantaruco
babhuḥ /
upavanāntalatāḥ pavanāhataiḥ kisalayaiḥ salayair iva pāṇibhiḥ
//35//

Having for song the buzzing of the bees which charms the ear, and lovely flowers for their teeth's shine, the creepers in the grove looked beautiful with their sprouts shaken by

27. For a similar image, see also Bhaṭṭ. II, 6.

the wind, which were similar to hands performing the movements of a dance.

Such are the situations in which the creeper-women are most usually depicted. As we see, they are based on a careful observation of nature, and then developed in a highly fanciful way to become stock-images of Sanskrit poetry. Still with respect to the creeper-woman image, Māgha in his Śiś. spring description managed to achieve a certain degree of originality, for in VI, 11-12 he does not compare the creeper to a woman, but a woman to a creeper, with the technique of inversion which is so typical for him. The two following verses are spoken by a lover to his mistress in order to scare her from the bees and make her seek the protection of his arms, which ultimately happens in verse 13.

idam apāsya virāgi parāgiṇīr alikadambakam amburuhāṁ tatīḥ /
stanabhareṇa jitastabakānamannavalate valate 'bhimukhaṁ tava //11//
surabhiṇi śvasīte dadhatas tṛṣaṁ navasudhāmadhure ca tavādhare /
alam aler iva gandharasāv amū mama na saumanasau manaso mude //12//

O you who have defeated by the weight of your breasts the young creeper bent under its clusters of flowers, this swarm of bees is flying in your direction, having lost its passion and (therefore) left the rows of lotuses covered with (dusty) pollen.

Like for the bee, the fragrance and the savour of the flower is not enough for my heart's joy, for I am thirsty for your sweet-smelling breath and your lower lip which is as fresh as nectar.

As we see, the opposite of what takes place usually is happening here, for it is a woman who is actually present in the text who is compared with an imaginary creeper:[28] her breasts are likened to clusters of flowers, her sweet breath to the perfume of the flower and her lower lip to fresh nectar. By doing this, her lover, who is speaking here, explains in a fanciful way why the bees are flying towards her. We can only conjecture about these two verses that the poet Māgha realized that the actual subject of description of these spring descriptions was not nature in spring, as is usually admitted, but woman herself, and thus consciously produced this inversion between the thing compared and that with which it is compared.

As we can see by the above-quoted verses, creepers are undoubtedly one of the most common spring-element to be likened to a woman. But we can find a series of other spring phenomena which are also, though more sporadically, compared to women in these descriptions. Thus for instance in Kum. III, 25, the southern region is compared to a woman who has been forsaken by her lover the sun:

kuberaguptāṁ diśam uṣṇaraśmau gantuṁ pravṛtte samayaṁ vilaṅghya |
dig dakṣiṇā gandhavahaṁ mukhena vyalīkaniḥśvāsam ivotsasarija ||25||

As the hot-rayed (sun), ahead of his time, was setting out to go towards the region governed by Kubera (i.e.: the North), the southern region emitted with her mouth a perfumed breeze, similar to a sigh of sorrow.

This way of representing the changes of seasons by the course of the sun is already found in a verse of the R. winter description (III, 15, 8). But here, since it is winter, the sun is visiting the southern hemisphere, and it is therefore the northern region which is compared to a sorrowing traveller's wife:

sevamāne dṛḍhaṁ sūrye diśam antakasevitām |
vihīnatilakeva strī nottarā dik prakāśate ||8||

Since the sun is assiduously visiting the region inhabited by Antaka (i.e.: the South), the northern region no longer shines, like a woman who has removed her *tilaka*.

28. This is already the case in Ragh. IX, 46 (quoted above) where the women's arms are likened to creepers (*bhujalatā*).

In the first verse, the region abandoned by the sun is compared to a woman who has been forsaken by her lover and reveals her sorrow by sighing. In the second verse, the northern region is likened to a widow whose husband's soul has departed to the South, the abode of the dead (Autak=Yama, the god of Death), and who removes her *tilaka* as a sign of her widowhood.[29]

Verse IX, 38 of the Ragh. spring description again contains a somewhat similar idea, but this time in connection with another natural phenomenon, namely the spring-night:

> *upayayau tanutāṁ madhuhaṇḍitā himakarodayapāṇḍumukhacchaviḥ /*
> *sadṛśam iṣṭasamāgamanirvṛtiṁ vanitayānitayā rajanīvadhūḥ //38//*

> Diminished by spring, the skin of her face paled by the rise of the moon, the night-bride became thin, like a woman who has not obtained the pleasure of the desired union.

Here again, a natural spring-phenomenon, namely the fact that the nights grow shorter, is interpreted in a fanciful way: the night is compared to a woman who is pining away and growing thin due to unrequited love, and whose face has become pale, presumably due to the additional suffering of having to watch in solitude the rise of the moon.[30]

In Ragh. IX, 37, it is this time the longish ponds of the houses which are, probably on account of their shape, compared to women:

> *śuśubhire smitacārutarānanāḥ striya iva ślathaśiñjitamekhalāḥ /*
> *vikacatāmarasā gṛhadīrghikā madakalodakalolavihaṁgamāḥ //37//*

29. Kālidāsa seems to have been fond of this image, for we again find this way of representing the change of seasons by the course of the sun (but this time without comparison with a woman) in the Ragh. spring description (IX, 25) and in the Ragh. summer description (XVI, 44), where again the northern region is likened to a woman, but this time a happy one since the sun is coming back to her in this season.

30. In the Ragh. summer description (XVI, 45) we find once again a similar idea. This time, the night-woman is growing thin due to remorse, because she quarrelled with her lover, the day.

Similar to women whose mouths are embellished by smiles and whose jingling zones are loosened, the oblong house-ponds were beautiful with their blooming day-lotuses and with the birds desiring water which emitted intoxicated cries.

Before Kālidāsa, this very same comparison between a pond and a woman can be found in the spring description of Aśvaghoṣa's *Buddhacarita,* where the wives of the Buddha try to make him forsake his wish to lead a hermit's life by describing to him the charms of the vernal season:

dīrghikāṁ prāvṛtāṁ paśya tīrajaiḥ sinduvārakaiḥ /
pāṇḍurāṁśukasaṁvītāṁ śayānāṁ pramadāṁ iva //IV, 49//

Look at this oblong pond hiden in *sinduvāraka*-trees growing on its banks: it looks like a reclining young woman clad in a white dress.

Here the oblong pond is compared to a reclining woman and the trees with their white flowers growing on its banks are her white dress. In the Ragh. verse, it is through different attributes that the two things are compared: here the blooming day-lotuses, being white, are likened to mouths embellished by smiles, and therefore also endowed with a white shine due to the teeth; the intoxicated cries of the birds are the jingling sound of the girdles, which is rendered by an onomatopy in the last pada: *madakalodakalola*... Moreover, these girdles are loose (*ślatha*), which is an obvious erotic allusion, for the untying of the girdle is always considered as a decisive step in the amorous play.[31] The fact that the girdles are untied and therefore do not stress the waist also increases the similarity with the shape of a pond. May be the birds themselves which "desire the water and produce intoxicated cries" can be considered as the lovers of these pond-women, but this comparison is not explicitely made. Thus we see that Kālidāsa's verse possesses a richness and erotic quality which is lacking in Aśvaghoṣa's verse, which is of course also much shorter.

As we can see, whenever a spring-element is likened to a woman, the reference is usually to a woman who is in well-

31. See for instance Kum. VIII, 4 and 14.

defined love situation : either separated from her lover, like the spring-night or the southern region, or united with him, like the creepers embracing the trees or kissed by a bee. In the rarer cases where no lovers are alluded to, the natural phenomenon is nevertheless described as highly attractive and alluring by itself, as is the case for the creeper-dancer or the pond-women, for instance. We thus see that such comparisons unmistakably aim at producing the amorous feeling in these descriptions.

There are also some verses which compare certain natural elements not to a woman, but only to some part(s) of her body. This happens in Kir. X, 33 :

muhur anupatatā vidhūyamānaṁ viracitasaṁhati dakṣiṇānilena /
alikulam alakākṛtiṁ prapede nalinamukhāntavisarpi paṅkajin-
yāḥ //33//

Agitated by the southern wind which was steadily blowing, and arranged in a compact group, the swarm of bees which was undulating on the edge of the face of a pond-lotus, assumed the appearance of a lock of hair.

Here the lotus is of course likened to a woman's face, and the swarm of bees is her flowing hair.[32] The southern wind could moreover well be the woman's lover who takes pleasure in tousling her hair. Although the comparison with a woman is not explicitely formulated here, the poet, with the help of these two natural elements, very skilfully contrived to draw the picture of a woman which he could visualize in nature.

We shall now turn to a verse of the Bhaṭṭ. spring description (VI, 81), which falls into a sub-category of the woman-creeper image, only here it is but a part of the plant, namely its leaves, which are compared to a woman's fingers :

avaśyāyakaṇāsrāvāś cārumuktāphalatviṣaḥ /
kurvanti cittasaṁsrāvaṁ calatparṇāgrasambhṛtāḥ //81//

Gathered on the edge of trembling leaves, the dripping dew-drops, as splendid as charming pearls, make the mind melt.

32. In Ragh. IX, 44 too, a swarm of bees is compared to a woman's hair.

The link between the dripping (*āsrāvaḥ*) of the dew-drops and the mind which is melting (or literally, flowing together) (*citta-saṁsrāvam*) is obvious. The dew-drops are explicitly compared to pearls, and we can deduce without much risk of erring that the trembling leaves are the fingers on which the pearls are placed as ornaments. This sight most certainly reminds Rāma of Sītā. We see that this verse manages to render very accurately the link between the object seen by the hero and the effect it produces on his mind.

In the R. spring description too, we find instances when a certain natural element is likened to some part of a woman's body. But here, the allusions are never to women in general or to an indetermined woman, but to Sītā only, for the obvious reason that she is the only woman present in Rāma's heart :

> *padmakośapalāśāni draṣṭuṁ dṛṣṭir hi manyate /*
> *sītāyā netrakośābhyāṁ sadṛśānīti lakṣmaṇa //30//*
>
> Verily Lakṣmaṇa, the eyes desire to see the petals of the lotus-buds, which are similar to the eye-lids of Sītā's eyes.
>
> Or also :
>
> *padmakesarasaṁsṛṣṭo vṛkṣāntaravinihsṛtaḥ /*
> *niḥśvāsa iva sītāyā vāti vāyur manoharaḥ //31//*
>
> Mingled with filaments of lotuses and released from inside the forest, a charming wind is blowing, similar to Sītā's breath.

Sometimes even, certain spring characteristics are not compared to some parts of a woman's body, but to certain ornaments, as we can see for instance in Ragh. IX, 41, where the *tilaka*-tree is compared to the *tilaka* on a woman's forehead, or also in Ragh. IX, 44, where the clusters of flowers are likened to pearls adorning the hair.

As we can see, there is an overwhelming mass of data on this subject in the texts we are studying here and which we have but sparingly quoted. The instances in which the poets compare either explicitely or implicitely certain natural phenomena to a woman or parts of her body, are indeed numerous. Nevertheless we must note that there are some cases (very few indeed) where certain characteristics of nature are likened not to women but to men. This is the case in Kum. III, 39 for instance, where the trees appear as the lovers of the creeper-women, or in Kum. III, 25, where it is the sun which is represented as the lover of the unfortunate southern region. But in these two instances, it it obvious that the trees or the sun do not at all form the main subject-matter upon which the verses are built, but only serve as attributes which further the feminization of the creepers or southern region.

In one verse of the R. spring description, we also find trees which are compared to men, and form this time the main subject of the verse :

> *puṣpitāgrāṁś ca paśyemān karṇikārān samantataḥ /*
> *hāṭakapratisaṁcchannān narān pītāmbarān iva //11//*
>
> And look on all sides at the *karṇikāra*-trees with their blooming tips, entirely enveloped in gold, which resemble men clad in yellow.

But as we can see this image is not at all erotic, and therefore does not come into contradiction with our thesis. In the Bhaṭṭ. spring description, we again come across trees which are likened to men, this time to dancers :

> *vātāhaticalacchākhā nartakā iva śākhinaḥ /*
> *duḥsahā hā parikṣiptāḥ kvaṇadbhir aligāyakaiḥ //85//*
>
> The trees whose branches are agitated due to the onslaught of the wind, similar to dancers, surrounded by buzzing bees which are the singers, are alas unbearable (to me).

This verse cannot but remind us of verse IX, 35 of the Ragh. spring description, quoted above, in which the creepers are likened to dancers. Here in the Bhaṭṭ. verse, the fact that the masculine trees give rise to unbearable suffering and love-longing in Rāma produces a slightly incongruous image, certainly less appropriate and felicitous than the creeper-woman image.

There is one more instance in which a tree is likened to a man, namely in Śiś. VI, 10 :

samabhisṛtya rasād avalambitaḥ pramadayā kusumāvaciciṣayā /
avinaman na rarāja vṛthoccakair anṛtayā nṛtayā vanapādapaḥ
//10//

With an unmanly manliness, the forest-tree, whom a lady had approached out of love and caught hold of with a desire to pluck its flowers, did not bend down (to her) and, its great height being in vain, did not shine.

In this verse, it is the manly-looking forest-tree which becomes an object of desire for the woman who catches it "with a desire to pluck its flowers", which according to Mallinātha means nothing else than "with a desire to make love" (*riraṁsayā*). But the tree's apparent manliness is only an illusion created by its great height, for, with a stiffness typical of trees, it does not bend down to reciprocate the lady's embrace and is therefore called unmanly. As Mallinātha says in his commentary : "the one who does not melt even when a girl takes him by the hand, he is but a eunuch" (*yaḥ kāntākaragṛhīto'pi na dravati sa napuṁsaka eva*). The image of the eunuch is of course supported by the terms "*anṛtayā nṛtayā*" (with an unmanly manliness). But another type of character could also be underlying in this tree which remains unmovable and does not yield to offers of love, namely, the type of the ascetic as we have seen it in Śiva and Arjuna. If this three is the ascetic who remains so to say firmly rooted in his *tapas,* then it becomes obvious that the woman who approaches it "out of love" and "with a desire to pluck its flowers" is nothing but spring the temptress finally revealed in her true form.

We can thus say that although the spring-woman equivalence is most obviously apparent in all our descriptions, and revealed by the various means and techniques which we have discussed above, it is only in Māgha's text that the common identity between woman and spring is consciously realized and brought about : spring finally drops its mask and appears in its true nature of a woman.

Grīṣma (Summer)

If spring, as we have seen, is the season dedicated to love, summer can be said to be its absolute antithesis in this respect. This does not imply that erotic scenes do not occur in summer descriptions : as usual, they are among of the poets' favourite themes. But they take place *in spite of* summer, whereas in spring descriptions they were very clearly provoked by the season. In summer, love is always described as weakened, like for instance in Ragh. XVI, 50 or XIX 46, or even totally annihilated and destroyed as Ragh. XVI, 51 symbolically shows.

The reason for this state of affairs is of course the extreme heat of the Indian summer, which forms the background of most verses. But in our texts, this heat is rarely stressed or described directly and realistically. Whenever the poets seek to render the sensation of heat, they rather prefer to do it indirectly by the means of some image, like for instance in Ragh. XVI, 51 by the burning of the god of Love.

In this respect, we must note that the disagreeable nature of summer is certainly responsible for its being scarcely treated in our texts.[1] For we must keep in mind that these season descriptions mostly allude to the beautiful and agreeable aspects of each season, and that therefore the poets must have found little indeed to inspire them in the scorching Indian summer. As a natural consequence of this, the poets, instead of dwelling on the disagreeable side of things, have preferred to describe the various means by which the heat can be avoided, such as baths, etc..., and this is the theme which forms the major part of these descriptions.

We shall now examine with the help of examples how the poets managed to render the sensation of intense heat in these verses. In the Śiś. summer description for instance, we find one verse (VI, 22) which depicts by means of a comparison the intense light and heat of this season "where the shine of the *śirīṣa*-pollen becomes similar to (that of) the manes of the sun's

1. It is only in the Ragh. that we find a full description of summer (XVI, 43-53) and in the Ragh. cycle of seasons, two verses are of course dedicated to it, like to the other seasons (XIX, 45-46). But otherwise, summer only appears in the Kir. and Śiś. cycles of seasons, where, as compared to other seasons, it is described in very few verses: Kir. X, 36 and Śiś. VI, 22-24 and 71.

horses" (*raviturangatanūruhatulyatāṁ dadhati yatra śirīṣarajo-rucaḥ*).[2] The sun's horses, which are called *haritaḥ*, are yellow or reddish in colour, and of course evoke immediately the shine and heat of sun itself, although the latter is not explicitely mentioned in this verse. Thus we see that although the actual subject of description here is just the yellowish pollen of the *śirīṣa*-flowers, the poet, by this comparison, manages to render tangible the blazing heat of the sun.

In the Ragh. summer description, we find another verse (XVI, 51) which uses the same indirect technique in order to depict the heat :

> *āpiñjarā baddharajaḥkaṇatvān mañjary udārā śuśubhe 'rjunasya /*
> *dagdhvāpi dehaṁ giriśena roṣāt khaṇḍīkṛtā jyeva manobhavasya// 51 //*
>
> Because of the particles of pollen sticking to it, the long shoot of the *arjuna*-tree shone with a reddish gleam, like the string of Manobhava's bow which Śiva, out of anger, reduced to pieces, though he had already burnt his (i.e. Manobhava's) body.

Here the image is one of fire, and everything evokes heat : *āpiñjarā* (reddish) is the colour of fire, and we also find the verbs *ruruce* (shone) and *dagdhvā* (having burnt). Moreover, Śiva's anger (*roṣa*) is also mentioned here, and anger is associated with the red colour and with heat (especially in Śiva's case, of course !). But it is very clear that the *arjuna*-tree (the element of reality upon which the comparison is built) is not really burning. The fire is only evoked by the comparison between the tree's long shoot, which is reddish due to pollen, and the shattered and burnt bow-string of Kāma. Thus there is no real forest-fire here, which would be a realistic way of describing the summer-heat, but it is only by a counter-effect of this comparison that the tree seems to be in flames.

The destruction of the god of Love by Śiva, which is alluded to in this verse, is indeed a very fitting theme for a summer

2. The *śirīṣa*-flowers are also mentioned in Ragh. XVI, 48.

description. For one of the most common topics of these passages is the weakening of love and desire due to the unbearable summer-heat. But the destruction of love need not always be as total and irremediable as in the above-quoted verse, for certain means were found to revive languishing sexual desires.[3] This is shown in the case of king Agnivarṇa in the Ragh. cycle of seasons (XIX, 46) :

> *yat sa bhagnasahakāram āsavaṁ raktapāṭalasamāgamaṁ papau /*
> *tena tasya madhunirgamāt kṛśaś cittayonir abhavat punarnavaḥ // 46 //*

> He drank wine with pieces of mango, mixed with red *pāṭala*-flowers, thanks to which his desire, weakened by the departure of spring, was again new.

This cocktail obviously serves as an aphrodisiac thanks to which the king's sexual power regains strength in spite of the heat.[4]

In Ragh. XVI, 50 it is the god of Love himself who, by means of a trick, manages to regain some of his lost power :

> *snānārdramukteṣv anudhūpavāsaṁ vinyastasāyantanamallikeṣu /*
> *kāmo vasantātyayamandavīryaḥ keśeṣu lebhe balam aṅganānām //50//*

> Love, which was weakened by the departure of spring, regained strength in the ladies' hair which was untied due to the wetness of the bath, and in which had been placed evening-jasmines, after keeping it in perfumed smoke.

In this verse, several means of escaping or at least attenuating the heat are mentioned. The jasmine-flowers (here evening-jasmines) are one of them, for they produce an impression of freshness by their delicious fragrance. We can note here that jasmines are the only summer-element to be mentioned in the

3. For the same theme, see Ṛtus. I, 8.

4. *Pāṭala*-flowers are also mentioned in connection with renewed desire in Śiś. VI, 23.

single verse dedicated to summer in the Kir. cycle of seasons (X, 36), where the personified summer is described as *viracita-mallikāvikāsaḥ* (adorned with blooming jasmines). We can therefore presume that they were the true symbol of the season for the poet Bhāravi. The above-quoted Ragh. verse mentions another means of attenuating the heat, which is actually the means par excellence, namely, baths. Bathing forms the subject matter of a great number of verses in these summer-descriptions.[5] Baths are of course refreshing, and they also provoke renewed sexual desire, as is well exemplified in Śiś. VI, 71 :

vapur ambuvihārahimaṁ śucinā ruciraṁ kamanīyatarā gamitā /
ramaṇena ramaṇy acirāṁśulatārucir aṅkam anīyata rāgamitā
//71//-

The lover took on his lap his beloved who, thanks to summer, had a shining body refreshed by the plays in the water (and) who had become even more adorable, shining like the creeper (-like) lightning and filled with love.[6]

Ragh. XVI, 46, which describes the drying ponds, also indirectly alludes to bathing women :

dine dine śaivalavanty adhastāt sopānaparvāṇi vimuñcad ambhaḥ /
uddaṇḍapadmaṁ gṛhadīrghikāṇāṁ nārīnitambadvayasaṁ babhūva //46//

As the water of the house-ponds, in which the stems of the lotuses were raised, was day by day leaving from below the

5. We must nevertheless note that descriptions of bath-scenes in rivers, etc..., though typical of summer, never occur in summer descriptions, for the reason that they constitute a separate poetic motif by themselves (see above Daṇḍin's definition of a *sargabandha*). Thus, in the Ragh., the description of Kuśa's bath in the Sarayū river immediately follows the one of summer, in a very natural way. And in both the Kir. and Śiś. we find the description of a bath in the river in *sarga* VIII.

6. A similar image can also be found in Ṛtus. I, 4 and Śiś. VI, 24.

steps of the moss-covered stairs, it (only) reached the height of the women's buttocks.[7]

Still with reference to bathing, verse XVI, 49 of the Ragh. bears testimony to the advanced techniques and incredible luxury to which the rich had recourse in order to attenuate the summer-heat :

yantrapravāhaiḥ śiśiraiḥ parītān rasena dhautān malayodbhavasya /
śilāviśeṣān adhiśayya ninyur dhārāgṛheṣv ātapam ṛddhimantaḥ //49//

The rich people spent the hot season in bath-houses with flowing water, lying on special stone-slabs which were surrounded by icy artificial streams and bathed in sandal-juice.[8]

This verse very strongly resembles verse I, 2 of the Ṛtus. summer description :

... kvacid vicitraṁ jalayantramandiram /
maṇiprakārāḥ sarasaṁ ca candanaṁ śucau priye yānti janasya sevyatām //2//

...somewhere a wonderful house with showers, different kinds of gems and juicy sandal-wood : these are the means, my dear, to which people have recourse in summer.

The elements mentioned in both verses are of course largely the same, only their names change. The *jalayantramandiram* of Ṛtus. has become *dhārāgṛheṣu* in Ragh., the *maṇiprakārāḥ* have become *śilāviśeṣān* and the *sarasaṁ candanam* has become *rasena malayodbhavasya.* But in spite of these variations in the vocabulary, which were facilitated by the richness of Sanskrit, the resemblance between the two verses is manifestly too great to be attributed to a mere coincidence.

7. This verse reminds us of verse IX, 37 of the Ragh. spring description, in which the *gṛhadīrghikās* themselves, due to their shape, are likened to women. Here, the image is so to say transposed to a vertical level, since the water is said to reach to the height of women's buttocks.

8. For more information on *yantras*, see V. Raghavan's study: *Yantras or Mechanical Contrivances in Ancient India.*

Some of the cooling elements enumerated in these two verses, namely sandal-wood and gems, also appear in two verses of the Ragh. (XVI, 43 and XIX, 45) which describe the summer-garb of the king's mistresses, which is of course designed to be as light and fresh as possible. In spite of some differences in the vocabulary and the description, these two verses are strikingly similar :

athāsya ratnagrathitottarīyam ekāntapāṇḍustanalambihāram /
niḥśvāsahāryāṁśukam ājagāma gharmaḥ priyāveśam ivopa-
deṣṭum //43//

Then summer arrived, as if to recommend to him for his beloved ones a dress (so light) that a (mere) sigh would make it fly up, with an upper garment set with precious stones and necklaces hanging on their very pale breasts.

taṁ payodharaniṣiktacandanair mauktikagrathitacārubhūṣa-
naiḥ /
grīṣmaveṣavidhibhiḥ siṣevire śroṇilambimaṇimekhalaiḥ
priyāḥ //45//

His beloved ones paid him homage by means of their summer-attire, with the sandal-paste anointing their breasts, the charming ornaments set with pearls and the gem-girdles hanging on their hips.[9]

There is one more thing which is always described as cool and to which people have recourse in summer in order to lessen the heat, namely, the moon. In Ragh. XVI, 53, both the moon and the king Kuśa are described as endowed with this beneficient influence.[10]

janasya tasmin samaye vigāḍhe babhūvatur dvau saviśeṣa-
kāntau /
tāpāpanodakṣamapādasevau sa codayasthau nṛpatiḥ śaśī ca
//53//

9. We can notice in Kālidāsa a certain predilection for describing the seasons by the dresses worn by women. In a verse dedicated to winter (XIX, 41) this theme appears as well.

10. We must note that this is the only place in the whole description where the king Kuśa is mentioned.

When this season was well-advanced, two things became specially agreeable to the people : the king and the moon, both capable of removing heat (or : suffering) when obedience is paid to their feet, and both at their rise.

Here there is a *śleṣa* on the word *tāpa*, which means "heat" when applied to the moon, and "suffering" in connection with the king.

We can thus make a list of all the means used in summer to allay the heat: baths, the moon, (in the Ragh. also the king Kuśa, but this is rather a text-specific element), jasmine-flowers, light dresses, sandal-juice or paste, precious stones or pearls. We can note here that most of these things were scientifically or rather medically approved and prescribed, for Caraka recommends the use of most of them during the hot season, in the section of his medical treatise which is dedicated to the seasons and the adequate activities during each of them.[11]

By the means of all these examples, we see that the theme of the heat is of course underlying in most of these verses (for without heat all these cooling devices would be redundant), but it is hardly ever stressed and developed. What the poets preferred to dwell upon in these descriptions are the various devices invented by people to make the heat more bearable, with the very natural result that the general impression produced by these verses is one of coolness much more than of heat.

We must nevertheless note that this is not the case for all summer descriptions. The second part of the Ṛtus. summer description (I, 10-28) for instance, does stress the summer-heat and the suffering it provokes in various creatures. This is not to say that this description is necessarily more realistic that the ones we find in our texts, for certain verses describing the perturbed behaviour of the thirst-afflicted animals in this season (the frog seeking shelter under the snake's hood (I, 18) and the snake under the peacock (I, 13)), are indeed highly fanciful and

11. Baths are recommended in VI, 32, the moon (or more precisely sleeping under the moon) in VI, 30, flowers (jasmines are not specifically mentioned) in VI, 32, sandal-wood in VI, 30 and gems and pearls in VI, 31.

do certainly not denote a close observation of nature.

Nevertheless, the sensation of intolerable and oppressive heat, with all its inconveniences, is thus rendered and stressed very successfully. The same holds true for Bāṇa's summer description in his *Harṣacaritam* (Ucchvāsa II), which gives a truly terrifying picture of summer with its scorching winds and deadly forest-fires.

We must of course note that in both these passages (the second part of the Ṛtus. description as well as the summer description in Bāṇa's text), the scene is set in wild nature, where very few means are available to lessen the heat-sensation. The first part of the Ṛtus. summer description (I, 1-9) on the other hand is set in a more mundane atmosphere, and it is this aspect of the summer season, as it is lived in the courts and palaces, that our poets have chosen to depict, thus giving us a, if not unrealistic, at least very partial view of the situation. The reason for this choice is certainly their distaste for depicting disagreeable or coarse things, and since it is obvious that most of these costly means of attenuating the heat were totally out of the reach of the lower strata of society and exclusively reserved to the rich (the term *ṛddhimantaḥ* (rich) is mentioned in Ragh. XVI, 49) and the kings, it follows naturally that the scene of these summer descriptions is limited to courts and palaces.[12]

Thus, rather than describing crudely the inconveniences of the hot season, our poets have chosen to stress only its positive aspects, as is very nicely illustrated by Ragh. XVI, 52:

manojñagandhaṁ sahakārabhaṅgaṁ purāṇaśīdhuṁ navapāṭalaṁ ca /
saṁbadhnatā kāmijaneṣu doṣāḥ sarve nidāghāvadhinā pramṛṣṭāḥ //52//

12. It seems at first sight that we cannot say much about Bhāravi's position in this respect, due to the paucity of information given about summer in the single verse which is dedicated to it in the Kir. (X, 36). But we must note that the only typical estival element he mentions in this verse are the jasmines, which count among the things used to produce a cooling sensation. We can therefore safely assume that Bhāravi follows the same tradition as Kālidāsa in his view of the hot season.

All the sins (it commits) against lovers are swept away by the hot season which brings the mango-shoot with its delicious perfume, old wine and fresh *pāṭalas*.

The elements mentioned in this verse are of course the same as those enumerated in Ragh. XIX, 46, which enter into the composition of Agnivarṇa's aphrodisiac drink. Thus what the poet means here is that summer of course brings heat, which is detrimental to the lovers' desire, but it brings at the same time all the necessary remedies to renew that desire, and it is this last, more positive aspect, which alone must be remembered. Moreover, as we can see in this verse, as well as in all our descriptions, the only real problem caused by the summer-heat is the weakening of love-desire, which, as compared for instance with the very real disasters occasioned by droughts for beasts and men, is of course but a petty problem, reserved to the class of the idle rich.

Varṣāḥ (*The Rains*)

The rainy season is certainly one of the most spectacular of all Indian seasons, and this is reflected in literature: the scene takes place in the sky, which thus becomes the stage upon which the monsoon drama is enacted, and the violent downpour of the rain, the sudden gusts of cold wind, the impressive black clouds with their thunder and lightning, all these natural phenomena become the main protagonists of the performance. The opening verses of the passage dedicated to the rains in the Bhaṭṭ. (VII, 1-3) give us for example a very vivid and indeed dramatic description of the onset of the monsoon, in which all the above-mentioned elements appear:

tataḥ kartā vanākampaṁ vavau varṣāprabhañjanaḥ /
nabhaḥ pūrayitāraś ca samunnemuḥ payodharāḥ //1//

tarpaṇaṁ prajaniṣṇūnāṁ sasyānām amalāṁ payaḥ /
rociṣṇavaḥ savisphūrjā mumucur bhinnavad ghanāḥ //2//

nirākariṣṇavo bhānuṁ divaṁ vartiṣṇavo 'bhitaḥ /
alaṁkariṣṇavo bhāntas taḍitvantaś cariṣṇavaḥ //3//

Then, the stormy monsoon-wind blew, making the forests shake; clouds rose up, filling the sky.

As if torn asunder, the bright clouds with their thunder released pure water, satiating the growing crops, (the clouds) which obstruct the sun, dwell in all parts of the sky, adorning (it), wandering about and shining with their lightning.

The monsoon is of course a violent season, during which the natural elements are unleashed. In our texts, this violence is reflected by various means. It can be described directly, like in the above-quoted verses from the Bhaṭṭ., in which the monsoon-wind is said to "make the forests shake" (*kartā vanākampam*) (VII, 1) and the clouds are said to be "as if torn asunder" (*bhinnavad*) (VII, 2). These expressions render very strikingly the general commotion which accompanies the monsoon, but they are comparatively few. If for instance we contrast the descriptions of the rains in our texts with the Ṛg-vedic Parjanya hymn, we must admit that the latter renders the violence of this season much more powerfully. The authors of our texts have mostly preferred to render this violence in an indirect way, by the means of comparisons and metaphors. To illustrate this procedure, we can quote here two verses from the R. monsoon description, in which the commotion in the sky is rendered by images which evoke violence. In the first one, the sky with its lightnings and thunder is likened to a person who is being whipped (the lightnings are compared to golden whips) and thus emits moans (the thunder):

kaśābhir iva haimībhir vidyudbhir iva tāḍitam /
antaḥstanitanirghoṣaṁ savedanam ivāmbaram //IV, 27, 11//

The sky with the sound of its internal thunder (or: groaning) seems to be suffering, as if it were beaten by the lightnings which resemble golden whips.

In R. IV, 27, 20 the whole atmospheric scene is likened to a battle[1]: the clouds become fighting elephants, the lightnings are compared to banners and the cranes to garlands:[2]

1. Verse 28 of the same passage contains a practically similar image.

2. The cranes fly in a circle, that is why they are likened to garlands hanging in the sky. This image is developed in the following verse, 21.

vidyutpatākāḥ sabalākamālāḥ śailendrakūṭākṛtisaṁnikāśāḥ /
garjanti meghāh samudīrṇanādā mattā gajendrā iva saṁyuga-
stāḥ //20//

With the lightnings for banners and the cranes for garlands, similar in their appearance to the peaks of lords of mountains[3], the clouds thunder with an excited roar, similar to lords of elephants engaged in battle.

The monsoon is not only depicted as violent, it also provokes violent, or at least sudden, compulsive and forceful reactions in various creatures. Thus, a common-place of these descriptions is that the peacocks start dancing in an intoxicated way at the onset of the monsoon, and their loud cries are also often mentioned in this context.[4] More aggressively, the elephant in R. IV, 27, 29 is immediately roused to a fighting mood when he hears the thunder, taking it for the cry of a rival.[5] As far as human beings are concerned, love itself is sometimes not devoid of a certain violence in this season, as can be seen in the two following verses from Ragh. and Śiś.:

vigrahāc ca śayane parāṅmukhīr nānunetum abalāḥ sa tatvare /
ācakāṅkṣa ghanaśabdaviklavās tā vivṛtya viśatīr bhujāntaram
//XIX, 38//

And he did not hasten to get reconciled with the women who, because of a quarrel, were turning their backs towards him on the bed: he waited until, scared by the thunder of the clouds, they would turn around and fall into his arms.[6]

praṇayakopabhṛto 'pi parāṅmukhāḥ sapadi vāridharāravabhī-
ravaḥ /
praṇayinaḥ parirabdhum athāṅganā vavalire valirecitamadhya-
māḥ //VI, 38//

3. This comparison with static mountain-peaks does of course not very well fit into the dynamic context of a battle.

4. See also below, pp. 159-60.

5. See also below, p. 160.

6. This verse also reveals an interesting aspect of Agnivarṇa's character : *nānunetum abalāḥ sa tatvare/ ācakāṅkṣa...*(he did not hasten to get reconciled with the women (but) waited...). This gives of the king the image of a cunning and calculating man, who is moreover very well informed of the gallant advantages that the rainy season can procure him.

Although they were angry with their lovers and turning the other side, the women, suddenly scared by the thunder of the clouds then turned over in order to embrace their lovers, their waists being thus freed of their folds.[7]

As we see, the love-making mood in these two verses is introduced by the sudden and violent fear of the thunder. It is here a purely impulsive and physiological reaction, and not a subtly and psychologically produced one, as it mostly happens in the spring descriptions for instance.

Also in the cases when the lover is separated from his beloved one, like for example in the Bhaṭṭ. monsoon description, love-longing turns to aggressiveness and bitterness under the influence of the season, as is well shown by Rāma's grudging invectives against the whole creation.[8]

Thus all these various reactions to the monsoon, be it dancing and singing in the case of the peacocks, desiring to fight for the elephant, making love, or finally anger in Rāma's case, are only different facets of one and the same urge to give vent to one's pent up flow of energy. The violence in the sky releases violent passions in the earthly creatures, which are manifested in different ways according to their species and situation in life.

We shall now turn to what we consider to be the most characteristic feature of these monsoon descriptions, namely the various interactions which take place between the sky and the earth. These interactions can function at different levels. Firstly, there are what we call purely physical interactions, like when the rain falls from the sky onto the earth, the wind sweeps down from the clouds, or inversely, when the vapour rises up from the hot earth, etc... A second type of interaction occurs when a heavenly phenomenon is compared to an earthly one, or to a human being, like for instance a cloud to a mountain. The third type of interaction consists in the influence

7. Māgha was visibly inspired by Kālidāsa's verse. We must note that the same image can already be found in the Ṛtus. monsoon description (II, 11), but this verse lacks the important element introduced by Kālidāsa, namely that the women are looking the other side, and only turn over to embrace their lovers when they are scared by the thunder.

8. See also below.

the atmospheric phenomena exert on the lives of various creatures on earth, animals as well as men, the latter being mainly depicted with relation to their amorous activities. To illustrate this, we can quote here a verse from the Śiś. which represents all these three types of interactions.

> *nijarajaḥ paṭavāsam ivākirad dhṛtapaṭopamavārimucāṁ diśām /*
> *priyaviyuktavadhūjanacetasām anavanī navanīpavanāvaliḥ*
> //37//

> The row of the forests of young *nīpa*-trees, which provokes sadness in the minds of the wives who are separated from their beloved ones, spread its own pollen, similar to perfumed powder, on the regions of the sky which were enveloped in clouds looking like veils.

The first type of interaction is here represented by the upward movement of the *nīpas*' pollen towards the sky. The second type appears in the comparison between clouds and veils, as well as in the implicit comparison between the regions of the sky and women, the whole image being that of women (the row of *nīpa*-trees) spreading perfumed powder (the pollen) on other women (the regions of the sky). Finally, the third type of interaction is revealed by the expression "which provokes sadness in the minds of the wives who are separated from their beloved ones" (*priyaviyuktavadhūjanacetasām anavanī*). Of course here it is the row of *nīpa*-trees which has this effect, and not an atmospheric phenomenon. But the theme of the influence of the monsoon-nature on people's minds is nevertheless present here.

We shall now examine more in details and with the help of examples the different kinds of physical interactions that occur between the sky and the earth during the rainy season. We can distinguish three different types of physical interactions: a downwards one, an upwards one, and one that functions in both directions. The rain comes of course into the first category. We can for instance refer to the above-quoted verse from the Bhaṭṭ (VII, 2) in which the rain-water establishes a link between the clouds in the sky and the earth which it fertilizes. Another atmospheric element which is frequently described as coming down from the clouds is the wind. This theme is illustrated by R. IV, 27, 8, by means of a poetic fancy:

> *meghodaravinirmuktāḥ kahlārasukhaśītalāḥ |*
> *śakyam añjalibhiḥ pātuṁ vātāḥ ketakigandinaḥ ||8||*
>
> The winds which are released from the bellies of the clouds, which are nicely cool due to the water-lilies and rendered fragrant by the *ketaki*-flowers can be drunk in the cupped hands.

The opposite kind of interaction, namely an upward one, is rendered in another poetic fancy expressed in very similar terms, in R. IV, 27, 4;

> *śakyam ambaram āruhya meghasopānapaṅktibhiḥ |*
> *kuṭajārjunamālābhir alaṁkartuṁ divākaram ||4||*
>
> Having ascended the sky by means of the rows of clouds serving as a ladder, it is possible to adorn the sun with garlands of *kuṭaja* and *arjuna* flowers.

The third type of physical interaction, which goes both up and down can be found in one of the opening verses of the R. monsoon description :

> *navamāsadhṛtaṁ garbhaṁ bhāskarasya gabhastibhiḥ |*
> *pītvā rasaṁ samudrāṇāṁ dyauḥ prasūte rasāyanam ||3||*
>
> After drinking the water of the oceans, the sky begets this elixir of life (i.e. : the rain), the foetus carried during nine months by the rays of the sun.

First, the water of the ocean is sucked up by the sky, and, after an "incubation" period of nine months, is again released upon the earth, thus performing an up and down movement. The term *rasāyana* designating the rain is of course particularly well-chosen, for the rains can really be said to be an elixir of life for the parched earth. This verse, which denotes a sure scientific knowledge about the formation of rain, obviously refers to a human pregnancy, since the rain, when it sojourns in the sky, is called a "foetus" (*garbham*), and it is carried during nine months by the sun's rays.

In the same passage, verse 7 also illustrates this double interaction :

eṣā gharmapariklisṭā navavāripariplutā /
sīteva śokasaṁtaptā mahī bāṣpaṁ vimuñcati //7//

The earth, which has been tormented by heat and is (now) flooded by new rain, emits vapour, like Sītā, tortured by grief, sheds tears.

Here again, the interaction functions in both directions : the rain falls from the sky upon the earth, and as a consequence, vapour rises up to the sky from the hot surface of the earth. The comparison between the earth emitting vapour and Sītā shedding tears, which is here rendered possible by the *śleṣa bāṣpam*, which can mean both vapour and tears, is of course inspired by Rāma's own preoccupations. One can wonder whether this verse did not inspire Kālidāsa for verse V, 23 of his Kum., which describes Pārvatī practising penance during the rainy season :

nikāmataptā dvividhena vahninā nabhaścareṇendhanasaṁbhṛ-, tena ca /
tapātyaye vāribhir ukṣitā navair bhuvā sahoṣmāṇam amuñcad ūrdhvagam //23//

Extremely burnt by two kinds of fires, the one which moves in the sky (i.e. : the sun) and the one which feeds on fuel when she was sprinkled with new rain at the end of summer she emitted, along with the earth, a vapour which was rising.

The situation of these two heroines is of course different : Sītā is not exposed to the rains, but only her tears are compared to the vapour which rises from the earth. Umā, on the other hand, is much more directly compared and indeed assimilated to the earth, for she finds herself in exactly the same situation as the earth itself, exposed first to the scorching heat and now to the rains. Nevertheless, the comparison between the earth and Sītā is without doubt also a very apt one, for after all Sītā means a "furrow", and she is said to be the daughter of the earth. The goddess Pārvatī is of course even much more than that : she is the earth itself. To this effect, we can only quote the beautiful analysis given of this verse by S. Lienhard[9] : "A princess who is a perfect yoginī. But she is more. The "highland of her breast"[10] hints at the fact that she is a power of nature. She is the daughter of Himālaya not only in name. Or is she more than that ? In the popular religion, Umā is the mother-goddess. The very word Umā, despite the fanciful etymology that Kālidāsa gives it, is simply an ancient word for mother. She is the goddess of the earth and fertility. And so her appearance is described as a sort of double, and anthropomorph, of the earth. The stream ris.s from her silent body just as it rises from the parched earth when the monsoon breaks. The rain courses down her just as it courses over the face of the earth we walk on, softening it and making it able to bear our crops."

We shall now turn to the second category of interactions, the ones which consist in comparing an atmospheric phenomenon to an earthly object or person. In this case, the aim is to achieve a poetic comparison which would highlight the nature of the first by means of the latter. But it is probably also more than that : it is a way of explaining the unknown, or at least unexplainable and ungraspable, by the known. Of course, the nature of these atmospheric phenomena was not entirely unknown even in those days. Does not Kālidāsa in Meghadūta I, 5 describe the cloud as a "mixture of smoke, light, water and wind" (*dhūmajyotiḥsalilamarutāṁ saṁnipātaḥ*) ? We can nevertheless safely assume that comparing these sky phenomena toe earthly ones was a way of bringing them into the realm of th familiar.

As mentioned above, we can divide these comparisons into two categories : the ones which compare heavenly phenomena or objects to the phenomena or objects belonging to the earth[11]

9. In : "A history of classical poetry, Sanskrit, Pali, Prakrit", p. 174.

10. The "highland of her breast" (*payodharotsedha*) is referred to in the following verse, V, 24. (My note)

11. Thus,among this first category, we find the sky compared to the ocean (R. IV, 27, 17) or to a *tamāla*-tree (Śiś. VI, 28). The clouds are compared to mountains (R, IV, 27, 2; 17; 20 and 31); to stairs (R. IV, 27, 4); to antelope-skins (R. IV, 27, 10); to elephants (R. IV, 27, 20 & 28;

and the ones which compare them to human figures. In this case, the comparisons usually offer a closer link with the context. These comparisons are rarely found in isolated units, but mostly several pairs of compared objects appear together in order to form a full picture, as we have for instance seen above in R. IV, 27, 20, where several pairs of comparisons concur in order to form the thunder-storm-battle image.

Among the first category, we find for instance the following verse from the R. monsoon description, in which the sky with its clouds is likened to the ocean with its mountain-islands, thus forming a perfectly symmetrical image in which the two appear as reflections of each other :

> *kvacit prakāśaṁ kvacid aprakāśaṁ nabhah prakīrṇāmbudha-*
> *raṁ vibhāti /*
> *kvacit kvacit parvatasaṁniruddhaṁ rūpaṁ yathā śāntamahāṇa-*
> *vasya //17//*

Sometimes visible, sometimes invisible, the sky, with its scattered clouds, looks like the form of a great and calm ocean which is here and there obstructed by mountains.

In verse 31 of the same R. passage, the very common comparison between clouds and mountains, this time terrestrial ones, occurs again, and forms once again a symmetrical image which is here reinforced by the syntactical parallelism of the verse :

> *nīleṣu nīlā navavāripūrṇā megheṣu meghā pravibhānti saktāḥ /*
> *davāgnidagdheṣu davāgnidagdhāḥ śaileṣu śailā iva baddha-*
> *mūlāḥ //31//*

The black clouds filled with new rain, which are attached to (other) black clouds, look like mountains burnt by forest-fires, whose base is linked to (other) mountains burnt by forest-fires.

Śiś. VI, 26); to veils (Śiś. VI, 37). The rain-drops are compared to pearls (R. IV, 27, 30). The thunder is compared to the cry of an elephant (R. IV, 27, 28 & 29); to the sound of drums (Śiś. VI, 31). The lightning is compared to golden whips (R. IV, 27, 11); to a banner (R. IV, 27, 20 & 28); to a creeper (Kir. X, 19); to a cluster of buds (Śiś. VI, 28). Finally the cranes, when they are flying in the sky, are compared to garlands (R. IV, 27, 20 & 21).

Here, the comparison is not only based on the massive shape of the two objects which are compared, but also on their colour, which is black : the clouds are black because they are full of water, and the mountains because they are calcinated by forest-fires, which is of course slightly incongruous in the context of a monsoon description.

Once again the similarity of colour forms the base of a somewhat unusual comparison between the dark monsoon-sky with its lightning and a *tamāla*-tree with its white cluster of buds, in Śiś. VI, 28 :[12]

> *drutasamīracalaiḥ kṣaṇalakṣitavyavahitā viṭapair iva mañjarī /*
> *navatamālanibhasya nabhastaror acirarocir arocata vāridaiḥ*
> //28//

> Similar to a cluster of buds which is sometimes revealed and sometimes hidden by the branches which are agitated by a swift wind, the lightning shone, (sometimes revealed and sometimes hidden) by the clouds (agitated by a swift wind) of the sky which looked like a young *tamāla*-tree.[13]

By means of the above-quoted verses, we have seen examples of atmospheric elements being compared with earthly ones. But in the Śiś. monsoon description, we twice find the opposite device which consists in comparing objects belonging to the earth to celestial ones, in a process of inversion of which Māgha seems to have been particularly found.[14] This procedure appears for instance in VI, 34, in which the *ketaka*-flower is likened to

12. The *tamāla*-tree, whose name signifies "which has a dark bark" is black, whereas its flowers are white. If the comparison between the sky and the tree is unusual, the one between the lightning and a vegetal element is a very common one. The terms *vidyullatā* or *taḍillatā* (lightning-creeper), (see e.g. Kir. X, 19), which can be considered as dead metaphors, are usual designations of the lightning, due to its forked, creeper-like shape.

13. *Drutasamīracalaiḥ* applies here both to the branches and to the clouds. Likewise, *kṣaṇalakṣitavyavahitā* applies at the same time to the cluster of buds and to the lightning.

14. Already in the context of spring descriptions we have come accross this kind of inversions which are typical of Māgha : whereas creepers are usually likened to women, he likens women to creepers. (See e.g. Śiś. VI, 11-13).

the moon, a comparison inspired both by its white colour and its curved shape :

dviradadantavalakṣam alakṣyata sphuritabhṛṅgamṛgacchavi ketakam |
ghanaghanaughavighaṭṭanayā divaḥ kṛśaśikhaṁ śaśikhaṇḍam iva cyutam[15] //34//

The *ketaka*-flower, as white as an elephant's tusk, wherein shone the colour of a bee (which looked like an) antelope, resembled a piece of the moon with thin tips, fallen from the sky under the impact of masses of black clouds.[16]

Likewise, in verse VI, 36, the bees are compared to shooting stars, because they are carrying the white pollen of the jasmines :

navapayaḥkaṇakomalamālatīkusumasaṁtatisaṁtatasaṅgibhiḥ |
pracalitoḍunibaiḥ paripāṇḍimā śubharajobharajo 'libhir ādade //36//

Similar to shooting stars, the bees which are always stuck to clusters of *mālatī* flowers which are adorned by drops of fresh water, have acquired absolute whiteness due to their loads of bright pollen.

As we see, here again the comparison is inspired by colours. This is the case for all three verses we quoted from the Śiś. monsoon description (VI, 28, 34 and 36). The basic colours, especially in VI, 28 and 34, appear to be black and white. In both cases, the black colour is inspired from the cloudy monsoon-sky which produces an all-pervasive atmosphere of dark-

15. This verse is remarkable from the point of view of alliterations. In the third *pada*, the expression *ghanaghanaughavighaṭṭanayā* immediately evokes the sound of the thunder, although this monsoon-element is not explicitely mentioned in this verse. Moreover, the terms *bhṛṅga* and *mṛga* are not only very similar phonetically speaking, but here the bee (*bhṛṅga*) on the white flower actually passes for the antelope (*mṛga*) which is supposed to be seen on the moon.

16. Again, the violence of the monsoon is perceptible here, since the moon, or rather a piece of it, is said to be "fallen from the sky under the impact of masses of black clouds".

ness. Is the monsoon itself not called *varṣārātri*, the "night of the rains" ?[17] On this black background, the only colour which can be clearly visible is of course white, and this whiteness can be seen in the cluster of buds-lightning, the *ketaka*-moon and the shooting stars-bees.[18]

We shall now turn to the second category of comparisons, namely the ones in which an atmospheric element is likened to a human being. This kind of comparisons tends to be more closely linked with the context and thus more unique, and therefore cannot be submitted to broader categorizations.

Thus, verse IV, 27, 12 of the R. monsoon description contains a comparison which could only appear in this text :

nīlamvghāśritā vidyut sphurantī pratibhāti me /
sphurantī rāvaṇasyāṅke vaidehīva tapasvinī /12//

The trembling lightning on the background of the black clouds looks to me like the unfortunate Vaidehī trembling in the lap of Rāvaṇa.

As we see, this verse does not only establish comparisons between the cloud and Rāvaṇa and the lightning and Sītā, but it also probably refers to one main episode of the story, that in which Rāvaṇa ravishes Sītā and flies away with her to Laṅkā.

In verse VI, 27 of the Śiś., we find another such closely context-dependent comparison : here the blue cloud with its rainbow is likened to the body of Kṛṣṇa with his garments and earrings of various colours :

anuyayau vividhopalakuṇḍaladyutivitānakasaṁvalitāṁśukam /
dhṛtadhanurvalasya payomucaḥ śabalimā balimānamuṣo vapuḥ
//27//

The colourfulness of the cloud which bears the circle of the rainbow imitated the body of the Destroyer of Bali's pride (i.e. : of Kṛṣṇa), whose garment was united with the mass of

17. This term appears for instance in R. IV, 29, 1.

18. Verse VI, 35 from Śiś. is also significant in this respect, for it is a monochrome in white.

brilliance of his ear-rings made out of gems of various colours.[19]

Kṛṣṇa is of course the hero of the Śiś., and in the same way Sītā and Rāvaṇa are two main protagonists of the R. story. Thus we see that the comparisons which appear in these two above-quoted verses are directly inspired by the context, and so very specific.

In the R. monsoon description, we find three verses which compare the sky to a suffering person (IV, 27, 5; 6; and 11). Here the link with the context is less narrow, but it is nevertheless clear that these images are directly dictated by Rāma's depressed state of mind. This is of course particularly obvious in verse 6 which likens the sky to a love-sick person. Since we have already quoted verse 11 above, as an illustration of the violence of this season, we shall only quote here verses 5 and 6 :

saṁdhyārāgotthitais tāmrair anteṣv adhikapāṇḍuraiḥ /
snigdhair abhrapaṭacchedair baddhavraṇam ivāmbaram //5//
mandamārutaniḥśvāsaṁ saṁdhyācandanarañjitam /
āpāṇḍujaladaṁ bhāti kāmāturam ivāmbaram //6//[20]

The sky seems to have dressed its wounds with pieces of cloth which are the unctuous clouds rising on the redness of the twilight, which have a coppery colour and are very pale on the edges.

The sky, having for sighs the slow winds, red with the sandal-paste of the twilight and having palish clouds, looks like a love-sick person.

In both these verses, the red colour of the twilight is used, but for a different purpose : in the first verse, due to its red colour, the sky seems to be wounded and bleeding, and the clouds are the bandages which are patched on it. In the second verse, the redness of the twilight is compared to sandal-paste.

19. In Ṛtus. II. 5, the earth forms the object of a somewhat similar comparison, for, with all its different colours, it is compared to woman adorned with jewels.

20. The terms *rāga* (5) and *rañjita* (6) used in both these verses refer of course to the red colour, but also to love-passion.

As we have seen above in the context of summer descriptions, sandal-wood is a well-known remedy against heat, and it is also used by love-sick people in order to allay the fever of love-longing. In this verse, the pale clouds are most likely the complexion of the love-stricken lover, who has become pale due to excessive love-longing.

As we see, the three verses from the R. monsoon description, which we have quoted above, all reflect the emotional state of Rāma. In verse 12, the violence of the thunder-storm reminds him of the violence done to his wife Sītā by the demon Rāvaṇa. In verses 5 and especially 6, his love-sickness is projected onto the atmosphere. But in the same R. passage, we also find such comparisons which are less directly dependent on the context, such as in verse 10 for instance. Here of course the basis of the comparison is not an atmospheric phenomenon, but the mountains, which are compared to learned brahmins. Nevertheless, one element belonging to the sky also appears here, namely the clouds, which are likened to the ascetics' antelope-skins:

> *meghakṛṣṇājinadharā dhārāyajñopavītinaḥ |*
> *mārutāpūritaguhāḥ prādhītā iva parvatāḥ ||10||*
>
> Bearing black clouds for antelope-skins, invested with sacred threads which are streams, the mountains, with their caves full of wind, resemble learned brahmins.

The monsoon is the season when all the wandering ascetics have to give up their peregrinations because of the rain which makes the paths impracticable. Then they come together in order to chant the Vedas. This is what verse 34 of the same passage tells us, in a purely descriptive way:

> *māsi prauṣṭhapade brahma brāhmaṇānāṁ vivakṣatām |*
> *ayam adhyāyasamayaḥ sāmagānām upasthitaḥ ||34||*
>
> In the month of *Prauṣṭhapada* has arrived this reading-meeting of the brahmins who sing the *sāman* and desire to recite the Vedas.

We can therefore safely deduce, from verse 34, that the "caves full of wind" (*mārutāpūritaguhāḥ*) in verse 10 produce a sound which is likened to the chanting of the Vedas, although this comparison is not explicitely mentioned in this verse.

In the same category of comparisons as the above-quoted verse, namely the ones which have a loose link with the context and the plot of the story, we find the following verse from the Śiś. (VI, 25), which is the opening verse of the passage dedicated to the rains in this cycle, and thus appropriately describes the onset of the monsoon. With the help of numerous *śleṣas*, this verse likens a row of clouds to a woman, rather an unusual comparison, more specifically to the *abhisārikā* type of heroine, namely the one who goes to meet her lover, who is here represented by a mountain. In this verse, all the epithets can at the same time be applied to the row of clouds or to the woman. The lightnings are her eyes and the clouds (*payodhara*) are her breasts (also *payodhara*):

> *sphuradadhīrataḍinnayanā muhuḥ priyam ivāgalitorupayodharā* |
> *jaladharāvalir apratipālitasvasamayā samayāj jagatīdharam* ||25||

> Suddenly, without waiting for its turn, a row of clouds approached the mountain, with its continuously shining and agitated lightnings and its big filled clouds, just like (a woman) approaches her lover according to their rendezvous, with her continuously shining and agitated eyes and her plump breasts which do not hang down.

We shall now turn to the third and last kind of interactions between the sky and the earth during the monsoon-season, that is, the influence that the sight and sound of certain atmospheric elements exert on the lives, behaviour, mood and thoughts of various earthly creatures.

The influence of the atmospheric elements is for instance very clear in the case of peacocks, birds which are extremely typical of monsoon descriptions, and truly symbolize this season, which is supposed to be their mating-time, in the same way as the cuckoo is the symbol of spring.[21] As we said above, the rains

21. The peacocks are mentioned in all the passages dedicated to the rainy season in the texts studied here. Thus we find allusions to them in in the following verses: R. IV, 27, 18; 23; 24; 25. Bhaṭṭ. VII, 8. Ragh. XIX, 37. Kir. X, 23 and Śiś. VI, 31; 72 and 73.

usually provoke their frenzied singing and dancing. Thus in Śiś. VI, 73, the sight of the rain-clouds makes them sing:

kuṭajāni vīkṣya śikhibhiḥ śikharīndraṁ samayāvanau ghanama-
dabhramarāṇi /
gaganaṁ ca gītaninadasya giroccaiḥ samayā vanaughanavada-
bhram arāṇi //73//

Having seen the *kuṭaja*-flowers full of intoxicated bees on the ground near the hill, and *having seen the sky with its clouds full of water*, the peacocks emitted loud cries, similar to the notes of a song.

In the same passage, in verse 31, it is the thunder which this time provokes their dancing. Here the thunder is likened to the sound of drums, the idea being that the peacocks interpret it as a kind of music and feel tempted to dance:

jaladapaṅktir anartayad unmadaṁ kalavilāpikalāpikadamba-
kam /
kṛtasamārjanamardalamaṇḍaladhvanijayā nijayā svanasaṁ-
padā //31//

A row of clouds which had defeated by the perfection of its own thunder the sound of a multitude of drums rubbed with ashes, made the intoxicated troup of the softly cooing peacocks dance.

This verse immediately reminds us of a very similar, but so to say inverted, verse from the Kir. autumn description (IV, 16). Here, since it is autumn, there is of course no real thunder, but the peacocks, hearing the sound of the churning, which is likened to the sound of drums, interpret it as the thunder:

vrajājireṣv ambudanādaśaṅkinīḥ śikhaṇḍinām unmadayatsu
yoṣitaḥ /
muhuḥ praṇunneṣu mathāṁ vivartanair nadatsu kumbheṣu
mṛdaṅgamantharam //16//[22]

...while, near the stables, the jars which were repeatedly beaten by the rotation of the churning rod produced a deep

22. This verse belongs to a group of four verses (*kapālaka*) forming a syntactic whole (IV, 14-17).

sound like a drum and excited the females of the peacocks who imagined that it was the clouds' thunder...[23]

The image of an animal which is deluded by a certain sound can also be found in the R. monsoon description (IV, 27, 29), where it is an elephant who, this time actually hearing the thunder, takes it for the trumpeting of a rival:

mārgānugaḥ śailavanānusārī saṁprasthito megharavaṁ niśamya /
yuddhābhikāmaḥ pratināgaśaṅkī matto gajendraḥ pratisaṁnivṛttaḥ //29//

The travelling Indra of elephants who is walking along the path, following mountains and forests, having heard the thunder of the clouds and suspecting a rival elephant, turns around furious, eager to engage in battle.[24]

If, as we have seen in the above-quoted verses, animals can be affected by certain sights or sounds typical of the monsoon, the influence of this season is more frequently depicted with relation to human beings, and, among them, with greater predilection as usual, with relation to lovers. For in many of our texts, the primary concern of the poet was not so much to describe nature in a particular season as to depict the people's various amorous activities and moods. To this effect, we can quote here verse X, 19 of the Kir.:

sajalajaladharaṁ nabho vireje vivṛtim iyāya rucis taḍillatānām /
vyavahitarativigrahair vitene jalagurubhiḥ stanitair digantareṣu //19//

The sky shone with its clouds full of water, the brilliance of the creeper-like lightnings was intensified and spread in the directions along with the thunder, heavy with water, *which removes love-quarrels.*

23. A similar image of the deluded peacocks can also be found for instance in Ragh. I, 39 (not in a season description context), where these birds, hearing the deep sound of Dilīpa's chariot, start dancing, taking it for the thunder.

24. A similar image can be found in the autumn description of the Bhaṭṭ. (II, 9), where a lion, hearing the echoes of his own roars, takes them for the roars of another lion.

Here is a verse which describes the natural spectacle of the monsoon as it appears in the sky, with various elements such as clouds, thunder and lightnings, and the description could have remained at this level. But one more, very important element is added here: the thunder is described as that which "removes love-quarrels" (*vyavahitarativigrahair*). And it is precisely this influence exerted, if not by the thunder then by some other atmospheric phenomenon, on the lover-folk, which forms the main topic of our monsoon descriptions, at least in the Ragh., Bhaṭṭ., Kir. and Śiś. passages.[25] The main reason for the predilection for this topic is that the monsoon, somewhat similarly to spring, is a season of love. After the long summer heat which smothered all love-desire, the rainy season brings a new coolness in the atmosphere, and with it, a renewal of desire. This theme appears for instance in Kir. X, 21, in the second part of the verse: *nava iva vibabhau sacittajanmā gatadhṛtir ākulitaś ca jīvalokaḥ* (the world of living beings was like new, full of love, all firmness gone, and agitated). The same theme appears once again in the following verse, but in a more disguised way:

vyathitam api bhṛśaṁ mano harantī pariṇatajambuphalopabhogahṛṣṭā /
parabhṛtayuvatiḥ svanaṁ vitene navanavayojitakaṇṭharāgaramyam //22//

Charming excessively even an afflicted heart, a young female cuckoo, very happy after enjoying the ripe fruit of the *jambu*-tree, spread around her song, which was delightful on account of the melody which her throat arranged in an ever new way.

If the *jambu*-fruit seems to be typical of the rainy season,[26] the cuckoo on the other hand is rather unusual in this context, for, as we have seen above, this bird is the symbol of spring.

25. We have quoted above, in the context of our discussion on the violent aspect of the monsoon, two verses (Ragh. XIX, 38 and Śiś. VI, 38) which precisely illustrate the thunder's ability to remove love-quarrels.

26. See for instance R. IV, 27, 19 & 27.

The reason for its presence here is certainly that with respect to love, the rainy season is in a way a renewal of spring. Its song, which is described as *navanavayojitakaṇṭharāgaramyam* (delightful on account of the melody which her throat arranged in an ever new way), a surprising description for the extremely monotonous and repetitive song of the cuckoo, must also be interpreted in the same light. What is meant here is probably not to be taken too literally in the sense that the song actually contains diverse melodies, but rather that after the forced interval of summer, the cuckoo, which here certainly symbolises love, is singing once again.

In the light of what has been said above, it is therefore not surprising to find in these monsoon descriptions a great number of verses which depict the love-feelings aroused in the lover-folk by the rainy season, and especially by certain atmospheric phenomena. We have seen above the effect of the thunder on offended women, but other monsoon elements too can provoke love-desire. Thus in Śiś. VI, 40, the (feigned) fear of the lightning prompts a group of young girls to stay with their lovers:

> *aramayan bhavanād aciradyuteḥ kila bhayād apayātum anicchavaḥ /*
> *yadunarendragaṇaṁ taruṇīgaṇās tam atha manmathamantharabhāṣiṇaḥ //40//*

Then the group of young girls who were stottering out of love pleased the group of Yadu princes by refusing to leave the house, allegedly out of fear of the lightning.

In verse 26 of the same passage, monsoon clouds prompt a woman to go and meet her lover. Here again, fear seems to be mixed with desire, for the cloud is described as *gajakadambakamecakam* (as dark as a group of elephants), a slightly disquietening image:

> *gajakadambakamecakam uccakair nabhasi vīkṣya navāmbudam ambare /*
> *abhisasāra na vallabham aṅganā na cakame ca kam ekarasaṁ rahaḥ //26//*

Which faithful lover was not visited by his woman, nor loved in secret, when in the month of *Nabhas* she saw, high up in the sky, a fresh cloud as dark as a group of elephants ?

If, as we have just seen, the monsoon clouds provoke feelings of love in the young women and make them go and meet their lovers, the same monsoon element has a much more destructive effect on women when the beloved object is far away, as we can see in verse 29 of the same passage:

paṭalam ambumucāṁ pathikāṅganā sapadi jīvitasaṁśayam eṣyatī /
sanayanāmbusakhījanasaṁbhramād vidhurabandhur abandhuram aikṣata //29//

The wife of the traveller, whose relatives were worried due to the agitation of her friends whose eyes were full of tears, looked at the inauspicious group of clouds and was immediately certain of death.

The wind coming from the clouds is one more element of the monsoon which provokes intense feelings of love, as is illustrated by Śiś. VI, 39. This time the effect of this natural element is not depicted with relation to women, but to men:[27]

vigatarāgaguṇo 'pi jano na kaś calati vāti payodanabhasvati /
abhihite 'libhir evam ivoccakair ananṛte nanṛte navapallavaiḥ //39//

The young shoots (or: the young libertines) danced as if the bees had loudly proclaimed this truth: "Which person, even if he is freed of his red colour (or: of his passion) is not moved when the wind from the rain-clouds is blowing?"

This verse demonstrates Māgha's perfect mastery of the art of double meaning (*śleṣa*), for it describes at the same time young shoots and young libertines, the expressions *vigatarāga-*

27. One more verse in this passage (Śiś. VI, 30) describes the effect of the monsoon wind, this time on travellers and on women in general.

guṇa, calati and *navapallava* having different meanings depending on which of the two they concern.

As we have seen above in some verses from the Śiś., the monsoon-elements are sometimes mentioned with reference to love-in-separation situations (VI, 29 and 30). In this respect, is is noteworthy that in the R. rains description, which is of course also a *vipralambha-śṛṅgāra* situation, Rāma's own grief is hardly stressed, unlike what happened for instance in the same text's spring description. There are of course indirect allusions to his sorrow, like in the three verses which liken the sky to a suffering person (IV, 27, 5; 6; and 11) and can certainly be considered as projections of Rāma's own suffering onto the natural elements. Otherwise we find direct references to his unhappiness only in two verses (IV, 27, 38 & 39), in the last part of the passage which is actually no longer dedicated to the description of the monsoon properly speaking, but in which Rāma analyzes his present situation.

In the Bhaṭṭ. monsoon description on the other hand, the situation is very different. Except in the three introductory verses, which we quoted above (VII, 1-3), from verse 4 onwards, when Rāma himself is describing the season, every verse without exception contains his laments and criticisms. Thus we find in each verse the mention of the negative effects that certain elements of the monsoon have on him or on unhappy lovers in general:[28] *pavanaḥ śaminām api klamitvaṁ kurute 'tyarthaṁ* (the wind causes to languish excessively even restrained people) (5); *saṁjvāriṇeva manasā dhvāntam āyāsinā mayā...duḥsaham* (the obscurity is unbearable to me who am exhausted by my mind which is as if feverish) (6); *kurvanti...vidyutaḥ paridevinam* (the lightnings make me lament) (7); *rāgiṇam pīḍayanti janaṁ dhārāḥ* (the rain tortures the lover-folk) (9); *kuryād yoginam apy eṣa sphūrjāvān parimohinam / tyāginaṁ sukhaduḥkhasya parikṣepy ambhasām ṛtuḥ //10//* (This thundering season which sheds water

28. Here we are taking into account not only the influence that the atmospheric phenomena have on our hero, but also other monsoon-elements which do not belong to sky. For the function of all the monsoon-characteristics which are mentioned here is essentially the same, namely to aggravate Rāma's mental suffering.

would disturb even an ascetic who has abandoned happiness and unhappiness) (10); *cātakaḥ...nikṛntann iva mānasam* (the *cātaka* seems to tear (my) heart) (11).

Thus we see that this passage of the Bhaṭṭ. gives us a vision of the monsoon which is distorted by the depressed state of mind of the hero. There is moreover a fundamental difference between this description and the other season descriptions we find in the R. and the Bhaṭṭ. For if Rāma often complains of the torture that certain seasons make him undergo due to his separation from Sītā, he nevertheless always depicts these seasons as agreeable and beautiful in themselves. If they have a negative effect, it is only due to his own depressed state of mind, and not because they are intrinsically bad. In the present monsoon description on the other hand, Rāma describes in thoroughly negative epithets some of the characteristics of the rains. Thus is verse 6, the obscurity is described as "harmful" (*drohin*); in verse 7, the *cātaka*-birds, which are supposed to feed only on rain-drops, are said to be "howling" (*parirāṭin*) and "attacking" (*abhyāghātin*); in 8, the peacocks are said to be "unbearable" (*aśakyāḥ*); in verse 9, the falling rain seems to be full of hatred (*dveṣiṇya iva*); in 11, the *cātaka*-birds are described as "distrustful" (*aviśrambhin*) and "boasting" (*vikatthin*). But the most negative kind of description is certainly reserved to the frogs, in verse 12:

pralāpino bhaviṣyanti kadā nv ete 'palāṣiṇaḥ /
pramāthino viyuktānāṁ hiṁsakāḥ pāpadardurāḥ //12//

But when will these wicked frogs, who are so malicious and chattering, and torment separated lovers, become free of desire?

As we see, there is a great difference between this passage and other rain descriptions in which the monsoon is described in a more "classical", that is, positive way, and Bhaṭṭi has certainly shown a great deal of originality in making his hero describe the season in such negative terms. The poet here has particularly stressed the psychological aspect of the problem: Rāma resents the whole season as negative and even harmful due to his dejected mental state. In these verses where he himself describes the season, he indeed loses all traces of his divine character. He is just like an ordinary human being, and seems even more prone to self-pity and lamenting than the average man.

In this section dedicated to the rainy season, we have traversed through three successive phases of analysis which have brought us ever closer to human concerns. The first kind of interactions between the sky and the earth, namely the purely physical ones, are utterly outside and beyond human scope. Among the second type of interactions, the comparisons between elements belonging to the sky and elements belonging to the earth, the ones which liken elements of the sky to human beings denote already a closer affinity to the world of men. Finally, the third type of interactions, namely the direct influence that the monsoon atmosphere has on people, prompting them to certain actions, lies of course at the core of human concerns. In our last passage from the Bhaṭṭ., we see that the rainy season does not even prompt Rāma to undertake any kind of action, but it only provokes feelings and thoughts in him, which he naturally expresses in words. Thus in this section we have followed a process of ever deepening interiorization, from the outer unlimited expanse of sky and earth right into the human soul.

Śarat (*Autumn*)

In the texts we are studying here, autumn is a season which is not represented in an homogeneous way. We can distinguish two major trends in the descriptions of this season. It is, on the one hand, the epic season of heroism and military prowess and expeditions. This trait is mainly found in the Ragh. autumn description (IV, 14-24), and also to some extent in the R. autumn description (IV, 29) and in the second, shorter description of this season in the Bhaṭṭ. (VII, 14-17). In these passages, the underlying theme is that after the violence of the monsoon, the natural elements have calmed down, but on the other hand, men resume their warlike activities after the forced rest of the rainy season.

The other way of depicting autumn is mainly found in the

first, major autumn description of the Bhaṭṭ. (II, 1-20), as well as in the *sarga* dedicated to this season in the Kir. (IV). In these two passages, autumn is described in an idyllic rural and pastoral setting.

We shall now examine the first manner in which this season is represented, since it is found in the earlier texts. In these descriptions, autumn is in many respects represented as the antithesis of the rainy season. For the monsoon is a time during which the natural elements are unleashed, and thus certain verses in monsoon descriptions very aptly liken the celestial commotion to a battle-scene. But autumn on the other hand brings about a renewed calm for nature. Thus, one atmospheric characteristic which announces the beginning of autumn is the sky which is again clear, freed of its rain-clouds. This is mentioned in three introductory verses of the R. autumn description (IV, 29, 1; 2 & 6): *vimukte gagane ghanaiḥ* (the sky being freed of its clouds) (1); *paṇḍuraṁ gaganaṁ dṛṣṭvā* (having seen the pale sky) (2); *dṛṣṭvā ca vimalaṁ vyoma gatavidyudbalāhakam* (and having seen the pure sky from which the lightnings and clouds hvae departed) (6). In these examples, we can observe a trait which appears in an even more pronounced way in a series of other verses (22-26) of the same passage, namely, the description of certain typical monsoon characteristics which have now disappeared with the onset of autumn.[1] The consequence of this way of describing the season is that these passages are ultimately more evocative of the rainy season than of autumn itself. Verse 24 for instance, which compares the clouds to elephants, is very similar to verses which can be found in monsoon descriptions. The only difference is that here the elephants are no longer intoxicated (*vimada*), since the clouds have lost their speed:

nīlotpaladalaśyāmāḥ śyāmīkṛtvā diśo daśa /
vimadā iva mātaṅgāḥ śāntavegāḥ payodharāḥ //24 //

The clouds which are as dark as the petals of blue lotuses,

1. We encounter also in other autumn descriptions verses illustrating the same technique of enumerating monsoon-elements which have now ceased to exist. See for instance Kir. IV, 23 or Ṛtus. III, 12.

after having darkened the ten directions, have (now) calmed their speed, like elephants who are no longer intoxicated.

Likewise, verse 25 describes the monsoon-winds which have now stopped blowing:

jalagarbhā mahāvegāḥ kuṭajārjunagandhinaḥ /
caritvā viratāḥ saumya vṛṣṭivātāḥ samudyatāḥ //25//

Having moved around, the roused rain-winds which are pregnant with water, which possess a great speed and are fragrant with *kuṭaju* and *arjuna* flowers, have (now) stopped, o gentle one.

Since all these turbulent manifestations of the monsoon have now relented, what is typical of autumn is nature's new-found calm, serenity and purity. Thus, the orb of the moon is pure (*vimalaṁ candramaṇḍalam*) (R. IV, 29, 2); the mountains are washed of their dirt and shine, as if anointed with moon-rays (*nirmalāś...anuliptā ivābhānti girayaś candraraśmibhiḥ*) (R. IV, 29, 27); the lakes, whose water is calm, are shining (*prasannasalilāḥ...vibhānti salilāśayāḥ*)...(R. IV, 29, 29). Likewise, the rivers which were swelled with water during the monsoon and produced a huge noise[2] are now calming down, as the amount of water is reducing. This is described in verse 28 of the R. autumn description, where the rivers are compared to women:

darśayanti śarannadyaḥ pulināni śanaiḥ śanaiḥ /
navasaṁgamasavrīḍā jaghanānīva yośitaḥ //28//

The autumn-rivers reveal their sand-banks little by little, like women who are shy at the first union (little by little reveal) their hips.

This verse which contains one of the very rare erotic allusions of these R. season descriptions knew a great success with later writers, for we find similar images in the Ragh. cycle (XIX, 40) as well as in the Kir. autumn description (IV, 6 and 12).

If the agitation of nature has stopped at the departure of the monsoon, human activity on the other hand, which was

2. See R. IV, 27, 36.

very much hindered during the rains, starts again with autumn. In the R. monsoon description, when Rāma was forced to give up temorarily his quest for Sītā, a number of verses mention the impossibility of travelling, like for instance the first part of verse IV, 27, 40: *ayātrāṁ caiva dṛṣṭvemāṁ mārgāṁś ca bhṛśadurgamān* (and having seen the impossibility of travelling and the roads which are absolutely impracticable...). In autumn on the other hand the roads dry up and the traffic can start again, as is illustrated in verse IV, 18 of the Kir. autumn description:

papāta pūrvāṁ jahato vijihmatāṁ vṛṣopabhuktāntikasasya-sampadaḥ |
rathāṅgasīmantitasāndrakardamān prasaktasaṁpātapṛthakkṛtān pathaḥ ||18||

He went along roads which had lost their former winding course, in whose vicinity the abundance of crops had been eaten by bulls, on which the hardened mud bore lines (made) by the chariot-wheels, and which had become distinct due to the continuous traffic.

Another important human activity which starts again in autumn is military warfare, which had also come to a forced halt in the monsoon, as is illustrated by verse IV, 27, 33 of the R. monsoon description:

vṛttā yātrā narendrāṇāṁ senā pratinivartate |
vairāṇi caiva mārgāś ca salilena samīkṛtāḥ ||33||

Having performed its expedition, the army of the kings is returning. Enmities as well as roads are made equal by the rains.

But now, the time has come again for kings to launch new expeditions, as Rāma tells his brother in verse IV, 29, 30 of the autumn description:

anyonyaṁ baddhavairāṇāṁ jigīṣūṇāṁ nṛpātmaja |
udyogasamayaḥ saumya pārthivānām upasthitaḥ ||30||

Now, gentle prince, has arrived the time to undertake (expeditions) for the kings who are desirous of victory and have contracted hostile relations with each other.

This aspect of autumn is of course of supreme importance to Rāma, who has been impatiently waiting for the arrival of this season during the long monsoon months, eager to resume his search for Sītā. The autumnal season rouses all his martial spirits and provokes his anger towards Sugrīva who is slow in keeping his promise of helping him to find his beloved wife. In the corresponding passage of the Bhaṭṭ., Bhaṭṭi makes his hero say: *kurvanti kopanaṁ tārā maṇḍanā gaganasya mām* (the stars which adorn the sky make me angry) (VII, 16). This is an excellent formulation, for the stars are by themselves a peaceful and serene sight, and do not usually provoke bellicose feelings in their beholders. But since here they announce, by their very visibility, that the rains have stopped, they provoke aggressive feelings in Rāma who is eager to set out for his expedition.

Thus, we see that autumn is a double-sided season, bringing about quietness for nature, but warlike activities for mankind. This is also the main theme of the Ragh. autumn description (IV, 14-24), which describes at the same time the autumnal season and the king Raghu, who has just succeeded his father Dilīpa on the throne. Just like the season itself, Raghu symbolizes at the same time power and peacefulness. Thus, in two verses of this description, Raghu is compared, or at least put on the same plane, as the sun and the moon, the first symbolizing power, for it is regaining strength at the departure of the rains, and the second, with its pure autumn shine, symbolizing calm and serenity:

nirvṛṣṭalaghubhir meghair muktavartmā suduḥsahaḥ /
pratāpas tasya bhānoś ca yugapad vyānaśe diśaḥ //15//

The radiant power of Raghu, as well as that of the sun, simultaneously pervaded the quarters, unbearable because their path had been cleared of the clouds which were light after shedding all their water [3]

3. There is probably a pun here on "*laghubhir meghair*" (the light clouds) which could also mean "the insignificant or weak masses", presumably of Raghu's enemies.

prasādasumukhe tasmiṁś candre ca viśadaprabhe /
tadā cakṣuṣmatāṁ prītir āsīt samarasā dvayoḥ //18//

Then, those who have eyes felt an equally delightful affection for both the king, who had a benevolent face, and the moon, which had a pure shine.[4]

If these two verses can be contrasted with one another, for each one of them illustrates an opposite aspect of the season, verses 16 and 21, on the other hand, each illustrate the two aspects at the same time, for in both the king Raghu symbolizes warlike power, whereas in 16 Indra, who deposits the rain-bow and in 21 the constellation Agastya, which brings clearness to the waters, symbolize the new-found peacefulness of nature in autumn:

vārṣikaṁ saṁjahārendro dhanur jaitraṁ raghur dadhau /
prajārthasādhane tau hi paryāyodyatakārmukau //16//

Indra abandoned the rain-bow and Raghu took up the bow of victory. For both of them alternately take up their bow in order to serve the well-being of the people.

prasasādodayād ambhaḥ kumbhayoner mahaujasaḥ /
raghor abhibhavāśaṅki cakṣubhe dviṣatāṁ manaḥ //21//

At the rise of the great hero born of a jar (i.e.: the constellation Agastya), the waters become clear. (But at the rise) of Raghu, the minds of his enemies, fearing defeat, became troubled.

Through these comparisons with the luminaries, Indra and Agastya, a very lofty and exalted portrait of this king is achieved. But of course, such hyperbolic and flattering comparisons are common place in Sanskrit poetry, and nearly every king is described in a similar way.[5] But here, by describing these natural elements with their typical autumnal character-

4. In the same poem, verse XVI, 53, which is part of the summer description, contains a very similar image.

5. For instance, Raghu's father, Dilipa, is likened to the moon in I, 12, to the sun in I, 18 and to Indra in I, 26.

istics, the poet very skilfully manages to bring about and stress the double-sided aspect of this season.

If the sun, the moon, Indra and Agastya are Raghu's equals, the more humble characteristics of autumn must be satisfied with trying to imitate the king's glory. This is the case for the personified autumn itself, in verse 17,[6] as well as for the bulls in verse 22:

madodagrāḥ kakudmantaḥ saritāṁ kūlam udrujaḥ /
līlākhelam anuprāpur mahokṣās tasya vikramam //22//

Maddened by intoxication, the great humped bulls, tearing the shores of the rivers, imitated his valor which is (just) a playful sport.[7]

Still other typical characteristics of autumn pay homage to the king by spreading his renown and glory, either in a concrete way like the female guardians of the rice-fields in verse 20 (see below), or in a metaphorical way like the swans, stars and lotuses in verse 19, which are all endowed with the white colour for fame is usually associated with whiteness in Sanskrit poetry (a *kavi-samaya*).

haṁsaśreṇīsu tārāsu kumudvatsu ca vāriṣu /
vibhūtayas tadīyānāṁ paryastā yaśasām iva //19//

The munificence of his glory seemed to be spread in the flocks of swans, the stars and the waters full of lotuses.[8]

Thus, we see in these verses, again expressed in a highly hyperbolical way, that it is thanks to the power and the fame of the king that nature itself is beautiful: in verse 17, autumn spreads her beauties merely out of desire to emulate the king. Likewise the bulls display their strength because they wish to

6. Quoted in the section on personifications.

7. This verse finds an echo in Kir. IV, 11, which also describes a bull tearing the shores of the rivers in the pride of his intoxication.

8. The idea that autumn spreads the glory of the hero can also be found in Kir. IV, 21, where the Yakṣa tells Arjuna : *iyaṁ......jayaśriyaṁ pārtha pṛthūkarotu te śarat* (may this autumn enhance the glory of your victory, o son of Pṛthā).

imitate him, and it is only due to his glory that the swans, stars and lotuses are white. This obviously implies that without Raghu, the earth would be a sterile and desolate place indeed, and that this king very concretely deserves the appellation of *mahībhṛt* (bearer of the earth).

Finally, the autumnal season provokes bellicose feelings in Raghu and incites him to set out on an expedition of conquest which will lead him through the whole of India:

> *saritaḥ kurvatī gādhāḥ pathaś cāśyānakardamān /*
> *yātrāyai codayāmāsa taṁ śakteḥ prathamaṁ śarat //24//*
>
> Autumn, which makes the rivers fordable and dries up the mud on the paths, incited him to start on an expedition, before his own energy (did so).

Here again we see that by itself, by its mere presence, autumn provokes war-like feelings in the hero, as we had already noted above in the case of the Bhaṭṭ. verse (VII, 16) in which Rāma says that the stars make him angry.

Thus we see that the idea of autumn being the season of expeditions is a prominent theme of many autumn descriptions. We must also note that altough this theme is not stressed in the first Bhaṭṭ. autumn description (in sarga II), nor in the Kir. autumn description (in sarga IV), this idea is nevertheless also underlying there, for in both cases autumn arrives at the precise moment when the two heroes, Rāma and Arjuna, start their journey which will lead them to fight with Rākṣasas and Śiva disguised as a Kirāta, respectively.

We shall now turn to the second way in which the autumnal season is described in our texts. This appears mainly in the Bhaṭṭ.'s first and main autumn description, as well as in the Kir. autumn description of *sarga* IV. In these two indeed strikingly similar passages[9], the season is described in the natural surroundings of fields and villages. The two heroes, Rāma and Arjuna, are also depicted in similar circumstances,

9. Usually, critics are of the opinion that Bhaṭṭi must have imitated Bhāravi, (see for instance Raghavan, p. 78) but it is not our aim to enter into this controversy here.

for they are both travelling and thus watch, like the spectators of a drama, the landscape pass by in front of their eyes. Moreover, they both observe the scene with equal enthusiasm, and their aesthetic delight is repeatedly stressed in both texts by expressions such as *tutoṣa paśyan* or *nananda paśyan* (he was delighted to see...).

Not only are the objects of description and the attitude of the two observers similar in both passages, but there is also a striking likeness in the pastoral atmosphere which emanates from these two autumn descriptions: in either case, these rural scenes are depicted with an aura of childlike innocence, harmlessness and indeed nearly religious purity and auspiciousness. We must note here that this kind of descriptions of simple rural life is quite unusual in Sanskrit poetry, except in the *gāthā* genre. On the other hand, descriptions of life in *āśramas* or hermitages are quite frequent, the best-known example being that of the *Abhijñānaśākuntalam* of Kālidāsa. Thus it seems that the atmosphere of holiness of these hermitages has in turn been transferred to the villages, in which, to the eyes of the poets, life must have seemed singularly simple and artless, so unlike in towns or courts. And there are indeed in both passages direct comparisons between the villages they describe and hermitages, which sustain this point.

We can here ask the question, why do these unusual descriptions of village-life occur here in the context of these autumn discriptions? One answer could be that autumn, as a direct outcome of the rains, is the season of ripening crops, fruits and fertility of the soil in general, and as such can best be described in the natural surroundings of fields and villages.

Thus, the growing crops are for instance described in Bhaṭṭ. II, 13:

digvyāpinīr locanalobhanīyā mṛjānvayāḥ sneham iva srajantīḥ /
ṛjvāyatāḥ sasyaviśeṣapaṅktīs tutoṣa paśyan vitṛṇāntarālāḥ //13//

He was pleased to see rows of different (varieties of) crops which were spread in (all) directions, pleasing to the sight, clean, which seemed to distill viscosity, stretched in a straight way, with their interstices cleared of grass.

We see that perfect order and cleanliness is reigning here. In the Kir. autumn description, the allusions to crops, especially to rice-fields and rice-plants are extremely numerous. The importance of this element of the season is revealed by the fact that rice-fields are mentioned in the first two opening verses of the passage. We shall here quote verse IV, 2 as an illustration:

> *vinamraśāliprasavaughaśālinīr apetapaṅkāḥ sasaroruhāṁbhasaḥ /*
> *nananda paśyann upasīma aa sthalīr upāyanībhūtaśaradguṇa-*
> *śriyaḥ //2//*

> He was pleased to see in the vicinity of villages natural grounds which were beautiful due to the multitude of bowing ears of rice, which were free of mud, whose water was endowed with lotuses, and whose abundance of autumnal qualities had become a present (for him).

Here again, the cleanliness and purity of nature after the cessation of the rains is stressed, since the ground is described as "free of mud". One more element which is typical of autumn is mentioned in this verse, namely the lotuses which grow in the water of the rice-fields. A great number of verses is dedicated to these flowers in both passages. Thus the Bhaṭṭ. autumn description dedicates not less than eight verses out of twenty to the lotuses. Lotuses are indeed a striking characteristic of the autumnal season, which is described as *paṅkajalakṣaṇā* (characterized by lotuses) in Ragh. IV, 14. The reason for the special conspiciousness of these flowers in autumn is that they have not been blooming during the long "night of the rains", and reappear now in great numbers with the renewed autumn sunshine. Thus in Bhaṭṭ. VII, 17, the sun is called the "nourisher of lotuses": *āpyāyitāram...kamalāni ravim.* The reason for the prominence of lotus-flowers in these autumn descriptions lies not only in the fact that they are indeed numerous in this season, but also in the long-established idea that they are a symbol of purity, and as such in harmony with the atmosphere which pervades these autumn descriptions. The lotus is the *paṅkaja*, the "mud-born one", but is unaffected in its purity and beauty by the mud and dirt surrounding it, and as such can be considered to be a true symbol of the autumnal season which is also born from the mud of the rains, but shines free of mud in its renewed sunshine.

Since they grow in the water of the rice-fields, lotuses are often described along with rice-plants. In Kir. IV, 26 and 34, the sight of the ripe and heavy rice-stalk bowing over the lotus-flower growing in the waters beneath it inspires the Yakṣa with two different images in which both vegetal elements are personified:

amī pṛthustambabhṛtaḥ piśaṅgatāṁ gatā vipākena phalasya śālayaḥ /
vikāsi vaprāmbhasi gandhasūcitaṁ namanti nighrātum ivāsitot-palam //26//

These rice-plants which carry heavy ears and have become tawny due to the ripening of their grains, are bending down as if to smell the blue lotus which is blooming in the water of the fields and is revealed (only) by its perfume.[10]

asāv anāsthāparayāvadhīritaḥ saroruhiṇyā śirasā namann api /
upaiti śuṣyan kalamaḥ sahāmbhasā manobhuvā tapta ivābhipāṇ-ḍutām //34//

Disregarded by the lotus-flower who is showing a supreme indifference (towards him), although he is bowing his head, this rice-plant, drying up along with the water, is becoming very pale, like one who is tortured by love.[11]

This way of personifying the lotus as a woman is also found in a verse from the Bhaṭṭ. autumn description, but this time the flower's lover is not a rice-plant, but a bee:

prabhātavātāhatikampitākṛtiḥ kumudvatīreṇupiśaṅgavigraham /
nirāsa bhṛṅgaṁ kupiteva padminī na māninī saṁsahate 'nyasaṅgamam //6//

10. Since this lotus is a blue one (*asita*), it is naturally invisible in the blue water, and thus its presence is revealed only by its perfume.

11. For the clarity of the translation, we have taken the liberty to use the pronoun "he" with reference to the rice-plant, which is obviously personified as the unhappy lover of the indifferent lotus-flower, *saroruhiṇī*, a feminine.

The day-lotus, whose form was agitated by the onslaught of the morning-breeze, was pushing away, as if angry, the bee whose body was tawny due to the pollen of the night-lotus: a proud woman does not tolerate (her lover's) union with another.

Here, the lotus, which is shaken by the wind, does not allow the bee to land on it, and is therefore compared to a jealous woman who is pushing away her unfaithful lover when he comes back in the morning after spending the night with another woman, that is, with the night-lotus as far as the bee is concerned, and whose body still bears traces of his mistress' yellow make-up paste, namely the pollen of the night-lotus.[12]

In the Kir. verse IV, 26, quoted above, the blue colour of the lotus gave rise to the image. Differently coloured lotuses can provoke diverse images, like for instance in Bhaṭṭ. II, 2, where the red lotuses are likened to a fire, their petals being the flames and the bees hovering around them, the smoke:

taraṅgasaṅgāc capalaiḥ palāśair jvālāśriyaṁ sātiśayāṁ dadhanti /
sadhūmadīptāgnirucīni rejus tāmrotpalāny ākulaṣaṭpadāni //2//

Displaying the superior beauty of a flame by means of their petals which were trembling due to the contact with the waves, the red lotuses, around which bees were swarming, shone with the brilliance of a smoking and blazing fire.

In the same passage, verse II, 18 again mentions lotuses, this time white ones, in order to create a colour-effect:

sitāravindapracayeṣu līnāḥ saṁsaktapheneṣu ca saikateṣu /
kundāvadātāḥ kalahaṁsamālāḥ pratīyire śrotrasukhair ninādaiḥ //18//

The rows of royal swans, as white as jasmine-flowers, which were hiding in the masses of white lotuses and on the sand-banks covered with foam, were recognized only by their songs which are delightful to hear.

12. A very similar image can be found in Kir. X, 34, in the context of the spring description (quoted above in the section dedicated to spring).

All the elements of the verse, and not only the lotuses, contribute here to produce a picture of absolute whiteness.[13] The *kalahaṁsa*-swans themselves are white, and also the jasmines, the lotuses and the sand-banks which are moreover covered with white foam. On this white background, the birds are of course totally invisible.[14]

The swans, which form the main subject-matter of this verse, are as typical of autumn as the peacocks are of the rains. Whereas the peacocks, with their bright plumage, exuberant singing and unrestrained dancing, embody the spirit of the colourful rainy season, the pure white swans, considered to be sacred birds, the birds of Brahmā, correspond equally well to the calm and limpid atmosphere of autumn. Moreover, although they are said to sing beautifully, as in the above-quoted verse, the swans are never described as dancing like the peacocks, a decidedly lower sort of activity, usually reserved to courtesans. Both kinds of birds have this in common, that they are supposed to sing melodiously only during their mating period, namely the rainy season for the peacocks and autumn for the swans. This forms the subject-matter of the following verse from the Kir. autumn description :

vihāya vāñcchām udite madātyayād araktakaṇṭhasya rute śikhaṇḍinaḥ /
śrutiḥ śrayaty unmadahaṁsamihsvanaṁ guṇāḥ priyatve 'dhikṛtā na saṁstavaḥ //25//

Having lost its longing for the high-pitched cry of the peacock whose voice has lost its sweetness at the departure of his intoxication, the ear turns towards the song of the love-enflamed swan : in generating liking, qualities come first, not acquaintance.

Magha also deals with the same theme in two verses of his cycle's autumn description (VI, 44-45). It is interesting to note

13. This is also the case in Ragh. IV, 19 (quoted above), in which both swans and lotuses are mentioned.

14. From this point of view, this verse is reminiscent of R. III, 15, 27, in the winter description, where the cranes are said to be recognizable only by their cries, because the rivers are shrouded in mist.

that just like the above-quoted verse of Bhāravi, Māgha's verses also contain an *arthāntaranyāsa* (exemplification) in the last *pada*. Verse 45 imagines a rivalry between the two birds:

> *tanuruhāṇi puro vijitadhvaner dhavalapakṣavihaṁgamakūjitaiḥ /*
> *jagalur akṣamayeva śikhaṇḍinaḥ paribhavo 'ribhavo hi suduḥ-sahaḥ //45//*

> The feathers of the peacock, whose cries had been surpassed in his presence by the songs of the white-winged bird (i.e. : the swan), fell down as if out of envy : a humiliation caused by the enemy is very hard to bear.

On the other hand, in the section of his cycle of seasons which is dedicated to autumn, Bhāravi describes as equally agreeable the songs of both these birds, in verse X, 25 :

> *samadaśikhirutāni haṁsanādaiḥ kumudavanāni kadambapuṣpa-vṛṣṭyā /*
> *śriyam atiśayinīṁ sametya jagmur guṇamahatāṁ mahate guṇāya yogaḥ //25//*

> The cries of the intoxicated peacocks combined with the songs of the swans, and the forests of *kumudas* combined with the rain of *kadamba*-flowers obtained an extreme splendour : the union of things which possess a great quality (leads to) a great quality.

But we must note that in the four verses (X, 24-27) dedicated to autumn in this cycle, right from the moment when the rainy season takes autumn by the hand, in verse 24, like in a marriage ceremony, these two seasons continue to be depicted together, intermingling the elements which are typical of each.[15] Thus, in the above-quoted verse, the *kumudas* are typical of autumn, whereas the *kadamba*-flowers belong to the rainy season. Bhāravi's obvious aim in doing so was to avoid any kind of repetition, since he had already extensively dealt with autumn in *sarga* IV.

Another kind of animal which appears predominantly tn the

15. The technical term for this is *ṛtu-saṁdhi* : union of two seasons.

Kir. autumn description, and which is very closely linked with rural life, is the cow.[16] Like the ripening crops, cows are a symbol of the fertility of autumn, as we can see for instance in verse 10 :

> *upāratāḥ paścimarātrigocarād apārayantaḥ patituṁ javena gām /*
> *taṁ utsukāś cakrur avekṣaṇotsukaṁ gavāṁ gaṇāḥ prasnutapīva-raudhasaḥ //10//*

> The herds of cows which were returning late in the evening from their pasture-grounds to the stable, unable to run fast because their udders were swollen and dripping with milk, and which were longing (for their calves), filled him with the desire to watch them.[17]

The udders of these cows are dripping because they are longing for their calves. Mallinātha, in his commentary, writes : *prasnuta-pīvaraudhasaḥ* means : *vatsasmaraṇāt sravatpīnāpīnāḥ* : their fat udders are flowing because they remember their calves. This is a common-place idea in Sanskrit poetry, and is not only applicable to cows, but to women as well.

In verse IV, 32, the cows are depicted in the company of their calves :

> *jagatprasūtir jagadekapāvanī vrajopakaṇṭhaṁ tanayair upeyuṣī /*
> *dyutiṁ samagrāṁ samitir gavām asāv upaiti mantrair iva saṁhitāhutiḥ //32//*

> This group of cows which is the cause of the world and the sole purifier of the world obtains its full splendour when it joins the calves near the stables, like an oblation accompanied by *mantras.*

Here again, the fertility of the cows is stressed : they are the cause of the world. In his commentary, Mallinātha says : *āhutir api jagadprasūtir jagadekapāvanī ca* : an oblation is also the cause of the world and the sole purifier of the world. And he goes on to quote Manusmṛti III, 76 :

16. The following Kir. verses have cows for their central theme : IV, 10; 31 and 32. They are also mentioned in IV, 12 and 13. Bulls appear in IV, 11 and 18.

17. Verse IV, 31 is practically identical to this verse.

agnau prāstāhutiḥ samyag ādityam upatiṣṭhate |
ādityāj jāyate vṛṣṭir vṛṣṭer annaṁ tataḥ prajāḥ ||

An oblation correctly thrown into the fire reaches the sun. From the sun, the rain is born, from the rain, food, and from there, offspring."

Thus we see that very concrete aims of the oblation are stressed here : to produce rain and, hence fertility for the earth, which in turn will yield food and generate fertility in the people.[18]

At the same time, this comparison drawn from the realm of the sacrifice stresses the holiness and sacred character of the cows, which reaches its highest point when they are in the company of their offspring. In this respect, the cow, even much more so than the lotus and the swan, truly symbolizes the purity of the autumnal season.

If the Bhaṭṭ. autumn description does not mention cows, it does on the other hand dedicate a verse to the cowherds :

viyogaduḥkhānubhavānabhijñaiḥ kāle nṛpāṁśaṁ vihitaṁ dadadbhiḥ |
āhāryaśobhārahitair amāyair akṣiṣṭa puṁbhiḥ pracitān sa goṣṭhān ||14||

He saw cattle-stations inhabited by men who did not know the experience of suffering due to separation, who paid in time the prescribed royal tax, who were devoid of artificial beauty, and without treachery.

We find a strikingly similar verse in Kir. IV, 13 :

gatān paśūnāṁ sahajanmabandhutāṁ gṛhāśrayaṁ prema vaneṣu bibhrataḥ |
dadarśa gopān upadhenu pāṇḍavaḥ kṛtānukārān iva gobhir ārjave ||13||

Near the cows, the son of Pāṇḍu saw cowherds who had with their cattle the same relation as with brothers, (litt.

18. In *sarga* II of the Ragh., Dilīpa serves the divine cow Nandinī, in order to obtain a son. This is an example of a cow can actually cause fertility.

who had gone towards a relation of same birth with their cattle), who felt for the forests the affection which is (usually) linked with a home, and who were so to say imitated by the cows in their honesty.

The details and the formulation of these two verses are of course different, but they give the same image of the perfect bucolic happiness enjoyed by these simple and honest people, who live in total harmony with nature. Verse IV, 19 of the Kir. again evokes a similar atmosphere, and this time we find an explicit comparison with hermitages, which of course enhances the purity of these simple villages :

janair upagrāmam anindyakarmabhir viviktabhāveṅgitabhūṣa-
nair vṛtāḥ /
bhṛśaṁ dadarśāśramamaṇḍapopamāḥ sapuṣpahāsāḥ sa niveśa-
vīrudhaḥ //19//

Near the villages, he intensely looked at bushes (which served as) houses, which were endowed with the laughter of flowers, similar to hermitage-bowers, and inhabited by people whose behaviour was irreproachable, and whose expressions, gestures and ornaments were special.

Here, the bush-houses are likened to hermitage-bowers, for the latter are also made out of leaves.

In the Bhaṭṭ. autumn description, the verse immediately following the one depicting the cowherds, which we quoted above, describes the cowherdesses:

strībhūṣaṇaṁ ceṣṭitam apragalbhaṁ cārūṇy avakrāṇy api
vīkṣitāni /
ṛjūṁś ca viśvāsakṛtaḥ svabhāvān gopāṅganānāṁ mumude
vilokya //15//

He was delighted to see the cowherdesses' modest behaviour, this ornament of women, their charming though not crooked glances, and their honest nature, which inspired confidence.

As we see here, even the women are described as honest and devoid of artifices, which is very rare in Sanskrit poetry. We are very far from the typical feminine tricks and coyness which the poets are usually so fond of describing. The following verses describes the same women engaged in the activity of churning the milk:

*vivṛttapārśvaṁ rucirāṅgahāraṁ samudvahaccārunitamba-
ramyam /
āmandramanthadhvanidattatālaṁ gopāṅganānṛtyam anandayat
tam //16//*

He was filled with joy to see the cowherdesses' dance, in which their sides were twisted and charming movements were made, which was delightful because their shapely buttocks were moving up and down, and whose rythm was given by the low sound of the churning.

These women are of course not really dancing, but churning the milk, and the movements they make while churning are very similar to a dance. Nevertheless, the activity of churning is very much side-tracked, for the poet describes actually the dance (*nṛtyam*).

An extremely similar description occurs in the Kir., but more at length, since the poet dedicates four verses (IV, 14-17) to the description of this scene:

*paribhramanmūrdhajaṣaṭpadākulaiḥ smitodayā darśitadanta-
kesaraiḥ /
mukhaiś calatkuṇḍalaraśmirañjitair navātapāmṛṣṭasarojacāru-
bhiḥ //14//*

*nibaddhaniḥśvāsavikampitādharā latā iva prasphuritaika-
pallavāḥ /
vyapoḍhapārśvair apavartitatrikā vikarṣaṇaiḥ pāṇivihārahāri-
bhiḥ //15//*

*vrajājireṣv ambudanādaśaṅkinīḥ śikhaṇḍinām unmadayatsu
yoṣitaḥ /
muhuḥ praṇunneṣu mathāṁ vivartanair nadatsu kumbheṣu
mṛdaṅgamantharam //16//*

*sa mantharāvalgitapīvarastanīḥ pariśramaklāntavilocanotpalāḥ /
nirīkṣituṁ nopararāma ballavīr abhipranṛttā iva vārayoṣitaḥ
//17//*

He could not stop looking at the cowherds' wives, whose plump breasts were slowly moving up and down, whose lotus-eyes were tired due to the exertion and who looked like dancing courtesans. (17)[19]

With their faces which were flurried by their whirling hair similar to bees, whose budlike teeth were reddened by the shine of their swaying golden ear-rings, and which were as charming as lotuses touched by the morning sun-shine. (14)

Whose lower lips were trembling due to suppressed sighs (and made them look) like creepers on which one single shoot is quivering, and whose buttocks were twisted by the pulling (of the rope of the churning stick) which made their sides turn in opposite directions, and which was charming due to the playful movements of the hands (15)

While, near the stables, the jars, which were repeatedly beaten by the rotation of the churning-rod, produced a deep sound like a drum and excited the peahens who imagined that it was the thunder. (16)

The Kir. description is of course much longer than that of the Bhaṭṭ. but many elements are very similar, if not identical, in both.[20] Most strikingly, in both descriptions the *gopīs* are said to be dancing: in the Kir., they are even compared to dancing courtesans (*abhipranṛttā iva vārayoṣitaḥ*). A slight touch of court-life seems here to have crept into this pastoral scene.

There is yet another kind of activity in which the village women are described with special predilection, namely, when they are guarding the ripening rice-fields. This scene is very typical of autumn descriptions, and appears in no less than

19. For the clarity of the translation, we are translating first the last verse of the series (IV, 17).

20. In the Bhaṭṭ. we have *vivṛttapārśvam*, and in the Kir. *vyapoḍhapārśvair*. In the Bhaṭṭ. we find the expression *rucirāṅgahāram*, and in the Kir. *pāṇivihārahāribhiḥ*. In the Bhaṭṭ. we have *samudvahaccārunitambaramyam* and in the Kir. *mantharāvalgitapīvarastanīḥ* (here the difference lies in the fact that the breasts of the *gopīs* are moving up and down, not their buttocks, like in the Bhaṭṭ.-verse). The sound of the jars is also similarly described in both verses: we find *āmandramanthadhvani* in the Bhaṭṭ. and *mṛdaṅgamantharam* in the Kir.

three texts, namely, the Ragh., the Kir. and the Śiś. Here is the verse from the Ragh. autumn description:

ikṣucchāyaniṣādinyas tasya goptur guṇodayam /
ākumārathodghātaṁ śāligopyo jagur yaśaḥ //IV, 20//

Sitting in the shade of the sugar-canes, the female rice-guardians sang, right from the stories of his childhood, this protector's (i.e. : Raghu's) glory, which was born from his qualities.

This subject then reappears in the Kir. autumn description, but developed in three verses (IV, 7-9), which are mainly concerned with describing the beauty of the rice-guardian:

manoramaṁ prāpitam antaraṁ bhruvor alaṁkṛtaṁ kesarareṇu-ṇāṇunā /
alaktatāmrādharapallavaśriyā samānayantīm iva bandhujīvakam //7//
navātapālohitam āhitaṁ muhur mahānivešau paritaḥ payo-dharau /
cakāsayantīm aravindajaṁ rajaḥ pariśramāmbhaḥpulakena sarpatā //8//
kapolasaṁśleṣi vilocanatviṣā bibhūṣanyantīm avataṁsakot-palam /
sutena pāṇḍoḥ kalamasya gopikāṁ nirīkṣya mene śaradaḥ kṛtārthatā //9//

The son of Pāṇḍu thought that autumn had fulfilled its aim, when he saw the female rice-guardian who was uniting the charming *bandhujīvaka*-flower which was placed between her eye-brows and adorned by the very fine pollen of its stamina, with the beauty of her bud-like lower lip which was red with lac. Who was increasing the brilliance of the lotus-pollen, red like the new sun, which was repeatedly being deposited all around her large breasts because of the spreading horripilation provoked by the sweat. And who was decorating with the lustre of her eyes the lotus serving as ear-ornament which was touching her cheek.

Finally, we encounter once again the same theme in the Śiś. autumn description:

> *vigatasasyajighatsam aghaṭṭayat kalamagopavadhūr na mṛga-*
> *vrajam /*
> *śrutatadīritakomalagītakadhvanim iṣe 'nimiṣekṣaṇam agrataḥ*
> //VI 49//

In the month of Iṣa (september-october), the female rice-guardian had no need to chase away the flock of deer (which were standing) in front of her, because they had lost all desire to eat the crops and listened without blinking to the sound of the sweet melody she was singing.

Here, the motif of the rice-guardian is combined with another theme, the one of the deer who are so fascinated by her song that they forget to eat the crops. This verse may well have been inspired by the following verse from the Kir. autumn description:

> *kṛtāvadhānaṁ jitabarhiṇadhvanau suraktagopījanagītaniḥsvane /*
> *idaṁ jighatsām apahāya bhūyasīṁ na sasyam abhyeti mṛgīka-*
> *dambakam //33//*

This flock of does, giving up their great desire to eat and concentrating their attention on the sound of the sweet-voiced cowherdesses' song, which surpasses the cries of the peacocks, does not go near the fields.

The image of a deer which is captivated by a song can also be found, though in a different context, in the Bhaṭṭ. autumn description:

> *dattāvadhānaṁ madhulehigītau praśāntaceṣṭaṁ hariṇaṁ*
> *jighāṁsuḥ /*
> *ākarṇayann utsukahaṁsanādān lakṣye samādhiṁ na dadhe*
> *mṛgāvit //7//*

Desiring to kill the deer who was fixing his attention on the song of the bees, and had ceased to move, the hunter, listening to the cries of the amorous swans, could not keep his concentration on his target.

Here, the image functions on two levels: the deer is listening to the song of the bees and therefore not bewaring of the hunter who is watching it, but the hunter himself is so captivated by the cries of the swans that he cannot fix his attention on the deer either. We see that these verses accentuate the atmosphere of hermitage-like peacefulness of these autumn descriptions, in which no violence takes place: the rice-guardians do not have to chase away the deer, and even the hunter is so taken away by one of the typical beauties of autumn, the song of the swans, that he loses all desire to kill.

Thus we can say that these autumn descriptions of the Bhaṭṭ. and the Kir. present us a highly idealized and idyllic view of life in the country. Nature in autumn is beautiful, serene and purified, and likewise men (and even women!) lead an honest, simple and happy life, devoid of any of the vices and corruption of town-life. Even the cows are said to be honest in Kir. IV, 13! Thus nature and man, in their peacefulness, are in perfect unison and harmony with each other. In this respect, these two descriptions are of course very different from the previously discussed autumn descriptions, as they appear mainly in the Ragh. and also in the R., where nature is indeed also described as peaceful during this season, but where this very peacefulness forms a sharp contrast with the renewed war-like activities of mankind.

Hemanta (Winter)

The R. is the only one among the texts we are studying here which dedicates a full description to winter (III, 15). Otherwise, this season appears only in the cycles.

The R. winter description focuses entirely on the description of nature in this season, which is not surprising, since Rāma, Sītā and Lakṣmaṇa are spending winter in the wilderness, on the shores of the Godāvarī-river. Therefore Lakṣmaṇa, who is here making the description, very naturally describes what he sees around him. In his Ragh. cycle of seasons, Kālidāsa dedicates only one verse to *hemanta* (XIX, 41), which mainly describes the seducing and erotic effect that the harem-women's winter-clothes have on the king Agnivarṇa. The Kir. cycle of seasons dedicates two verses to winter (X, 28-29), but here winter appears mixed with spring, and even strongly overwhelmed by this season. Thus, in X, 28 we have of course "a few snow flakes" (*virala-tuṣāra-kaṇaḥ*), but at the same time blooming *phalinīs* and *kundas* (28), as well as *lavalī*-creepers and *lodhras* (29), and all these flowers obviously evoke spring. Thus these two verses are not really representative of winter.[1] In his Śiś., Māgha dedicates a greater number of verses to this season (VI, 55-61; 77). The main theme here is the erotic aspect of the hivernal season, for these verses mainly describe the effect that the cold has on lovers.

In the R., the most striking characteristic of winter is the cold, and all the cosnequences it brings about: the world is hardened with frost: (*nīhāraparuṣo lokaḥ*) (5); the waters cannot be tasted (because they are too cold) (*jalāny anupabhogyāni*) (5); the mount Himavān is now very obviously "himavān" (endowed with snow): *suvyaktaṁ himavān himavān giriḥ*) (9); the days are frosty, bitter cold and windy: (*sanīhārāḥ paṭuśītāḥ samarutāḥ... divasā* (11); the nights have to be spent under a roof, they are cold and pass with a lengthened duration: (*nivṛttākāśaśayanāḥ... śītā vṛddhatarā yāmās triyāmā yānti sāṁpratam*) (12); the west-wind blows twice as cold in this season: (*pravāti paścimo vāyuḥ kāle dviguṇaśītalaḥ*) (15). As a natural consequence of this, the fire, as well as the sun, are pleasant: (*subhago havyavāhanaḥ*) (5), (*subhagādityāḥ*) (10). As we mentioned above, this description is centered mainly on nature in this season. People are hardly mentioned: only in verse 6 there is a reference to "good people" (*santaḥ*) who are performing oblations, and verse 7 mentions the subjects of kings (*janapadāḥ*) as well as kings who are engaged in expeditions. Even animals hardly figure in this passage. Only birds appear in two verses (III, 15, 16 and 22), and what matters here is not so much their physical presence as their cries:

bāṣpacchannāny araṇyāni yavagodhūmavanti ca /
śobhante 'bhyudite sūrye nadadbhiḥ krauñcasārasaiḥ //16//

With the singing curlews and herons, the forests, which are

1. As Bhāravi writes in X, 28 : *guṇam asamayajaṁ cirāya lebhe... tuṣārakālaḥ* (the cold season obtained for a long time an untimely quality).

covered with mist and full of barley and wheat, shine as the sun is rising.

And also:

bāṣpasaṁcchannasalilā rutavijñeyasārasāḥ /
himārdravālukais tīraiḥ sarito bhānti sāmpratam //22//

With their water covered with mist and the herons recognizable (only) by their cries, the rivers are beautiful now with their shores whose sand is humid with snow.

Since the fog is covering everything, only the cries of the birds can be heard. Thus, the herons are said to be "recognizable only by their cries" (*rutavijñeyasārasāḥ*) in verse 22, and as such seem to have a "disembodied" existence. The overall atmosphere of these verses is that of a great solitude and nearly total absence of movement and visibility: thus, in both above-quoted verses, we find the terms *bāṣpa-cchanna* of *bāṣpa-saṁcchanna* (covered with mist). In this season, the forests are empty (*śūnyāraṇyāḥ*) (11) and somnolent, as if life is suspended for the time being : *prasuptā iva lakṣyante vipuṣpā vanarājayaḥ*: the flowerless rows of forests seem to be sleeping (21).

Generally speaking, the world seems to be transformed by winter, and things no longer appear to be what they really are. Thus the sun, which is characteristically weakened in this season, passes for the moon:

mayūkhair upasarpadbhir himanīhārasaṁvṛtaiḥ /
dūram abhyuditaḥ sūryaḥ śaśāṅka iva lakṣyate //18//

With its creeping rays veiled in snow and mist, the sun looks like the moon, (even) long after it has risen.

If the sun, with its dim light, looks like the moon, the latter luminary also undergoes certain changes in this season:

ravisaṁkrāntasaubhāgyas tuṣārāvṛtamaṇḍalaḥ /
niḥśvāsāndha ivādarśaś candramā na prakāśate //13//[2]

2. Here, we have preferred to keep the variant reading *āvṛta* instead of *aruṇa*, because it seems to be more consistent with the *upamā* : for a mirror does not become red (*aruṇa*) due to a breath, but so to say covered

The moon, whose splendour has been transferred to the sun and whose orb is covered with mist, no longer shines, like a mirror blinded by a breath.

The following verse once again takes up the same idea, but this time with a different comparison inspired by the context of the life of the speaker and of his companions:

jyotsnā tuṣāramalinā paurṇamāsyāṁ na rājate /
sīteva cātapaśyāmā lakṣyate na tu śobhate //14//

During the full-moon night, the moon-light, which is stained by snow, does not shine, and it looks like Sītā who is darkened by the sun, but it is lustreless (unlike her).

Thus, all the light and colour of this season seem to have taken refuge in the ripe rice-plants, which shine like gold:

kharjūrapuṣpākṛtibhiḥ śirobhiḥ pūrṇataṇḍulaiḥ /
śobhante kiṁcid ālambāḥ śālayaḥ kanakaprabhāḥ //17//

With their ears full of grains which look like *kharjūra*-flowers, the somewhat bent rice-plants shine with the splendour of gold.

Through these examples, we see that this R. winter description evokes in highly poetical and delicate terms the mysterious and somnolent atmosphere of the cold season.

The winter description of the Śiś. cycle of seasons, which is the only other important winter description found in these texts, is diametrically opposed to the R. passage in that it is mainly concerned with the activities of people in this season. These verses mainly describe the effect that the cold has on lovers. First of all, on separated lovers (VI, 55-56). Then, verse 57 describes a reconciliation, and finally verses 58 to 61 reflect love in union. Thus the cold season provides Māgha with a pretext to describe love in its various stages.

In this description, the most prominent characteristic of this season, and that which appears most frequently, is the icy-cold wind, which, according to R. III, 15, 15, blows from the West

(*āvṛta*) with a layer of vapour. Moreover, the reading *āvṛta* is quoted by poeticians, like for instance by Ānandavardhana in his *Dhvanyāloka*.

in this time of the year (*paścimo vāyuḥ*). This winter-wind is guilty of many crimes against the lover-folk. Thus, in verse 55 it burns the tearful eyes of the travellers' wives. In 56, it kills travellers who are separated from their beloved ones. In 58, it burns the wound on the lip of a lady, and in 60, it threatens women with the help of finger-like creepers, which personifies it to some extent.

The theme which constantly recurs in these verses dedicated to the winter-wind is the opposition between the icy-cold nature of this wind, and, rather surprisingly, the burning sensation it causes in lovers. Thus, verse VI, 55 describes in its first part the cold nature of this wind and the freezing effect it has even on deep rivers, but the second part describes the burning it causes, due to tears, to the eyes of travellers' wives:

> *gajapatidvayasīr api haimanas tuhinayat saritaḥ pṛṣatāṁ patiḥ |*
> *salilasaṁtatim adhvagayoṣitām atanutātanutāpakṛtaṁ dṛśām*
> //55//

> The winter (wind), this lord of water drops, covering with ice even rivers which are as deep as lords of elephants, gave rise to a flood of tears which caused an intense burning to the eyes of traveller's wives.

The next verse plays on the contrast between the icy nature of this wind and the power it has to kill travellers, but only if they remember their beloved's young, and more importantly *warm* breasts:

> ...
> *smṛtasayauvanasoṣmapayodharān satuhinas tu hinastu*
> *viyoginaḥ* //56//

> ...but when it (i.e. the wind) is freezing cold, it kills people who are separated (from the beloved one), when they remember the youth and warmth of her breasts.

Finally, in verse 58, the opposition between cold and warm plays on the whole of the verse:

> *bhṛśam adūyata yādharapallavakṣatir anāvaraṇā himamārutaiḥ |*
> *daśanaraśmipaṭena ca sītkṛtair nivasitenva sitena sunirvavau*
> //58//

bhṛśam adūyata yādharapallavakṣatir anāvaraṇā himamāru-taiḥ /
daśanaraśmipaṭena ca sītkṛtair nivasiteva sitena sunirvavau //58//

The exposed wound which was on the bud-like lower lip was severely burnt by the winter-winds, but when it was so to say clad, due to sighs of pleasure, in the white dress of the teeth's rays, it was completely refreshed.

Here, the contradiction lies in the fact that the cold winter-winds burn the wound, whereas the teeth's rays refresh it. For indeed, rays are usually associated with warmth, and moreover, they are likened to a dress here, which should also conduce to warmth.

Thus we see that it is not practicable to make generalizations or draw overall conclusions about the winter season, for the two important descriptions of this season which we find in our texts stress two totally different aspects of winter: the R. is concerned only with nature, and the Śiś. only with lovers in different amorous situations which are provoked by the cold.

Śiśira (The Cool Season)

Śiśira, or the "cool season", is undoubtedly the most ill-favoured of all seasons, since we do not find any full description dedicated to it in the texts we are studying here. It appears only in the cycles, and even there, as compared to some other seasons, very few verses are concerned with it.

At first sight, the nature of this season appears to be somewhat ill-defined. Etymologically speaking, *śiśira* means of course "cool season", and as such, it should bear some resemblance to winter. We shall now see in the texts in what way this season is actually described.

Kālidāsa, in the Ragh. cycle of seasons, dedicates only one verse each to *hemanta* and to *śiśira* (XIX, 41 & 42), whereas all other seasons are described in two verses. Prima facie, this already gives the impression that for this poet these two seasons are not markedly different, and that he is just making a concession to the established usage by mentioning once the term *haimana*, in XIX, 41, and once *śiśira*, in XIX, 42. And indeed, if we read the verse dedicated to *śiśira*, we find that the atmosphere it evokes is not very different from winter.

> *arpitastimitadīpadṛṣṭayo garbhaveśmasu nivātakukṣiṣu /*
> *tasya sarvasuratāntarakṣamāḥ sākṣitāṁ śiśirarātrayo yayuḥ* //42//
>
> Having for eyes lamps with a soft light placed in the inner appartements which were protected from the wind, the nights of *śiśira*, proper to all pleasures, became his witnesses.

Of course, the main aim of this verse is not the description of the climatic conditions during *śiśira*, for it is concerned with a more erotic subject-matter, but we can nevertheless gain the following information from it: *śiśira* seems to be a cold season, for the king spends the nights in the inner appartements, which are "protected from the wind". To make such a protection necessary, this wind must be a cold one, like the winter-wind.[1]

In the cycle of his Kir., Bhāravi also dedicates only one verse to *śiśira*. Here this season appears to be a hybrid between winter and spring:

> *katipayasahakārapuṣparamyas tanutuhino 'lpavinidrasinduvāraḥ /*
> *surabhimukhahimāgamāntaśaṁsī samupayayau śiśiraḥ smaraikabandhuḥ* //X, 30//
>
> Charming with a few mango-flowers, a little bit of snow and some rare blooming *sinduvāras*, *śiśira*, the only friend of Love[2], arrived, announcing the beginning of spring and the end of winter.

As we see, *śiśira* posseses "a little bit" of the qualities of the seasons which immediately precede and follow it : it has snow, like winter, and mango- and *sinduvāra*-flowers, like spring. Its intermediary position and transitory nature is moreover stressed by the compound *surabhimukhahimāgamāntaśaṁsī* (announcing

1. In the *Ṛtusaṁhāra* too, which describes *śiśira* more at length, this season appears like a cold season, endowed with snow, during which the nights must be spent inside.

2. Usually, spring is called the only friend of Love.

the beginning of spring and the end of winter). Thus, in this text, *śiśira* seems to be nothing but the transitory period between winter and spring. But we must note that in this cycle, even winter already appeared strongly mixed with spring. In this respect, *hemanta* and *śiśira* are therefore not described here in a markedly different way.

Māgha seems to be the only poet to make a clear distinction between winter and *śiśira* : whereas winter is described as a definitely cold season, *śiśira* appears as the transitory period between winter and spring, having qualities belonging to both. Thus in the verses he dedicates to *śiśira*, (VI, 62-66; 78), Māgha stresses the ambiguous nature of this season by describing it either like winter or like spring, alternating at every verse.

Thus, verse 62 underlines the spring-like aspects : the wind seems to be shouting angrily because of the buzzing of the bees, which are of course typical of spring. Moreover, it covers the *phalinīs* with buds. Verse 63 underlines the winter-like aspects: the sun is weak and the snow deep. Verse 64 again evokes spring characteristics, since it mentions the pollen of the *lodhra*-flowers. Verse 65, which is comparable to verse 61 of the winter description by its basic idea, which is that in the cold season women are more prone to love-making, accentuates of course the hibernal aspect. As for verse 66, it underlines the spring-like aspect of the season : there are bees, the *kundalatā* is opening, and the *lavaṁgamas* are in full bloom.[3]

Thus, the verses dedicated to *śiśira* in this cycle illustrate the fight which is going on at this time of the year between winter and spring, in which spring finally wins, since the last verse, 66, as well as verse 78 in the second cycle, underline the spring-like aspect of *śiśira*. Very often, images of conflicts appear in these verses : thus in 62, the wind shouts angrily (*āhitahuṁkṛtiḥ*) and threatens (*nirabhartsayata*) the young women. As for verses 63 and 64, they illustrate with the help of more direct images the fight which is going on between winter and spring. To this effect, verse 63 uses a proverbial expression :

3. In the second cycle, verse 78 also underlines the vernal aspect of this season, for it mentions the opening buds of the *lavalī*-creeper.

upaciteṣu pareṣv asamarthatāṁ vrajati kālavaśād balavān api |
tapasi mandagabhastir abhīṣumān na hi mahāhimahānikaro
'bhavat ||63||

When the enemies are powerful, even the strong one becomes, for the time being, incapable (of defeating them). Thus, in the month of *Tapas*, the sun, with its weak rays, could not diminish the deep snow.

Verse 64 contains an epic image :

abhiṣiṣeṇayiṣuṁ bhuvanāni yaḥ smaram ivākhyata lodhrarajaścayaḥ |
kṣubhitasainyaparāgavipāṇḍuradyutir ayaṁ tirayann udabhūd diśaḥ ||64||

A mass of *lodhra*-pollen, which possessed the dazzling whiteness of the dust provoked by an army, and which covered the horizon, arose, as if to announce that love was starting upon an expedition against the whole world.

The army of love is surely also the army of spring, since the *lodhra*-flowers bloom in this season. Thus, the mass of *lodhra*-pollen which is flying up indicates the imminent victory of this season over winter.

Through these examples, we see that it is impossible so give a list of things which are solely typical of *śiśira*, for all the motifs and elements which figure in these *śiśira* descriptions are also typical either of winter or of spring. The double nature of the season is very well illustrated by Kir. X, 30 (quoted above), in which Bhāravi attributes to *śiśira* "a little bit" of the characteristics of both winter and spring, thus depicting in a fairly realistic way the passage from one season to the other. This is far from being the case in Māgha's Śiś., in which the deep snow in verse 63 figures next to the blooming *lodhra*-flowers in 64. But it would certainly be vain to ask for realism in a cycle of seasons where all the seasons appear together, in a totally unrealistic way.

These examples all show that *śiśira* cannot be considered to be a separate and distinct season, since no element can be found which would be exclusively typical of it : it is either similar to winter, as in the Ragh. cycle of seasons, or at best the transitory period between winter and spring, as is shown by the Kir. and Śiś. cycles. This lack of typical characteristics certainly accounts for the fact that we do not find in these texts any descriptions dedicated solely to this season.

CHAPTER II

THE PECULIAR SEASON DESCRIPTION OF THE NAIṢADHACARITA

Now that we have determined some of the most typical traits and themes of each season, we shall turn to the passage of the Naiṣ. (I, 76-106) wherein, as it seems to us, appears a somewhat peculiar season description. We must note that none of the critics who wrote on the seasons consider this passage to be a season description.[1] This is obviously due to the fact that here the seasons are neither named nor announced, as it is the case in other season descriptions.[2] Nevertheless, verse 105, at the end of this passage, describes the forest Nala is visiting as being "filled with all the seasons" (*sarvartughane vane*). Should we then consider these words to be merely an empty phrase, or should we on the other hand take them seriously and deduce from them that there is really a description of all the seasons in these verses?

For several reasons, we would rather tend to adopt the second solution. First of all, from the point of view of poetic

1. Neither Renou nor Raghavan think that the Naiṣ. contains any season description. Raghavan does not mention the Naiṣ. at all, and Renou says in his essay "Un theme litteraire en sanskrit : les saisons" in *Sanskrit et culture,* on p. 150: "Il est notable que le *Naiṣadhīya*, seul du genre, et is enclin par ailleurs a decrire, ne presente rien." (It is noteworthy that the *Naiṣadhīya,* as the only one of its kind, and which is elsewhere so prone to describe, does not present anything (on the seasons)).

2. The only exception is *Madhu* (spring) who appears in verse I, 105 in his personified form of Kāma's friend.

and internal consistency, why should Śrīharṣa describe the forest in which Nala is taking a walk as being "filled with all the seasons", if he has not mentioned in the description of that same forest some of the characteristic attributes of each season? Secondly, taking into account the fact that this poet, as is shown all along his work, was extremely fond of digressions on all sorts of topics, it would seem strange indeed if he had not inserted a description of the seasons in his poem.

We shall now examine this passage and see whether it really contains certain characteristic traits of the different seasons. At first glance, while reading these verses, we see that they indeed describe plants, flowers and animals which are typical of certain seasons. As far as spring is concerned, we find the *kiṁśuka*-flower in verse 83, which appears already in the spring descriptions of the R. (IV, 1, 34), of the Ragh. (IX, 31) and of the Śiś. (VI, 21). There is also the *palāśa*-flower[3] in 84, which is found in Kum. III, 29 or Śiś. VI, 2. Verses 86 and 91 describe the *campaka*-buds which are mentioned in Śiś. VI, 5. Verses 88, 90, 100, 102 and 104 mention the cuckoo, a bird which is extremely typical of spring and can be found in numerous spring descriptions, for instance in Kum. III, 32, Ragh. IX, 47, Śiś. VI, 8. The blooming mango-tree in verse 89 is of course also typical of this season, and appears in Ragh. XIX, 43. Verse 92 describes the flower of the *nāgakesara*-tree, which is mentioned for example in Aśvaghoṣa's poem, the *Saundarananda*, in the context of the spring description, in VII, 9.[4] The blooming *aśoka*-tree in verse 101 is also typical of spring, being mentioned for instance in Kum. III, 26. Finally, the bees which appear in verses 86, 88, 89, 91, 93, and 102, and honey, which is mentioned in verses 85, 99 and 106, are depicted in innumerable verses of preceding spring descriptions.

As far as summer is concerned, we find the *pāṭala* flower in verse 95, which is extremely typical of this time of the year and is already found for instance in Ragh. XVI, 52 and XIX, 46, as well as in Śiś. VI, 23.

3. *Palāśas* and *kiṁśukas* are actually the same flowers, belonging to the tree Butea Frondosa.

4. This verse actually mentions a *nāga*-tree. But it is the same tree, Mesua Roxburghii, called by a slightly different name.

Typical of the rainy season are for instance the blooming *ketaka*-trees which appear in verses 78 to 81, and also 99. The flowers of this tree can already be found in R. IV, 27, 8 & 9, in Kir. X, 26 and in Śiś. VI, 34. The dancing peacocks in verse 102 are of course also extremely typical of this season, and appear in innumerable verses describing the rains in previous descriptions.

The elements which could represent autumn are on the other hand not easily discernible. We can nevertheless assume that fruits are typical of this season, since they are mentioned in the autumn description of the Bhaṭṭ. (II, 20) for example. In this passage of the Naiṣ., they are mentioned in a general way in verses 76, 77 and 98. Verses 82 and 83 describe more specifically the pomegranate fruit (*dāḍima*), and verse 94 mentions the *mālūra*-fruit, neither of which appears in any previous autumn description.

As for the cold seasons, we find traces of them in verse 97 and 99. In 97, it is said that the "leaves are whitened by frost" (*tuṣāra-pāṇḍura-cchadā*). But in the same verse we also find flowers (*kusumita*). The season described here could therefore be *śiśira*, which is often depicted as a mixture of winter and spring. But verse 99 is more surprising:

nṛpāya tasmai himitaṁ vanānilaḥ sudhīkṛtaṁ puṣparasair aharmahaḥ |
vinirmitaṁ ketakareṇubhiḥ sitaṁ viyogine 'datta na kaumudī-mudaḥ ||99||

The day-light, changed into ice by the forest-winds and into nectar by the juice of flowers (i.e.: by honey), rendered white by the pollen of the *ketakas*, did not give the joys of the moonlight to the king who was separated (from Damayantī).

The day-light changed into ice by the forest-winds evokes winter. But the fact that it is transformed into nectar by the flowers' honey evokes spring. As for the *ketakas*, they bloom during the monsoon. Finally, *kaumudī*, the moonlight, can also mean "full-moon night", and designates more specifically the full-moon night of the month of Kārttika, a month of autumn.

This verse is therefore a perfect hybrid, and alludes to four seasons at the same time, and not only to winter.

Now that we have ascertained that there really do figure in this passage elements which are typical of each season, it is time that we examine the nature of this description. There seem to be three major characteristics which dominate Śrīharṣa's idiosyncratic style in these verses.

First of all, this entire season description is made mostly with reference to the flora of the park Nala is visiting, little emphasis being given to the fauna, and none at all to atmospheric elements.

Secondly, and this is certainly one of the most striking characteristics of this season description, we see that Śrīharṣa did not follow the convention of representing the seasons one after the other, in the form of a cycle. Here all the seasons appear in total confusion.

Last but not least, the seasons in this forest are viewed through Nala's eyes, which give him a singularly distorted vision of reality, due to his acute love-longing. This is accomplished mainly on the basis of puns and unusual, especially morbid, comparisons.

As far as the first point is concerned, we can see in the above-mentioned list of elements which are typical of each season, that most of them are vegetal elements: trees, flowers and fruits. This state of affairs is already indicated in the very first verse of the passage: *tataḥ prasūne ca phale ca mañjule sa... vyalokayat kānanakāmanīyakam* (76): "then, *in the charming flowers and fruits,* he saw the beauty of the forest". It is of course not surprising that such emphasis should be given to the flora, for Nala is after all visiting a forest.[5] Other elements, such as birds, especially the cuckoo, are also mentioned in these verses, but they are few as compared to vegetal elements.

This way of representing the seasons by means of the plants which bear their flowers and fruits at certain times of the year

5. The fact itself that the hero is walking and observing what he sees is typical of many descriptions. Already in the R spring, monsoon and autumn descriptions, in all the Bhaṭṭ descriptions, as well as in the Kir. autumn description, the heroes observe (sometimes describe) and respond in various ways to what they see, which is also Nala's case here.

is of course to a certain extent typical of all season descriptions. But the extreme emphasis given by Śrīharṣa to vegetal elements, making them practically the sole object of his description, seems to have its parallel only in the spring descriptions of Aśvaghoṣa's two poems, the *Saundarananda* and the *Buddhacarita*, with which we are of course not dealing here.

We shall now turn to the second point, namely the extreme confusion in which the seasons appear in this passage. The authors of other cycles of seasons usually start with a certain season of their own choice (there did not seem to exist any fixed convention as to which season to start with), and then go on describing one season after the other, in their natural order of occurrence. But this is not the method of description adopted here by Śrīharṣa, for not only does he not "announce" the seasons, but they appear moreover in a totally erratic order.

Thus for instance, verses 78-81, describing the *ketaka*, represent the monsoon. Then verses 82-83 are presumably representative of autumn, since they mention fruits. But then, verses 84-92 all depict typical elements of spring, whereas we would expect to find winter and *śiśira* between autumn and spring. In the following verses, we probably have autumn in 94, summer in 95, spring in 96, *śiśira* in 97, etc...As we can see, the natural sequence of the seasons is not at all respected here. Moreover, certain verses evoke two seasons at the same time, like verse 102 which describes both the song of the cuckoo, which is typical of spring, and the dance of the peacock, a characteristic of the monsoon, or even four, like verse 99 which we quoted above.

What is more, if we read the above-mentioned list of elements which are typical of each season, we realize that there is an overwhelming mass of data concerning spring, but that the other seasons are only sparsely represented.[6] Spring is also the only season to be explicitely mentioned in this passage: verse 105 likens Nala to "Kāma following his friend Spring" (*madhuṁ*

6. The predominance of spring in these verses may account for the fact that special predilection is given to the flora, for spring is a season which is mainly manifested in the budding and flowering trees, unlike other seasons, like the rains, autumn or even winter, where atmospheric elements like clouds, rain, thunder,the moon, etc...play a greater role.

sa mitram...anusarann iva smaraḥ). Since nowhere in these verses do we read about any companion of the king who could represent spring, we must admit that *madhu* here is the actual season of spring as it appears in this forest.

We should not, of course, be surprised by the preference given here to the vernal season, for as we have seen, spring is the most romantic and erotic of all the seasons, and as such, it is best equipped to drive Nala to an extreme point of love-longing and despair.

This way of representing the seasons in a state of confusion is announced to a certain extent by Bhāravi's treatment of this theme in the Kir. cycle of seasons, wherein appear numerous *ṛtu-saṁdhis*: autumn is represented along with monsoon-characteristics, and winter is mixed with spring. But there the confusion is of course less extreme, and the seasons are moreover announced and appear one after the other, in their natural order.

In the Naiṣ., the fact that the seasons appear in such an intermingled way seems to be a direct and logical consequence of the idea that they are present together in this forest. This way of representing the seasons further increases the difficulty of this passage, and demands from the reader a good knowledge of the characteristic elements and themes of each season, in order to recognize which season is being described.

We shall now turn to the third and most important point which distinguishes this passage, namely, the distorted way in which Nala perceives this forest, due to his excessive love-longing. The fact that his state of mind is acutely pathological and verges at times on madness is revealed by various traits of his behaviour. Thus, he reacts in an excessive way at the most innocent and harmless sights, like for instance in verse 95 where, mistaking for Kāma's quiver a cluster of *pāṭala*-flowers, he "trembles, his mind blinded by fear" : *dhiyā bhayāndhayā sa... prakampitaḥ*. In verses 79 to 81, he addresses the most fanciful reproaches to a *ketaka*-tree, which is obviously unable to hear them. Talking to inanimate objects as if they were persons is a typical trait of madness induced by extreme love-longing. The example of the Yakṣa talking to the cloud in the *Meghadūta* is well-known. It is also the case for the king Purūravas in Kālidāsa's drama, the *Vikramorvaśīya*, who, in the fourth act, wanders in the wilderness, stricken with madness because of the disappearance of his beloved Urvaśī, asking various animals and objects whether they have seen her.

But most strikingly, Nala's pathological state is revealed by the fact that he interprets everything he sees in a very negative way. In reality, each and every one tries to please him : in verse 77, the trees offer him flowers and fruits as a gift of hospitality. Verse 102 says that "even in the forest, the triad "song, music and dance" honored him" : *vane 'pi tauryatrikam ārarādha tam.*[7] In 103, parrots and *sārika*-birds, which have been specially trained to this effect, praise him and in 106, the forest-wind serves him. But all this is to no avail, as verse 104 explains :

itīṣṭagandhāḍhyam aṭann asau vanaṁ pikopagīto 'pi śukastuto 'pi ca |
avindatāmodabharaṁ bahiś paraṁ vidarbhasubhrūvirahena nāntaram ||104||

As he was thus walking in this wood which was rich in agreeable fragrances, lauded by the cuckoos and praised by the parrots, he felt a supreme abundance of exterior joy (or : perfume), but no interior joy, due to his separation from the beautiful eye-browed (Damayantī) of Vidarbha.

Thus we can say that only the very first and last verse of this passage describe the facts "objectively" : I, 76-77 and 102-106. Otherwise, this forest is viewed through Nala's eyes, which deform reality to a great extent. This distortion of reality is revealed in two ways : either by erotic images, or else, by extremely morbid if not frankly disgusting ones. Thus, certain verses are erotic, but not because they depict couples of lovers, but because Nala, whose thoughts are constantly fixed on Damayantī, interprets in an erotic way the forms of certain plants or fruits. Other verses have an excessively morbid tone, because Nala, with his brooding thoughts, imagines that all the plants and birds in this forest are trying to harm him, or separated lovers in general. In this context, Kāma himself appears as a

7. This verse can nevertheless have a double meaning if instead of reading *ārarādha* (honoured) we read *ā* (alas) and *rarādha* (hurt, tortured).

most evil personage, and many things are taken by Nala to be his arrows or other instruments with which he tortures unfortunate lovers. Many of these images, either erotic or morbid are contrived with the help of puns or *śleṣas*.

We shall now examine with the help of examples in what way this distortion of reality is achieved. In each case, we shall also underline the images which are very typical of certain seasons, and note, whenever it exists, the resemblance with some verses belonging to previous season descriptions. We shall first deal with the erotic aspect. Thus, in verse 85, Nala sees a creeper which he obviously mistakes for a woman :

navā latā gandhavahena cumbitā karambitāṅgī makarandaśī-
karaiḥ /
dṛśā nṛpeṇa smitaśobhikuḍmalā darādarābhyāṁ darakampinī
pape //85//

With both fear and interest, the king drank with his eyes a young and gently quivering creeper which was kissed by the breeze, whose branches (lit. limbs) were covered with sprays of honey, and whose buds were shining with flowers (or : smiles).

We have here the well-known creeper-woman image, which is extremely typical of spring, as we have seen above.[8] Spring is also without doubt the season which is alluded to here, since the creeper bears flowers and honey. Śrīharṣa has contrived a relatively original image in this verse, since the lover of the creeper is the wind, which is unusual.[9]

Verse 94 has an even more pronounced erotic flavour :

marullalatpallavakaṇṭakaiḥ kṣataṁ samucchalaccandanasāra-
saurabham /
sa vāranārīkucasaṁcitopamaṁ dadarśa mālūraphalaṁ paceli-
mam //94//

8. See for instance Kum. III, 39, Ragh. IX, 29, 35, 42, etc...

9. The usual lovers of creepers are trees and sometimes bees (see section on spring). The creeper-woman appears also in 97, again with the wind-lover, and in 106 where it is likened to a dancer, the wind being its teacher.

He saw a ripening *mālūra*-fruit, similar to the firm breast of a courtesan, which was wounded by the thorns of young sprouts which were playing in the wind (or : which was wounded by the nails of libertines who were as playful as the wind), and which exuded a perfume similar to sandal-wood juice (or: of sandal-wood juice).

Here, the erotic element is brought about with the help of *śleṣas*: *pallava* means at the same time "young sprout" and "libertine"[10], and *kaṇṭaka* designates any sharp object, therefore thorns in the case of the sprouts and nails in the case of the libertines. Thus this fruit is likened to a breast[11] which is being wounded by the lover's nails during amorous sports. Moreover, sandal-wood juice is usually applied to the breasts, precisely.[12]

But Nala's imagination is more often morbid than erotic. He attributes bad intentions to most of the plants and creatures he encounters in this forest, suspecting them mostly of harming, torturing and even killing separated lovers, to whose category he of course belongs. This is for instance the case for the mango-tree in verse 89:

rasālasālaḥ samadṛśyatāmunā sphuraddvirephāravaraṣahuṁ-kṛtiḥ /
samīralolair mukulair viyogine janāya ditsann iva tarjanābhi-yam //89//

He saw a mango-tree which emitted roars of anger with the buzzing of quivering bees, and which seemed to be desirous of giving the fear of a threat to separated lovers, with its buds swinging in the wind.

This verse contains images which can already be found in two verses from the Śiś. (VI, 60 and 62), concerning winter and

10. This verse evokes another verse by Māgha (VI, 39) quoted above in the section dedicated to the rainy season, in which appears the same *śleṣa* on *pallava*.

11. The same comparison between breasts and fruits can also be found in verses 1, 82 and 83.

12. Sandal-wood paste, due to its cooling effect, is usually applied in summer (see e.g. Ragh. XIX, 45). We could therefore see in this verse an allusion to the summer-season.

śiśira respectively, and which describe the actions of the wind. Verse 60 says:

> *dhṛtatuṣārakaṇasya nabhasvatas tarulatāṅgulitarjanavibhramāḥ /*
> *pṛthu nirantaram iṣṭabhujāntaraṁ vanitayānitayā na viṣehire*
> //60//

> The beloved could not bear the threatening movements of the fingers in the form of the trees' creepers, of the wind which carried snow-flakes, without tightly embracing the broad chest of her lover.

As for verse 62, it speaks of the "wind of the cool season which uttered angry roars with the buzzing of the bees which was increased due to their intoxication, and threatened the young women who were rejecting their lovers": *alinīravair madavikāsibhir āhitahuṁkṛtiḥ...nirabhartsayata priyān viyuvatīr yuvatīḥ śiśirānilaḥ.*

In the Naiṣ. verse, the subject of the action is of course the mango-tree and not the wind, and the season described therein is most likely spring, since this tree is budding. But otherwise, this verse contains the same images as the two Śiś. verses: like in Śiś. VI, 60, the tree threatens the lovers with the help of a vegetal element, here its buds, and like in Śiś. VI, 62 with the help of the buzzing of the bees. But in the Śiś. verses, these threats have for object to make the women reconcile with their lovers, whereas in the Naiṣ. verse, the mango-tree seems to act in this way out of pure malice, with the sole aim of aggravating the sufferings of separated lovers.

The cuckoo, this well-known symbol of spring, a bird which is elsewhere described as rather harmless, and favourable to lovers, also appears in this passage in a most evil guise.[13] Verse 88 already warns us with this detail: "whereas the forest heard from the cuckoo the fate of separated lovers": *pikād vane śṛṇvati...daśām...viyoginām.* Then in verse 90, we actually hear in the cuckoo's own words, what fate is reserved to these unfortunate ones:

13. Except in two verses at the end of the passage, I, 102 and 104, which, as we have seen, describe the facts more "objectively".

dine dine tvaṁ tanur edhi re 'dhikaṁ punaḥ punar mūrccha ca tāpam ṛccha ca /
itīva pānthāñ śapataḥ pikān dvijān sakhedam aikṣiṣṭa sa lohitekṣaṇān //90//

With sorrow, he looked at the red-eyed, twice-born[14] cuckoos, which seemed to be cursing the travellers thus: "Hey, you! Grow excessively thin day by day, swoon again and again and feel pain!"

We remember the verse from the Ragh. spring description (IX, 47) in which the cuckoos are also speaking. But what they are saying there is very different: *tyajata mānam alaṁ bata vigrahair na punar eti gataṁ caturaṁ vayaḥ.* (Abandon your sulkiness, enough of separations, once gone, youth, that charming age, never returns!) Whereas Kālidāsa's cuckoos encourage the women to yield to love and enjoy their youth, Śrīharṣa's cuckoos visibly enjoy and relish people's misfortunes. It is quite obvious that here Śrīharṣa makes a humorous allusion to Kālidāsa's verse.

The angry cuckoo reappears once again in verse 100, and this time his rage is directed at Nala himself:

ayogabhājo 'pi nṛpasya paśyatā tad eva sākṣād amṛtāṁśuṁ ānanam /
pikena rosāruṇacakṣuṣā muhuh kuhūrutāhūyata candravairiṇī //100//

The cuckoo, his eyes red with anger, seeing the face of the king which was obviously the moon itself, in spite of his separation (from Damayantī)[15], repeatedly called with cries of "*kuhū*" the night which is the enemy of the moon.

Here again, we find a *śleṣa*, this time on the term *kuhū*, which is of course an onomatopy of the cuckoo's song, but is also the name of the Vedic goddess of the moonless nights.

14. The term *dvi-ja* (twice-born) designates both birds and brahmins. It is used here because the cuckoos are obviously likened to irascible ascetics (hence the red eyes) who curse people at the slightest provocation.

15. i.e.: his face was still as beautiful as the moon, although he was in a state of extreme love-longing.

Here, in a poetic fancy, the poet imagine sthat the cuckoo, mistaking Nala's face for the moon, a sight which it seems to dislike, invokes, by crying "*kuhū*" the *amāvāsyā* night, the night without moon.

Thus we see that in these verses the cuckoo is depicted as an extremely disagreeable and even malicious character. We are very far here from the charming "female cuckoo whose voice is absolutely lovely", which chides women "like a dear friend" and manages to "extinguish their heavy anger", as it appears in Śiś. VI, 8, where its sole preoccupation seems to be people's happiness.

In his altered state of mind induced by his acute love-longing, Nala mistakes various objects, especially plants, for weapons of the god of Love, with which the latter is supposed to torture and kill unfortunate lovers suffering from separation. Thus, in verse 95 which we quoted above, he takes a bunch of *pāṭala*-flowers for Kāma's quiver. In 86, the rows of *campaka*-buds are likened to sacrificial lamps in honour of Kāma, in which the wayfarers are burnt like moths. In 92, a *nāgakesara*-flower, from which pollen is falling and around which bees are swarming, is likened to a grindstone from which sparks are flying because Love is whetting his arrows on it.

A great number of objects are compared to Kāma's arrows, especially flowers like in 87, where their name is not specified. In verse 83, with the help of a pun, the beaks of parrots (*śuka*) are likened to Kāma's *kiṁśuka*-flower arrows. In 93, a row of bees is compared to the god's arrows.[16] In 101, the *aśoka*-tree, in spite of its name which means "sorrowless", kills love-lorn travellers with its sprouts which are nothing but Kāma's arrows. Finally, in 84, it is the *palāsa*-flower which is compared to Love's arrow:

smarārdhacandreṣunibhe kraśīyasāṁ sphuṭaṁ palāśe 'dhva-
juṣāṁ palāśanāt /
sa vṛntam ālokata khaṇḍam anvitaṁ viyogihṛtkhaṇḍini kāla-
khaṇḍajam //84//

16. The god of Love seems to be really present in this verse, and not only in Nala's imagination, for he himself mistakes a row of bees for his own arrow. This comparison between a row of bees and Kāma's arrows appears already in Śiś. VI, 7, describing spring.

On a *palāśa*-flower loohing like the half-moon shaped arrow of Kāma and breaking the hearts of separated lovers, he saw the stalk (similar to) a piece of liver fixed to it, obviously due to the fact that it eats away the flesh of emaciated (lovers) who are travelling.

Here again, the image is of course based upon a *śleṣa*, the name of the flower, *palāśa*, which means "carnivorous", "eating flesh". Thus this flower is supposed to eat the flesh of the travellers who are of course pining away and becoming thin due to their unhappiness.

With this comparison between a vegetal element, here the stalk of the flower, and an anatomical part of the human body, the liver, this verse strongly reminds us of another verse from the Śiś. spring description:

sphuṭam ivojjvalakāñcanakāntibhir yutam aśokam aśobhata campakaiḥ /
virahiṇāṁ hṛdayasya bhidābhṛtaḥ kapiśitaṁ piśitaṁ madanāgninā //VI, 5//

Combined with the *campaka*-flowers which had the splendour of blazing gold, the open *aśoka*-flower looked like the flesh, turned brownish due to the fire of love, of the broken heart of separated lovers.

We see that with these two comparisons between the stalk and a liver, and between the *aśoka*-flower and the burnt and brownish flesh of the heart, these two verses are situated in the same morbid register.

By one more detail, this verse reminds us of another verse belonging to a spring description: the *palāśa*-flower is likened to the half-moon, here the half-moon shaped arrow of Kāma. In the spring description of the Kum. (III, 29), the same flowers are likened to the young moon. Moreover, they are also compared to nail-marks, which is already a somewhat cruel and morbid image.[17] As we can see, Śrīharṣa has reused in this

17. It is nevertheless clear that these nail-marks are made during love-sports.

verse images which can already be found in two preceding spring descriptions.

As for the *ketaka*-tree, it is certainly the one which is guilty of the greatest crimes against lovers. The *ketaka* is described in verse 78[18], and from verse 79 to 81, Nala addresses this tree, bitterly reproaching it of being the nefarious instrument of the god of Love:

viyogabhājāṁ hṛdi kaṇṭakaiḥ kaṭur nidhīyase karṇiśaraḥ smareṇa yat /
tato durākarṣatayā tadantakṛd vigīyase manmathadehadāhinā //79//

tvadagrasūcīsacivena kāminor manobhavaḥ sīvyati duryaśaḥ-paṭau /
sphuṭaṁ sa patraiḥ karapatramūrtibhir viyogihṛddāruṇi dāru-ṇāyate //80//

dhanurmadhusvinnakaro 'pi bhīmajāparaṁ parāgais tava dhūli-hastayan /
prasūnadhanvā śarasāt karoti mām iti krudhākruśyata tena ketakam //81//

"The one who burnt the body of Manmatha (i.e : Śiva) blames you because, sharp as you are due to your thorns, Love plants you like a barbed arrow into the hearts of separated lovers, and since it is difficult to remove you from there, you are the cause of their death."

"With the needle of your thorn for companion, Love stitches the two sheets which are the bad fortune of lovers. And it is obvious that with your saw-shaped leaves, Love acts cruelly towards this wood which is the heart of separated lovers."

"Though having hands which are wet due to the honey of his bow, the flowery-bowed one (i.e.: Kāma), powdering his hands with your pollen, hits me, who am attached to the

18. This verse contains an indirect comparison between the white *ketaka*-flowers with their bees, and the moon with its mark of the deer (here Śiva's moon). The same image is already found in Śiś. VI, 34, which we quoted above.

daughter of Bhīma, with his arrows", thus he angrily reprimanded the *ketaka.*

Thus we see that the *ketaka*-tree becomes the accomplice of the god of Love in manifold ways, lending him not only its thorns, which can most obviously be used as weapons, but even its saw-shaped leaves and its pollen, to help him torment separated lovers. Nevertheless, it is clear that the real culprit here, and in all these verses, is the god of Love himself, whom Nala perceives in such a negative light for the obvious reason that he is himself suffering due to unrequited love. Apart from Nala, the favourite victims of Kāma seem to be the general and unspecified crowd of lonely travellers or separated lovers, who are mentioned in a great number of verses. From this point of view, this passage reminds us of the Śiś. cycle of seasons, which also dedicates many verses to the type of the suffering separated lovers or travellers.

As we can see in the above-quoted verses, this passage does not only contain isolated elements, but also developed images which are typical of certain seasons, like the creeper-woman, speaking cuckoo, etc... Moreover, certain verses are visibly inspired from verses which belong to previous season descriptions.[19] It is interesting to note that Śrīharṣa was mainly influenced by Kālidāsa and Māgha.

But there is one point on which Śrīharṣa distinguishes himself in a marked way from his predecessors, namely by developing morbid, at times even disgusting images. This trait is of course already visible in the Śiś. cycle, like in verse VI, 5 which we quoted above, but no great stress is given to it. Śrīharṣa was the only one to develop to such an extent this morbid aspect in the context of a season description.

As we have seen in the above-quoted verses, there are innumerable images of torture, which echo of course Nala's own tormented state of mind: the *ketaka's* thorns become barbed arrows which pierce the hearts of lovers and its leaves become saws with which Kāma tortures their hearts (79-80). In 83, the

19. This is obviously the case for verse I, 78, 84, 85, 89, and 90, all quoted above.

parrots' beaks are likened to Love's arrows which "penetrate the red and broken heart" of a pomegranate-tree-damsel, quite a graphic image. In 84, which we quoted above, the *palāśa*-flower eats the flesh of lovers, and its stalk is likened to a piece of liver, a frankly repulsive image. And there are of course many more instances of lovers being killed mercilessly by certain objects, mostly plants, which are compared to Kāma's arrows. But the repulsive element can also appear in other contexts than Kāma's crimes, like for instance in verse 96: "He thought that a dark-hued *agastya*-tree, in this wood, which was putting forth blossoms, was Rāhu *vomiting* a bunch of digits of the moon..." (*munidrumaḥ korakitaḥ śitidyutir vane 'munā 'manyata siṁhikāsutaḥ...kalākalāpaṁ kila vaidhavaṁ* vaman).

Thus, by developing this kind of images which verge on the morbid and disgusting, Śrīharṣa has shown a temerity which does not lack genius, and he gives in a highly imaginative way a perverse coloration to his season description. By stressing the "horrible" aspect of the seasons, the author of the Naiṣ. has decidedly innovated as compared to the preceding poets who mostly describe the seasons in a "classical" way, namely by underlining their beauty. The consequence of this is that in this passage, the *vipralambhaśṛṅgāra-rasa* seems at times to tend towards the *bībhatsa-rasa*: the disgusting sentiment.

In spite of all the arguments we have given in favour of the theory that this passage is indeed a season description, one could object that the main aim of these verses is not the description of the various seasons as such, but rather the effect that the natural surroundings of this forest, in which certain seasonal elements of course appear, have on the love-lorn king. But the fact that Nala's reactions face to what he sees are given such importance is rather an argument in favour of the season description, than against it. For, as we have noted while studying other season descriptions, nearly all of them, with may be the sole exception of the R. winter description, do not describe the seasons in a "detached" or "impersonal" way, but on the other hand give a great importance to the attitude of either the hero himself or else of some other vaguely defined characters, face to the season which is described.

In this respect, the way in which Nala's behaviour is described in this passage is a direct echo of the way in which the *ādikāvya* itself, the R., depicts Rāma's emotional response to the seasons. Both heroes are of course in the same unfortunate situation, being separated from their beloved ones. But whereas Rāma, in spite of his sorrow, always underlines the beautiful aspects of the seasons, Nala's imagination on the opposite takes an excessively morbid turn. The way to this kind of attitude face to the seasons has of course already been paved to a certain extent by Bhaṭṭi's description of Rāma's behaviour during the rainy season, where, as we have seen, the hero sees everything very negatively due to his affliction. Nala's attitude is thus only one step further in the same direction.

Thus, on the basis of all that has been said above, and in spite of Śrīharṣa's many innovations, both from the point of view of the form, by representing the seasons in utter disorder, and from the point of view of the content, by developing morbid images, we can conclude without hesitating that this is indeed a season description, and that the words *sarvartughane vane* in verse I, 105 are not just an empty phrase.

CONCLUSION

To conclude, we shall briefly sum up the main points which have emerged out of our study of the seasons.

As we have seen in the first part, the number of the seasons was fixed to six in late Vedic times. Though there are are passages in the Veda, especially in the Ṛg-Veda, which look like season descriptions, the religious context is always predominant, and thus this theme cannot be said to have originated in Vedic literature. Rather, it might have come from folk-songs, and its first appearance in literature is in short lyrical poems, from which it was later 'borrowed' by *Mahākāvyas*. Three poeticians reveal and stress important aspects of these season descriptions : Bharata, who prescribes the use of the seasons in order to produce certain *rasas* (especially the sentiment of love); Daṇḍin, who stresses their importance in the context of *Mahākāvyas*, and Rājaśekhara, whose main contribution, except from writing a complete 'prescriptive' cycle of seasons, is on the *kavi-samaya* aspect of these season descriptions, that is, on their conventional nature.

We have seen in the second part that the season descriptions of the R. and of the six *Mahākāvyas* are written in various different meters, and that they are indeed often used to evoke certain *rasas*, the most common being the sentiments of love-in-union and in-separation. The form of the discourse, that is, the description being spoken by one character of the story, which is the rule in the R., was mostly abandoned by *Mahākāvya* writers for the narrative style. But in most cases, the attitude of the hero and his feelings face to the seasons remain all-important, as indeed they allow the harmonious insertion of such passages into the broader context. From Kālidāsa onwards, the seasons which are clearly personified are spring, either as male or female, and autumn, which always appears in a female guise.

In the third part, we have tried to see what are the main themes evoked by the descriptions of the various seasons : spring is the most erotic of all seasons, and it is systematically described as provoking love in all creatures. For this reason, it is mostly represented as a woman. Summer, on the other hand, is always said to destroy love, and thus, what is stressed in summer descriptions are the various means people resort to in order to alay the burning heat and resurrect love-desire. The monsoon descriptions mainly evoke the various interactions between the sky and the earth and the influence that the heavenly phenomena exert on earthly creatures. Autum either appears as the season for military expeditions, or on the other hand it is depicted in a bucolic rural setting which represents in a highly idyllic and idealized way the life of the villagers. No definite theme can be said to underlie in the descriptions of winter, excepting the cold, which is always stressed. As for *śiśira*, as we have seen, it does not seem to be a 'real' season, but it is either described like winter, or else, as the intermediary time between winter and spring.

Finally, we have seen that the Naiṣ. passage, although the seasons are not mentioned or at least systematically announced in it, should nevertheless be considered as a season description: it contains many characteristics and images which are typical of the various seasons, some of its verses are visibly inspired from previous season descriptions, and it general traits, such as *rasa*, narration, etc...., fit in very well with the overall trend of such descriptions.

BIBLIOGRAPHY

Primary Sources and Translations:

Acarya, Narayana Rama, *Naiṣadhīyacaritam*, Bombay 1952 (9th ed.).

Bhatt, G.H., *The Vālmīki-Rāmāyaṇa*, Baroda 1960-1975.

Bhattacharya, B., *Kāvyamīmāṁsā of Rājaśekhara*, Baroda 1934.

Cappeller, Carl, *Bhāravi's Poem Kirātārjunīya*, HOS vol. 15, Cambridge (Mass.) 1912, (transl.).

Devadhar, C.R., *Works of Kālidāsa*, vol. 2 Poetry, Delhi 1984, (transl.).

Durgaprasad (Pandit) and Kasinath Pandurang Parab, *The Kirātārjunīya of Bhāravi*, Bombay 1895.

Durgaprasad (Pandit) and Sivadatta (Pandit), *The Śiśupālavadha of Māgha*, Bombay 1933.

Handiqui, K.K., *Śrīharṣa's Naiṣadhacaritam*, Poona 1965 (3rd ed.), (transl.).

Hulzsch, Eugen, *Māgha's Śiśupālavadha*, Leipzig 1929, (transl.).

Johnston, E.H., *The Buddhacarita or Acts of the Buddha*, (text and transl.), Delhi 1972 (2nd ed.).

Johnston, E.H., *The Saundarananda of Aśvaghoṣa*, (text and transl.), Delhi 1975 (2nd ed.).

Karandikar, M.A. and Karandikar, S., *Bhaṭṭikāvyam*, (text and transl.), Delhi 1982.

Macdonell, A.A., *A Vedic Reader for Students*, Oxford 1917.

Nagar, R.S., *Nāṭyaśāstra of Bharatamuni*, Delhi 1988 (2nd ed.).

Norman, K.R., *The Elder's Verses I, Theragāthā*, (transl.), London 1961.

Oldenberg, H. and Pischel, R., *The Thera- and Therī-gāthā*, London 1966 (2nd ed.).

Roodbergen, J.A.F., *Mallinātha's Ghaṇṭāpatha on the Kirātārjunīya*, I-VI, Leiden 1984.

Scharpé, A., *Kālidāsa-Lexicon*, vol. I, Part III, 'Kumārasaṁbhava, Meghadūta, Ṛtusaṁhāra et incerta', Bruges 1958.

Scharpé, A., *Kālidāsa-Lexicon*, vol. I, part IV, 'Raghuvaṁśa', Bruges 1964.

Shastri, V.P.R.R., *Kāvyādarśa of Daṇḍin*, Poona 1970.

Stchoupak, Nadine and Renou, Louis : *La Kāvyamīmāṁsā de Rājaśekhara*, Paris 1946 (transl.).

Sukthankar Vishnu, S., *The Mahābhārata*, Poona 1933—1959.

Secondary Sources :

1. Works on Ṛtu:

Raghavan, V., *Ṛtu in Sanskrit Literature*, Delhi 1972.

Renou, Louis, 'Un theme littéraire en sanskrit: les saisons', in *Sanskrit et culture: l'apport de l'Inde à la civilisation humaine*, Paris 1950.

2. General works:

Brockington, John, *Righteous Rama: The Evolution of an Epic*, Delhi 1984.

Gonda, Jan, 'Vedic literature', in *A History of Indian Literature*, vol. 1, Wiesbaden 1975.

Gerow, *A Glossary of Indian Figures of Speech*, The Hague-Paris 1971.

Jacobi, Hermann, 'Die Epen Kālidāsa's', in *Kleine Schriften I*, p. 409 ff, Wiesbaden 1970.

Jacobi, Hermann, 'On Bhāravi and Māgha', in *Kleine Schriften I*, p. 447 ff, Wiesbaden 1970.

Lienhard, Siegfried, 'A history of classical poetry, Sanskrit, Pāli, Prākrit', in *A History of Indian Literature*, vol. 3, Wiesbaden 1984.

Renou, Louis, 'Sur la structure du kāvya', in *Journal Asiatique* 247, p. 1 ff, Paris 1959.

Sehnen, Renate, *Untersuchungen zur Komposition von Reden und Gespraechen im Rāmāyaṇa*, Reinbeck 1979.

Warder, A.K., *Indian Kāvya Literature*, Delhi 1972.

Zimmer, Heinrich, *Altindisches Leben*, Berlin 1879 (reed. Hildesheim-New York 1973).

Dictionaries referred to :

Apte, Vaman Shivram, *The Practical Sanskrit-English Dictionary*, Appendix I, 'Sanskrit Prosody', Delhi 1985.

Mayrhofer, Manfred, *Kurzgefasstes etymologisches Woerterbuch des Altindischen*, Heidelberg 1956.

Sir Monier-Williams, Monier, *A Sanskrit-English Dictionary*, Oxford 1979 (9th ed.)

Pokorny, Julius, *Indogermanisches etymologisches Woerterbuch*, Bern 1959.

INDEX OF QUOTED VERSES*

*Concerns only fully quoted verses.

अष्टादशोऽध्यायः कालविभागः ।

कालः काष्ठादिभेदभिन्नः । तथा च[1]—

काष्टा निमेषा दश पञ्च चैव त्रिंशच्च काष्ठाः कथिताः कलेति[2] ।
त्रिंशत्कलश्चैव भवेन्मुहूर्त्तस्तैस्त्रिंशता रात्र्यहनी समेते ॥

ते च चैत्राश्वयुजमासयोर्भवतः । चैत्रात्परं प्रतिमासं मौहूर्तिको दिवसवृद्धिः निशाहानिश्च त्रिमास्याः; ततः परं मौहूर्त्तिकी निशावृद्धिः दिवसहानिश्च । आश्वयुजात्परतः पुनरेतदेव विपरीतम् । राशितो राश्यन्तरसङ्क्रमणमुष्णभासो मासः, वर्षादि दक्षिणायनं शिशिराद्युत्तरायणं द्व्ययनः संवत्सर इति सौरं मानम् । पञ्चदशाहोरात्रः पक्षः । वर्द्धमानसोमः[3] शुक्लो, वर्द्धमानकृष्णिमा कृष्ण इति पित्र्यं मासमानम् । अमुना च वेदोदितः कृत्स्नोऽपि क्रियाकल्पः । पित्र्यमेव व्यत्ययितपक्षं चान्द्रमसम् । इदमार्यावर्त्तवासिनः कवयश्च मानमाश्रिताः । एवं च द्वौ पक्षौ मासः । द्वौ मासावृतुः । षण्णामृतूनां परिवर्त्तः संवत्सरः । स च चैत्रादिरिति

१ V adds this line. २ V कला तु. ३ V सोमशुक्लिमा, वर्धमानसोमकृष्णिमा.

दैवज्ञाः, श्रवणादिरिति लोकयात्राविदः । तत्र नभा नभस्यश्च वर्षाः, इष ऊर्जश्च शरत्, सहः[1] सहस्यश्च हेमन्तः, तपस्तपस्यश्च शिशिरः, मधुर्माधवश्च वसन्तः, शुक्रः शुचिश्च ग्रीष्मः । तत्र "वर्षासु पूर्वो वायुः" इति कवयः । "पाश्चात्यः, पौरस्त्यस्तु प्रतिहन्ता" इत्याचार्याः ।

तदाहुः—"पुरोवाता हता प्रावृट् पश्चाद्वाता हता शरत्" इति ।

तदाहुः—"प्रावृष्यम्भोभृताम्भोदभरनिर्भरमम्बरम् ।
[2]कादम्बकुसुमामोदा वायवो वान्ति वारुणाः ॥"

"वस्तुवृत्तिरतन्त्रं, कविसमयः प्रमाणम्" इति यायावरीयः ।

तदाहुः—"पौरस्त्यस्तोयदर्त्तोः पवन इव पतन्पावकस्येव धूमो
विश्वस्येवादि[3]सर्गः प्रणव इव परं पावनं वेदराशेः ।
सन्ध्यानृत्तोत्सवेच्छोरिव मदनरिपोर्नन्दिनान्दीनिनादः
सौरस्याग्रे सुखं वो वितरतु विनतानन्दनः स्यन्दनस्य ॥"

शरद्यनियतदिक्को वायुर्यथा—

"उषःसु ववुराकृष्टजडावश्यायशीकराः ।
शेफालीकलिकाकोशकषायामोदिनोऽनिलाः ॥"

"हेमन्ते पाश्चात्यो वायुः" इत्येके । "उदीच्य" इत्यपरे । "उभयमपि" इति यायावरीयः । तयोः पाश्चात्यः—

"भञ्जन्भूर्जद्रुमालीस्तुहिनगिरितटेषूद्गतास्त्वक्करालाः
रेवाम्भःस्थूलवीचीचयचकितचलच्चातकान् व्याधुनानः ।
पाश्चात्यो वाति वेगाद्धुततुहिनशिलाशीकरासारवर्षी
मातङ्गक्षुण्णसान्द्रस्नुतसरल[4]तरत्सारसारी समीरः ॥"

उदीच्यः—

"लम्पाकीनां किरन्तश्चिकुरविरचनां रल्लकांल्लासयन्तः
चुम्बन्तश्चन्द्रभागासलिलमविकलं[5] भूर्जकाण्डैकचण्डाः ।
एते कस्तूरिकैणप्रणयसुरभयो वल्लभा बाल्हवीनां
कौल्लूतीकेलिकाराः परिचयितहिमं वायवो वान्त्युदीच्याः ॥"

---

१ V सहाः. २ V कदम्ब. ३ V B & V C विश्वस्येवादिमार्गः. ४ V A & V B सरत्सारसारी. ५ V B & V C चन्द्रभागां विचितसुमनसः कुङ्कुमान् कम्पयन्तः.

शिशिरेऽपि हेमन्तवदुदीच्यः पाश्चात्यो वा । वसन्ते दक्षिणः । तदुक्तम्—

"[1]धुन्वंल्लङ्कावनालीर्मुहुरलकलता लासयन्केरलीना-
मन्ध्रीधम्मिल्लबन्धान्सपदि शिथिलयन्वेल्लयन्नागवल्लीः ।
उद्दामं दाक्षिणात्यो म(मि)लितमलयजः सारथिर्मीनकेतोः
प्राप्तः सीमन्तिनीनां मधुसमयसुहृन्मानचौरः समीरः ॥"

"अनियतदिक्को वायुर्ग्रीष्मे" इत्येके । नैर्ऋतः" इत्यपरे । "उभयमपि" इति यायावरीयः । तत्र प्रथमः—

"वात्याचक्रकचुम्बिताम्बरभुवः स्थूला रजोदण्डकाः
संग्रथ्नन्ति भविष्यदभ्रपटलस्थूणावितर्कं नभः ।
किं चान्यन्मृगतृष्णिकाम्बुविसरैः पात्राणि वीतार्णसां
सिन्धूनामिह [2]सूत्रयन्ति दिवसेष्वागामिनीं सम्पदम् ॥"

द्वितीयः—"सोऽयं करैस्तपति वह्निमयैरिवार्कः
साङ्गारविस्तरभरेव धरा समग्रा ।
वायुः कुकूलमिव वर्षति नैर्ऋतश्च
कार्शानवैरिव शरैर्मदनश्च हन्ति ॥"

किञ्च—

"[3]गर्भान्बलाकासु निवेशयन्तो वंशाङ्कुरान्स्वैर्निनदैः सृजन्तः ।
रजोऽम्बुदाः प्रावृषि मुद्रयन्तो यात्रोद्यमं भूमिभृतां हरन्ति ॥
स सल्लकीसालशिलीन्ध्रयूथीप्रसूनदः पुष्पितलाङ्गलीकः ।
दग्धोर्वरासुन्दरगन्धबन्धुरर्घत्ययं वारिमुचामनेहा ॥
वनानि नीलीदलमेचकानि धाराम्बुधौता गिरयः स्फुरन्ति ।
पूराम्भसा भिन्नतटास्तटिन्यः सान्द्रेन्द्रगोपानि च शाद्वलानि ॥
चकोरहर्षी रतिचारचौरो वियोगिनीवीक्षितनाथवर्त्मा ।
गृहान्प्रति प्रस्थितपान्थसार्थः कालोऽयमाध्मातनभाः पयोदैः ॥
या केलियात्रा [4]केरिकामिनीभिर्या तुङ्गहर्म्याग्रविलासशय्या ।
चतुःसमं यन्मृगनाभिगर्भं सा वारिदर्त्तोः प्रथमातिथेयी ॥

---

१ V चुम्बँल्लङ्का॰ २ V सूत्र. ३ V गर्भ. ४ V B & V C किल श्रामिनीभिः.

चलच्चटुलचातकः कृतकुरङ्गरागोदयः
सदर्दुररवोद्यमो मदभरप्रगल्भोरगः ।
शिखण्डिकुलताण्डवामुदितमद्गुकङ्काह्वयो
योगिषु घनागमः स्मरविषं विषं मुञ्चति ॥
दलत्कुटजकुड्मलः स्फुटितनीपपुष्पोत्करो
धवप्रसवबान्धवः प्रचितमञ्जरीकार्जुनः ।
कदम्बकलुषाम्बरः कलितकेतकीकोरक-
श्चलन्निचुलसञ्चयो हरति हन्त घर्मात्ययः ॥"

वर्षाः ॥

"[1]द्रागंग(क्त)र्जयन्ती विमदान्मयूरान्प्रगल्भयन्ती कुररद्विरेफान् ।
शरत्समभ्येति विकास्य पद्मानुन्मीलयन्ती कुमुदोत्पलानि ॥
सा भाति पुष्पाणि [2]निवेशयन्ती बन्धूकबाणासनकुङ्कुमेषु ।
शेफालिकासप्तपलाशकाशभाण्डीरसौगन्धिकमालतीषु ॥
सखञ्जरीटा सपयःप्रसादा सा कस्य नो मानसमाच्छिनत्ति ।
कादम्बकारण्डवचक्रवाकससारसक्रौञ्चकुलानुयाता ॥
उपानयन्ती कलहंसयूथमगस्त्यदृष्ट्या पुनती पयांसि ।
मुक्तासु शुभ्रं दधती च गर्भं शरद्विचित्रैश्चरितैश्चकास्ति ॥
क्षितिं खनन्तो वृषभाः खुराग्रै रोधो विषाणैर्द्विरदा रदन्तः ।
शृङ्गं त्यजन्तो रुरवश्च जीर्णं कुर्वन्ति लोकानवलोकनोत्कान् ॥
अत्रावदातद्युति चन्द्रिकाम्बु नीलावभासं च नभः समन्तात् ।
[3]सुरेभवीथी दिवसावतारो [4]जीर्णाभ्रखण्डानि च पाण्डुराणि ॥
महानवम्यां निखिलास्त्रपूजा नीराजना वाजिभटद्विपानाम् ।
दीपालिकायां विविधा विलासा यात्रोन्मुखैरत्र नृपैर्विधेयाः ॥
व्योम्नि तारतरतारकोत्करः स्यन्दनप्रचरणक्षमा मही ।
भास्करः शरदि दीप्रदीधितिर्बुध्यते च सह माधवः सुरैः ॥
केदार एव कलमाः परिणामनम्राः
प्राचीनमामलकमर्घति पाकनीलम् ।

---

1 V B प्रोम्मादयन्ती. V C प्रोन्मोदयन्ती. 2 V B & V C विशेषयन्ती. 3 V सुरे-
द्विवि सावतारा. 4 V B & V C जीर्णाब्जखण्डानि.

एर्वारुकं स्फुटननिर्गतगर्भगन्ध-
मम्लीभवन्ति च जरत्त्रपुसीफलानि ॥
गेहाजिरेषु नवशालिकणावपात-
गन्धानुभावसुभगेषु कृषीवलानाम् ।
आनन्दयन्ति मुसलोल्लसनावधूत-
पाणिस्खलच्छलयपद्धतयो वधूट्यः ॥
तीक्ष्णं रविस्तपति नीच इवाचिराढ्यः
शृङ्गं रुरुस्त्यजति मित्रमिवाकृतज्ञः ।
तोयं प्रसीदति मुनेरिव धर्मचिन्ता[1]
कामी दरिद्र इव शोषमुपैति पङ्कम्[2] ॥
नद्यो वहन्ति कुटिलक्रमयुक्तशुक्ति-
रेखाङ्कबालपुलिनोदरसुप्तकूर्माः ।
अस्यां तरङ्गिततनुतोयपलायमान-
मीनानुसारिबकदत्तै[3]करालफालाः ॥
अपङ्किलतटावटः शफरफाण्टफालोज्ज्वलः
पतत्कुररकातरभ्रमदभ्रमीनार्भकः ।
लुठत्कमठसैकतश्चलबकोटवाचाटितः
सरित्सलिलसंचयः शरदि मेदुरः सीदति ॥"

शरत् ॥

"द्वित्रिमुचुकुन्दकलिकस्त्रिचतुरमुकुलः क्रमेण लवलीपु ।
पञ्चषफलिनीकुसुमो जयति हिमर्त्तुर्नवावतरः ॥
पुन्नागरोध्रप्रसवावतंसा वामभ्रुवः कञ्चुककुञ्चिताङ्ग्यः ।
वक्त्रोल्लसत्कुङ्कुमसिक्थ[4]काङ्काः सुगन्धतैलाः कबरीर्वहन्ति ॥
यथा यथा पुष्यति शीतकालस्तुषारचूर्णोत्करकीर्णवातः ।
तथा तथा यौवनशालिनीनां कवोष्णतामत्र कुचा लभन्ते ॥
वराहवर्ध्राणि[5] नवौदनानि दधीनि सशर्कराणि[6] चात्र ।
सुकोमलाः सर्षपकन्दलीश्च भुक्त्वा जनो निन्दति वैश्रविश्राम्

१ V चित्तं. २ V मेघः. ३ V दन्त. ४ V सिक्थकाढ्याः. ५ B वर्ध्मा. A वघ्र
६ V ०रसानि.

अत्रोपचारः सलिलैः कवोष्णैर्यत्किञ्चिदत्र स्वदतेऽन्नपानम् ।
सुदुर्भगामत्र निपीड्य शेते स्वस्त्यस्तु नित्यं तुहिनर्त्तवेऽस्मै ॥
विमुक्तबर्हा विमदा मयूराः प्ररूढगोधूमयवा च सीमा ।
व्याघ्रीप्रसूतिः सलिलं सबाष्पं हेमन्तलिङ्गानि जयन्त्यमूनि ॥

सशमीधान्यपाकानि क्षेत्राण्यत्र [1]जयन्ति च ।
त्रिशङ्कुतिलका रात्र्यः पच्यन्ते लवणानि च ॥

उद्यानानां मूकपुंस्कोकिलत्वं भृङ्गस्त्रीणां मौनमुद्रा मुखेषु ।
मन्दोद्योगा पत्रिणां व्योमयात्रा हेमन्ते स्यात्सर्पदर्पक्षयश्च ॥
कर्कन्धूनां नागरङ्गीफलानां पाकोद्रेकः खाण्डे[2]वोप्याविरस्ति ।
कृष्णेक्षूणां पुण्ड्रकाणां च गर्भे माधुर्यश्रीर्जायते चाप्यपूर्वा ॥
येषां मध्येमन्दिरं तल्पसम्पत् पार्श्वे दाराः स्फारतारुण्यताराः ।
लीलावह्निर्निह्नुतोद्दामधूमस्ते हेमन्तं ग्रीष्मशेषं विदन्ति ॥"

इति हेमन्तः । हेमन्तधर्मः(र्मा) शिशिरः ।

विशेषस्तु—"रात्रिर्विचित्रसुरतोचितयामदै[3]र्घ्या
चण्डो मरुद्वहति कुङ्कुमपङ्कसाध्यः ।
तल्पस्थितिर्द्विगुणतूलपटा किमन्य-
दर्घन्ति चात्र विततागुरुधूपधूमाः ॥
आश्लेषिणः पृथुरतक्लमपीतशीत-
मायामिनीं घनमुदो रजनीं युवानः ।
ऊर्वोर्मुहुर्वलनबन्धनसंधिलोल-
पादान्तसंवलिततूलपटाः स्वपन्ति ॥
पानेऽम्भसोः सुरसनीरसयोर्न भाति
स्पर्शक्रियासु तुहिनानलयोर्न चात्र ।
नो दुर्भगासुभगयोः परिरम्भणे च
नो सेवने च शशिभास्करयोर्विशेषः ॥

१ न्ति च. २ B षाह. ३ V दीर्घा.

पुष्पक्रिया मरुबके जलकेलिनिन्दा
कुन्दान्यशेषकुसुमेषु धुरि स्थितानि ।
सौभाग्यमेणतिलकाद्व्रजतेऽर्कबिम्बं
काले तुषारिणि दहन्ति च चन्दनानि ॥
सिद्धार्थयष्टिषु यथोत्तरहीयमान-
सन्तानभिन्नघनसूचिपरम्परासु ।
द्वित्रावशेषकुसुमासु जनिक्रमेण
पाकक्रमः कपिशिमानमुपादधाति ॥
उदीच्यचण्डानिलताडितासु
[1]सुलीनमीनासु जलस्य मूले ।
नालावशेषाब्जलताखिदानीं
विलासवापीषु न याति दृष्टिः ॥
माद्यन्मतङ्गः पृषतैकतोषी
[2]पुष्यद्वराहो धृतिमल्लुलायः ।
दरिद्रनिन्द्यः [3]सधनैकवन्द्यः
स एष कालः शिशिरः करालः ॥
अभिनववधूरोषस्वादुः करीषतनूनपा-
दसरलजनाश्लेषक्रूरस्तुषारसमीरणः ।
गलितविभवस्याज्ञेवाद्य द्युतिर्मसृणा रवे-
र्विरहिवनितावक्त्रौपम्यं बिभर्त्ति निशाकरः ॥
स्त्रियः प्रकृतिपित्तलाः क्वथितकुङ्कुमालेपनै-
र्नितम्बफलकस्तनस्थलभुजोरुमूलादिभिः ।
इहाभिनवयौवनाः सकलरात्रिसंश्लेषितै-
र्हरन्ति शिशिरज्वरारतिमतीव पृथ्वीमपि ॥"

शिशिरः ॥

"चैत्रे मदर्द्धिः शुकसारिकाणां
हारीतदात्यूहमधुव्रतानाम् ।

---

१ V निलीनमीनासु. २ V B & V C पुष्यद्वराहा. ३ V C सधनैकनन्दकृष्णिमा.

पुंस्कोकिलानां सहकारबन्धुः
मदस्य कालः पुनरेष एव ॥
मनोऽधिकं चात्र विलासलास्ये
प्रेङ्खासु दोलासु च सुन्दरीणाम् ।
गीते च गौरीचरितावतंसे
पूजाप्रपञ्चे च मनोभवस्य ॥
पुंस्कोकिलः कूजति पञ्चमेन
बलाद्विलासा युवतौ स्फुरन्ति ।
स्मरो वसन्तेऽत्र नवैः प्रसूनैः
स्वचापयष्टेर्घटनां करोति ॥
पिनद्धमाहारजनांशुकानां
सीमन्तसिन्दूरजुषां वसन्ते ।
स्मरीकृते प्रेयसि भक्तिभाजां
विशेषवेषः स्वदते वधूनाम् ॥
अयं प्रसूनोद्धुरकर्णिकारः
पुष्पप्रपञ्चार्चितकाञ्चनारः ।
विजृम्भणाकोविदकोविदारः
कालो विकाशोद्यतसिन्दुवारः ॥
रोहीतकाम्रातककिङ्किराता
मधूकमोचाः सह माधवीभिः ।
जयन्ति शोभाञ्जनकश्च शाखी
सकेसरैः[2] पुष्पभरैर्वसन्ते ॥
यो माधवीमुकुलदृष्टिषु वेणिबन्धो
यः कोकिलाकलरुते[3] कथने च लाभः ।
पूजाविधिर्दमनकेन च यः स्मरस्य
तस्मिन्मधुः स भगवान्गुरुरङ्गनानाम् ॥

V रसवतां. २ V शेखर· ३ V रुतेः.

नालिङ्गितः कुरबकस्तिलको न दृष्टो
नो ताडितश्च चरणैः सुदृशामशोकः ।
सिक्तो न वक्त्रमधुना बकुलश्च चैत्रे
चित्रं तथापि भवति प्रसवावकीर्णः ॥

चैत्रे चित्रौ रक्तनीलावशोकौ
स्वर्णाशोकस्तत्तृतीयश्च पीतः ।
जैत्रं तत्त्रं तत्प्रसूनान्तरेभ्यः
चेतोयोनेः भूर्भुवःस्वस्त्रयेऽपि ॥

गूवाकानां नालिकेरद्रुमाणां
हिन्तालानां पाटलीकिंशुकानाम् ।
खर्जूराणां ताडताडी[1]तरूणां
पुष्पापीडन्यासहेतुर्वसन्तः ॥

वसन्तः ॥

विकाशकारी नव[2]मल्लिकानां
दलच्छिरीषप्रसवाभिरामः ।
पुष्पप्रदः काञ्चनकेतकीनां
ग्रीष्मोऽयमुल्लासितधातकीकः ॥

खर्जूरजम्बूपनसाम्रमोच-
प्रियालपूगीफलनालिकेरैः ।
द्वन्द्वानि खेदालसता[3]मु(म)पास्य
रतानुसन्धानमिहाद्रियन्ते ॥

स्रोतांस्यनम्भांसि सकूपकानि
प्रपाः कठोरेऽह्नि पान्थपूर्णाः ।
शुचौ [4]समभ्यर्थि(र्घि)तसक्तुपाने
प्रगे च सायं च वहन्ति मार्गाः ॥

यत्कायमानेषु दिनार्द्धनिद्रा
यत्स्नानकेलिर्दिवसावसाने ।

१ V द्रुमाणां. २ V मालिकानां. ३ V ०मपास्य. ४ समभ्यर्च्चितसक्तुधाने०.

यद्रात्रिशेषे सुरतावतारः
स मुष्टियोगो घनघर्ममाथी ॥
या चन्द्रिका चन्दनपङ्कहृद्या
या जालमार्गानिलवीचिमाला ।
या तालवृन्तैरुदबिन्दुवृष्टि-
र्जलाञ्जलिं सा शुचये ददाति ॥
कर्पूरचूर्णं[1] सहकारभङ्ग-
स्ताम्बूलमार्द्रक्रमुकोपक्लृप्तम् ।
हाराश्च तारास्तनुवस्त्रमेत-
न्महारहस्यं शिशिरक्रियायाः ॥
मुक्तालताश्चन्दनपङ्कदिग्धा
मृणालहारानुसृता जलार्द्राः ।
स्रजश्च मौलौ स्मि(सि)तचम्पकानां
ग्रीष्मेऽपि सोऽयं शिशिरावतारः ॥"

अत्र हि—"पच्यन्त इव भूतानि ताप्यन्त इव पांसवः ।
क्वथ्यन्त इव तोयानि ध्मायन्त इव चाद्रयः ॥
ऐणाः[2] स्थलीषु मृगतृष्णिकया ह्रियन्ते
स्रोतस्तनुत्वजनिता जलवेणिबन्धाः ।
ताम्यत्तिमीनि च सरांसि जलस्य शोषा-
त्तुद्धार[3]घट्टघटिकावलयाश्च कूपाः ॥
करभाः शरभाः सरासभा
मदमायान्ति भजन्ति विक्रियाम् ।
करवीरकरीरपुष्पिणीः
स्थलभूमीरधिरुह्य चासते ॥
सहकाररसार्चिता रसाला
जलभक्तं फलपानकानि मन्थाः ।

---

१ V चूर्णः. २ V एण्यः. ३ A ०द्वद्वारघट्ट०.

मृगलावरसाः शृतं च दुग्धं
स्मरसञ्जीवनमौषधं निदाघे ॥
जडचन्दनचारवस्तरुण्यः
सजलार्द्राः सहतारहारमालाः ।
कदलीदलतल्पकल्पनस्थाः
स्मरमाहूय निवेशयन्ति पार्श्वे ॥
ग्रीष्मे चीरीनादवन्तो वनान्ताः
पङ्काभ्यक्ताः सैरिभाः सेभकोलाः ।
लोलज्जिह्वाः [1]सर्पसारङ्गवर्गा
मूलस्रस्तैः पत्त्रिणश्चांसदेशैः ॥
हर्म्यं रम्यं चन्द्रिकाधौतपृष्ठं
कान्तोच्छिष्टा वारुणी वारिमिश्रा ।
मालाः कण्ठे पाटलामल्लिकानां
सद्यो ग्रीष्मं हन्त हेमन्तयन्ति ॥

ग्रीष्मः ॥

चतुरवस्थश्च ऋतुरुपनिबन्धनीयः। तद्यथा—सन्धिः, शैशवं, प्रौढिः, अनुवृत्तिश्च। ऋतुद्वयमध्यं सन्धिः। शिशिरवसन्तसन्धिर्यथा—

"च्युतसुमनसः कुन्दाः पुष्पोद्गमेष्वलसा द्रुमा
मनसि च गिरं गृह्णन्तीमे [2]गिरन्ति न कोकिलाः ।
अथ च सवितुः शीतोल्लासं लुनन्ति मरीचयो
न च जरठतामालम्बन्ते क्लमोदयदायिनीम् ॥"

वसन्तशैशवम्—

"गर्भग्रन्थिषु वीरुधां सुमनसो मध्येऽङ्कुरं पल्लवा
वाञ्छामात्रपरिग्रहः पिकवधूकण्ठोदरे पञ्चमः ।
किं च त्रीणि जगन्ति जिष्णु दिवसैर्द्वित्रैर्मनोजन्मनो
देवस्यापि चिरोज्झितं यदि भवेदभ्यासवश्यं धनुः ॥"

---

१ V सर्वसारङ्ग०. २ V किरन्ति.

वसन्तप्रौढिः—

"साम्यं सम्प्रति सेवते विचकिलं षाण्मासिकैर्मौक्तिकैः
कान्तिं कर्षति काञ्चनारकुसुमं माञ्जिष्ठधौतात्पटात् ।
हूणीनां कुरुते मधूकमुकुलं लावण्यलुण्टाकतां
लाटीनाभिनिभं चकास्ति च पतद्वृन्ताग्रतः केसरम् ॥"

अतिक्रान्तर्तुलिङ्गं यत्कुसुमाद्यनुवर्त्तते ।
लिङ्गानुवृत्तिं तामाहुः सा ज्ञेया काव्यलोकतः ॥

वर्षासु ग्रीष्मलिङ्गाब्जविकासानुवृत्तिः ।

यथा—"खं वस्ते कलविङ्ककण्ठमलिनं कादम्बिनीकम्बलं
चर्चां पारयतीव दर्दुरकुलं कोलाहलैरुन्मदम् ।
गन्धं मुञ्चति सिक्तलाजसदृशं वर्षेण दग्धा स्थली
दुर्लक्ष्योऽपि विभाव्यते कमलिनीहासेन भासां पतिः ॥"

एवमन्येऽपि ।

किञ्च—ग्रैष्मिकसमयविकासी कथितो धूलीकदम्ब इति लोके ।
जलधरसमयप्राप्तौ स एव धाराकदम्बः स्यात् ॥

यथा— "धूलीकदम्बपरिधूसरदिङ्मुखस्य
रक्तच्छटासुरशरासनमण्डनस्य ।
दीप्तायुधाशनिमुचो ननु नीलकण्ठ
नोत्कण्ठसे समरवारिधरागमस्य ॥"

जलसमयजायमानां जातिं यां कार्द्दमीति[1] निगदन्ति ।
सा शरदि महोत्सविनी गन्धान्वितषट्पदा भवति ॥

यथा—"स्थूलावश्यायबिन्दुद्यु(द्रु)तिदलितबृहत्कोरकग्रन्थिभाजो
जात्या जालं लतानां जरठपरिमलप्लावितानां जजृम्भे ।
नानाहंसोपधानं सपदि जलनिधेश्चोत्ससर्पापरस्य
ज्योत्स्नाशुक्लोपधानं[2] शयनमिव शशी नागभोगाङ्कमम्भः ॥

स्तोकानुवृत्तिं केतक्या अपि केचिदिच्छन्ति ।

---

[1] V कर्दमेन जनयन्ति. २ CB ०मुक्तोपधानं.

यथा— “असूच्यत शरत्कालः केतकीधूलिधूसरैः ।
पद्मातात्रैर्नवायातश्चरणैरिव वासरैः ॥”

शरद्भवानामनुवृत्तिरत्र
बाणासनानां सकुरुण्टकानाम् ।
हेमन्तवक्रे यदि दृश्यतेऽपि
न दृश्यते बन्धविधिः कवीनाम् ॥

हेमन्तशिशिरयोरैक्ये सर्वलिङ्गानुवृत्तिरेव । उक्तञ्च—“द्वादशमासः संवत्सरः, पञ्चर्तवो हेमन्तशिशिरयोः समासेन” [इति]।

मरुबकदमनकपुन्नागपुष्पलिङ्गानुवृत्तिभिः सुरभिः ।
रचनीयश्चित्रश्रीः किञ्चित्कुन्दानुवृत्त्या च ॥

यथा[1]—“गेहे वाहीकयूनां वहति दमनको मञ्जरीकर्णपूरा-
नुन्मादः पामरीणां मरुति मरुबकामोदिनि व्यक्तिमेति ।
सद्योभङ्गानुसारस्नुतसुरभिसिराशीकरः साहकारः
सर्पन्नम्भःशरावे रचयति च रसो रेचकीचन्द्र[2]काणि ॥”[1]

यथा वा[3]—“कुन्दे मन्दस्तमाले मुकुलिनि विकलः कातरः किङ्किराते
रक्ताशोके सशोकश्चिरमतिविकचे चम्पके कुञ्चिताक्षः ।
पान्थः खेदालसोऽपि श्रवणकटुरटच्चक्रमभ्येति धुन्वन्
सोत्कण्ठः षट्पदानां नवमधुपटलीलम्पटं कर्पटेन ॥”

यथा वा—“धुनानः कावेरीपरिसरभुवश्चन्दनतरून्
मरुन्मन्दः कुन्दप्रकरमकरन्दानवकिरन् ।
प्रियक्रीडाकर्षच्युतकुसुममामूलसरलं
ललाटे लाटीनां लुठितमलकं ताण्डवयति ॥”

एवमन्याऽप्यनुवृत्तिः ।

विचकिलकेसरपाटलिचम्पकपुष्पानुवृत्तयो ग्रीष्मे ।
तत्र च तुहिनर्तुभवं मरुबकमपि केचिदिच्छन्ति ॥

---

१ V adds this before गेहे. २ V चक्र. ३ V adds this here.

यथा—"कर्णे स्मेरं शिरीषं शिरसि विचकिलस्रग्लताः पाटलिन्यः
कण्ठे मार्णालहारो वलयितमसिताम्भोजनालं कलाच्योः ।
सामोदं चन्दनाम्भः स्तनभुवि नयने म्लानमाञ्जिष्ठपृष्ठे
गात्रं लोलज्जलार्द्रं जयति मृगदृशां ग्रैष्मिको वेष एषः ॥"

यथा च—"अभिनवकुशसूचिस्पर्द्धि कर्णे शिरीषं
मरुबकपरिवारं पाटलादाम कण्ठे ।
स तु सरसजलार्द्रोन्मीलितः सुन्दरीणां
दिनपरिणतिजन्मा कोऽपि वेषश्चकास्ति ॥"

एवमुदाहरणान्तराणि ।

ऋतुभववृत्त्यनुवृत्ती दिङ्मात्रेणात्र सूत्रिते[2] सन्तः ।
शेषं स्वधिया पश्यत नामग्राहं कियद्ब्रूमः ॥
देशेषु पदार्थानां व्यत्यासो दृश्यते स्वरूपस्य ।
तन्न तथा बध्नीयात्कविबद्धमिह प्रमाणं नः ॥
[3]शोभान्धोगन्धरसैः फलार्चनाभ्यां च पुष्पमुपयोगि ।
षोढा दर्शितमेतत्स्यात्ससममनुपयोगि [तथा[4]] ॥

यथा— यत्प्राचि मासे कुसुमं निबद्धं
तदुत्तरे बालफलं विधेयम् ।
तदग्रिमे प्रौढिधरं च कार्यं
तदग्रिमे पाकपरिष्कृतं च ॥
द्रुमोद्भवानां विधिरेष दृष्टो
वल्लीफलानां न महाननेहा ।
तेषां द्विमासावधिरेव कार्यः
पुष्पे फले पाकविधौ च कालः ॥

अन्तर्व्याजं बहिर्व्याजं बाह्यान्तर्व्याजमेव च ।
सर्वव्याजं बहुव्याजं निर्व्याजं च तथा फलम् ॥

---

१ BC म्लान० २ AC चि. ३ V B & V C शोभास्रग् V A शोभाध्र० ४ V तत्ससममनुपयोगि तथा.

लकुचाद्यन्तर्व्याजं तथा बहिर्व्याजमत्र मोचादि ।
आम्राद्युभयव्याजं सर्वव्याजं च ककुभादि ॥
पनसादि बहुव्याजं नीलकपित्थादि भवति निर्व्याजम् ।
सकलफलानां षोढा ज्ञातव्यः कविभिरिति भेदः ॥
एकद्वित्र्यादिभेदेन सामस्त्येनाथवा ऋतून् ।
प्रबन्धेषु निबध्नीयात्क्रमेण व्युत्क्रमेण वा ॥
न च व्युत्क्रमदोषोऽस्ति कवेरर्थपथस्पृशः ।
तथा कथा कापि भवेद् व्युत्क्रमो भूषणं यथा ॥
अनुसन्धानशून्यस्य भूषणं दूषणायते ।
सावधानस्य च कवेर्दूषणं भूषणायते ॥
इति कालविभागस्य दर्शिता वृत्तिरीदृशी ।
कवेरिह महान्मोह इह सिद्धो महाकविः ॥

इति राजशेखरकृतौ काव्यमीमांसायां कविरहस्ये प्रथमेऽधिकरणे
कालविभागो नाम अष्टादशोऽध्यायः ॥

समाप्तमिदं प्रथममधिकरणं कविरहस्यं काव्यमीमांसायाम् ॥

---

१ V कापेच्छादि.